ST. JAMES'S:
Theatre of Distinction

Other books by W. Macqueen-Pope

THEATRE ROYAL, DRURY LANE
HAYMARKET: THEATRE OF PERFECTION
GAIETY: THEATRE OF ENCHANTMENT
&c.

JOHN BRAHAM, the famous tenor, who founded the St. James's Theatre

ST. JAMES'S

THEATRE of DISTINCTION

By

W. MACQUEEN-POPE

With a foreword by

VIVIEN LEIGH

W. H. ALLEN

LONDON

1958

Made and printed in Great Britain by
Taylor Garnett Evans & Co. Ltd., Watford, Hertfordshire, for the publishers,
W. H. Allen & Co. Ltd., Essex Street, London, W.C.2

To

GILBERT MILLER

Complete Man of the Theatre,
who controlled the St. James's Theatre
for so many years with distinction and dignity,
and in whose heart its memory
will always be enshrined.

CONTENTS

		page
	Foreword by Vivien Leigh	9
	Introduction: Before the Doors Open	11
1	East Comes West	19
2	The Doors Open	28
3	From Bunn to Braddon	37
4	Bright Intervals and Deep Depressions	46
5	No Luck About the House	57
6	Success at Last	65
7	The Sun Shines	72
8	A Dramatist Comes Home	80
9	The Sun Sets Again	89
10	St. George for the St. James's	98
11	Light and Shade	109
12	Enter Oscar Wilde	118
13	Re-enter Pinero	125
14	Days of Glory	132
15	Romance—and Shakespeare	145
16	The New St. James's	154
17	The Age of Elegance	164
18	The Zenith	171
19	More Great Days	178
20	The Old Order Changeth	184
21	The New Era	190
22	The Last Years	201
23	The Curtain Falls	210
24	Other People's Memories	218
25	Personal Farewell	226
	Index	233

ILLUSTRATIONS

Frontispiece: JOHN BRAHAM

A famous triple partnership *facing page* 48

LADY ALEXANDER; MARION TERRY; ADA CAVENDISH „ 49

SIR HENRY IRVING; LILY HANBURY; LILY LANGTRY; H. B. IRVING „ 64

Three Alexander roles „ 65

GEORGE ALEXANDER; his double, JOHN THOROLD; as his own double „ 80

GEORGE ALEXANDER in four roles „ 81

MAUDE MILLETT; EVA MOORE with H. V. ESMOND; E. S. WILLARD; FAY DAVIS „ 96

Leading ladies „ 97

ALLAN AYNESWORTH; MATHESON LANG; SIR JOHNSTONE FORBES-ROBERTSON; HENRY AINLEY „ 144

GLADYS COOPER; MIRIAM CLEMENTS; MRS. PATRICK CAMPBELL; PHYLLIS NEILSON-TERRY „ 145

OWEN NARES; SIR GODFREY TEARLE; SIR GERALD DU MAURIER „ 160

CELIA JOHNSON with HUGH WILLIAMS; DIANA WYNYARD with EMLYN WILLIAMS; MICHAEL REDGRAVE and TOM GILL with VALERIE TAYLOR „ 161

PAUL SCOFIELD with JOY PARKER; with MAI ZETTERLING „ 192

RUTH DRAPER; HELEN HAYE with MARY KERRIDGE „ 193

SIR LAURENCE OLIVIER and VIVIEN LEIGH; ORSON WELLES and GUDRUN URE „ 208

A scene from *Caesar and Cleopatra*; St. James's Theatre „ 209

Most of the illustrations are from the author's private collection. Acknowledgment is gratefully made for others to Angus McBean, Vivienne Byerley (*of H. M. Tennent Ltd.*) *and* John Vickers.

FOREWORD

BY the time this book is published, the St. James's will have been pulled down. One of the oldest and most celebrated of London's theatres will have disappeared, after close on a century and a quarter's faithful and honourable service to the public. And, since we hear nothing of any scheme to make good this loss elsewhere in the West End, the number of theatres left to serve London audiences is accordingly still further diminished.

Mr. Macqueen-Pope's book is thus, alas, a memorial or obituary volume. It will remind readers today of much that was memorable in London stage history from the reign of William IV to that of Elizabeth II; and it will surely fill readers of the future with nostalgia and astonishment—nostalgia for the past, and astonishment at the apathy and levity with which our generation disposes of London's landmarks. For the death, or more correctly, the murder of the St. James's Theatre must be seen in the wider context of the ruin spread throughout the West End in the years since the First World War. One more building of historical and architectural importance is gone, one more place devoted to entertainment and the arts shut down.

None of us likes to admit defeat, and I think this may be especially true of the members of the theatrical profession. With us optimism must be an essential ingredient of our lives. No one puts on a play or takes up a part assuming that the production is bound to be a certain failure. In the same way it seemed incredible to all of us that so much enthusiasm, good faith and generous public support could fail to save the St. James's Theatre from destruction. The author of this book is a passionate partisan of the St. James's, with which he has had a long, practical connection during some of its greatest days. He rightly emphasises the vast size of the sum finally named as needed to save the building, a sum which grew and grew with a discouraging bean-stalk speed until it became the double of that originally suggested.

All that now remains of the St. James's is the traditions and the memories of those who went to see plays there, and of those who put them on or acted in them. In his affectionate and carefully detailed book, Mr. Macqueen-Pope has collated these memories and records, from the first days when Charles Dickens's friend Braham opened the new theatre for the Christmas season of 1835, on through its many vicissitudes to the great period of the Kendal management and the even more famous one of Sir George Alexander.

Every London theatre has its own atmosphere, charged with the struggles and successes of generations of acting people who have performed there. It is this essential atmosphere which Mr. Macqueen-Pope has captured in this book. It is all that now remains to us of the dear old St. James's Theatre, and every reader must agree that he has put every theatre-lover in his debt.

VIVIEN LEIGH

INTRODUCTION

Before the Doors Open

NOWADAYS, when people tear themselves away from their television sets, as they do on rare occasions in search of entertainment, they may say "Let's go out. Let's go to a show." An elder generation would have said "Let's go to the theatre," but it would have meant the same thing, an evening out; and with all the change it brought was then an event of importance. Now it is something which happens only occasionally, when there is a play of such importance or entertainment of such popularity that one just has to go.

The play and the theatre are interdependent: a play without a theatre in which to display itself is just so many words on paper lying on a manager's desk or hidden in an author's drawer; a theatre without a play in it is about the saddest sight in the world. It is a closed, derelict sort of place by day, with a rather shameful, hangdog air and no sign of life. By night it is a dark gap in a cavalcade of twinkling lights. But when a theatre finds its soul, which is a play, and the play finds its body, which is a theatre, then both of them achieve a unity which is viable.

If you do go to a theatre to see a play, it is long odds that you know all about the actors and actresses who are bathed in the glare of modern publicity and ballyhoo. It is generally long odds that you know little or nothing about the building in which you see them and their play. Theatres, as such, get little or no publicity, except when they are built and first opened, or when they die.

There are a few famous theatres still standing—Drury Lane and Covent Garden (even if one is now an opera-house); the Haymarket, Her Majesty's, and maybe the Adelphi and the Savoy—the last largely because of Gilbert and Sullivan. Once there were others equally famous, like the Gaiety and Daly's; but their fame did not save them, any more than the traditions of the Lyceum prevented the home of Irving being turned into a dance-hall.

Theatres don't make enough of themselves—there is little to remind the public of what happened in them. True, there is a plaque to Sir Herbert Tree on the *outside* of Her Majesty's, and *inside* St. Martin's is a little plaque recording the fact that Meggie Albanesi played there. *Inside* Drury Lane, too, there are statues and portraits; but for the passers-by nothing indicates that Drury Lane was the real starting point of the English theatre, where so much happened, where freedom was gained for the players, where Garrick, Kean, Siddons and so many more held sway. Outside this theatre stands a drinking-fountain to the memory of Sir Augustus Harris, erected by subscription from a host of people grateful to him for purveying illusion in the form they liked, by means of pantomime and melodrama. But what else is there? Does the Haymarket record the talents of Samuel Foote, who first made it famous? Is there any mention of William Terriss outside the Adelphi? Does the Savoy acclaim Gilbert and Sullivan? Will you find any mention of Peg Woffington or Quin at Covent Garden? Sir Charles Wyndham, it is true, has a theatre bearing his name and in which he played, and is also commemorated by a plaque inside the New Theatre; but is Gerald Du Maurier mentioned at Wyndham's?

Theatres do very little to commemorate their greatness and maybe that is why they do not catch the imagination of the public. But they are very important: they are the palaces of illusion. Their whole purpose, and the job of everyone connected with them, is illusion. That magic curtain, which conceals the mysteries and cuts the players off from the real life into which they should never enter, can only be achieved in a theatre. That proscenium arch which frames it—which ill-advised people want to destroy—is really the window of the land of illusion. Through it you gaze into a world so different from the one that encompasses you outside—a world of excitement, activity, danger, adventure, romance, music, melody, beauty and colour, and tragedy as well. What place except a theatre can give you that thrill, which even hard-boiled moderns feel when the house lights dim and the footlights blaze in that moment of delightful suspense before the blind of the window of illusion is raised and the magic of the theatre unfolds itself?

The cinema cannot give you that. A film just flicks on the screen after a long list of "credits" (which sometimes become discredits) has assailed the eye. A television set certainly cannot give it, for your mind is not cleared of what you have watched during the preceding half-hour, or your ears are still singing from the loud and insistent claims of the latest detergent—so appropriate an overture for a romantic programme! But the theatre can, and does. That is its magic. That is what makes it a place apart.

Every theatre has its own story. They are thronged with ghosts—but such pleasant ghosts—with the echoes of past successes and failures, memories of the men and women who performed in them and whose deeds still linger and make that impalpable but most precious thing called "atmosphere". It is an atmosphere that can be savoured if you take the trouble to find out something about it. The older theatres of course possess the most, but all theatres have some. A sort of electricity lingers in the air, generated by—sometimes—generations of endeavour to please and give delight. There is an aftermath of battles lost and won. If you are sensitive to environment, you will feel all that is a theatre. Sons and daughters of the theatre in the true line will tell you how you can sense it and how, after a big "first night", you can almost feel the reactions of that seemingly inanimate thing—the auditorium itself—to the emotion which has been spent there during the evening. Something of it always remains.

And there is another thing: a theatre is always a battlefield on which numerous combats have been fought—fought to a finish, without quarter asked or given. For every new play is a battle between audiences on the one side, and the allied forces of management, author, composer and players on the other. There may be lesser combats between leading players, between company and management, but it is always a battlefield, packed with warring elements. All that adds to the atmosphere. No other kind of building can produce quite the same thing.

Theatres are strange places and theatrical people are strange folk. There is very little sanity in a theatre, at least the sort of sanity which belongs to the ordinary world. These people of the playhouse are a race apart. They don't deal in an ordinary marketable commodity. They deal in something which may be of great value or worth nothing at all. And they can never predict which it will be. Commercial rules cannot enter a theatre: there is no such thing as goodwill. Money is poured out and may never pour in. For the theatre is not even a good gamble. It is a gamble with a gamble, and nobody knows much about it. It is a tremendous game of chance; but it is always a wildly exciting place, a place of mystery, thrill, romance, of hard work, bitter disappointment, and also of overwhelming joy and triumph.

Misguided folk who speak of the theatrical profession as "show business" reveal by that very phrase that they know nothing about it. It is not, and it never has been, a business. The theatre and its satellites—the cinema, the circus, the concert hall, and even radio and television—have nothing tangible to sell. Money is paid and nothing changes hands for it. There is nothing to be carried away, save perhaps memories of pleasure. If you look at this in the cold light of reason it is crazy. But then the theatre is a crazy place, full of crazy people.

There are several kinds of theatre and they grade themselves in their own way. Some have touched the fringe of sanity but only the very fringe. That was when certain theatres had real policies and sold "branded goods". You knew what you were to receive when you went there. That was when those theatres had a stable management and a man at the head who was called an actor-manager—a genus that doesn't really exist any more, although some use the title. But today there is not one who has a theatre where he is a permanent resident, which, no doubt, is one of the reasons why the theatre has declined. It has given up the only bit of certainty it ever possessed—the virtue of consistency. By that certainty it collected a following of people whose loyalty was staunch. They came primarily to see the actor-manager (or actress-manageress), and they came regularly because they felt at home there. The theatre became associated in their minds with real pleasure and satisfaction. It was the gateway to that illusion they loved, the only gateway through which they could enter. Even when the critics did not speak highly of the play (or word of mouth—very powerful then—had no praise for it), still a large proportion went to see their favourite (who could do little wrong in their eyes) and to spend an evening in a theatre they loved.

Those fortunate places became institutions. The public went to them irrespective of what was on, because they knew who was there. That is amply proved by the enduring success of those playhouses which dealt in continuity: Irving at the Lyceum, Tree at Her Majesty's, Cyril Maude at the Haymarket, Wyndham, first at the Criterion and then at the New, Bourchier at the Garrick. Likewise, the Gaiety as long as George Grossmith, Edmund Payne, Connie Ediss and Gertie Millar held sway. Ellaline Terriss and Seymour Hicks pursued the same policy at the Vaudeville and the Aldwych, William Terriss at the Adelphi, Gilbert and Sullivan at the Savoy, Sir Augustus Harris and Arthur Collins with their pantomimes and melodramas at Drury Lane. There was also Daly's, with its musical comedies, but less certain of success except when George Edwardes had resident players, like Marie Tempest, Letty Lind, Hayden Coffin, Huntley Wright and Rutland Barrington, as he did in the early days of the Sidney Jones light operas.

Later, Gerald Du Maurier showed what could be done in this respect at Wyndham's, and later still Tom Walls and Ralph Lynn at the Aldwych—practically the last of the long-resident actor-managerial régimes. Just as there are in the world of the Turf, horses for courses, so there are in the world of the Drama, players for theatres. And, like a gem in the above necklace of theatrical glory, shone the St. James's Theatre—when the actor-manager was in charge.

Playhouses which did not come under the sway of an actor-manager never achieved quite such a hold on the public imagination, and never the same fame. They had far more ups and downs. They would glitter when an actor-manager settled in for a period—as when Waller, and Hawtrey too, brought success to the Comedy, and Isabel Jay and the musical plays of Paul Rubens to the Prince of Wales's. It was the Bancrofts who transformed the Prince of Wales's into the leading comedy house in town. It was Samuel Foote, actor-manager, who injected popularity into the Little Theatre in the Haymarket, which was to pass down time as the Haymarket Theatre.

Those men and women knew their jobs. They worked on their productions with their own talents, as did Sheraton and Chippendale on their furniture and Gainsborough and Reynolds on their pictures. They were craftsmen. And they imposed their own powerful personalities on their playhouses, giving them in turn personalities of their own. These could be felt by theatre lovers and the result was all to the good. Those personalities varied, of course, or they would not indeed have been personalities at all. It is not easy to define, but it existed. There was, for instance, a sort of tingle of excitement at the Adelphi, a feeling of rich velvet at Daly's, and the rustle of silk at the Gaiety. There was a sense of good breeding and maybe a whiff of pomander at the Haymarket—there still is—a feeling of reverence at the Lyceum in Irving's days; and for the writer (who knew the building so well) a sheen of gold about Her Majesty's, and an aroma of the best Russian leather and good cigars (although smoking was never permitted there). Wyndham's and the New gave the impression that you were sure of enjoyment. There was a tang of champagne in the air. At the Aldwych one entered with a smile of anticipation. The Garrick, when Bourchier ruled, was virile and masculine. And, in the days of Sir George Alexander, at the St. James's, one had a sense of well-being, of refinement and satisfaction, a feeling that one was sitting at table with the most perfect host in the world . . .

Perhaps the St. James's Theatre, of all the London playhouses, was the one which most needed an actor-manager. When it had such leadership, it prospered and glowed. When it did not, it frequently failed and often closed. It had the right people for two periods; but the time when it really shone was under Sir George Alexander's rule. It had, one was told, many drawbacks: it was off the beaten track, it lay too far west, it was not in a main thoroughfare, it was not at all convenient. But when the right person came along those drawbacks just did not exist. Crowds converged on it, carriages (and later cars) discharged their loads of well-dressed, well-to-do people, who had come for a night of gladness and were sure of getting it. Above all others, the St. James's destiny was entwined with that of Alexander. Other great people, many indeed, played there, but he was beyond question the right man in the right place. Alexander and the St. James's Theatre were synonymous. He conferred upon it his own air of distinction, he made it resound to his fine mind and taste, and it responded because it was part of a distinguished area, with royalty as its neighbours and aristocracy all round. In truth, the St. James's became an aristocrat among theatres, and reflected in its heyday—the late Victorian and Edwardian epoch—all that was best in the life of this country.

Elegant and rich people filled its stalls, its dress circle and its two boxes. People of substance but less social standing booked for the upper circle, and the rest of the playgoers made for the pit and the gallery. They queued, and in those days the theatre was the only thing for which one did queue. But they did it with pleasure, for they were sure of their reward. While waiting, they talked and formed friendships, ate sandwiches, cakes, chocolates, read magazines and newspapers, watched the buskers. Some paid District Messenger boys to queue for them, they themselves arriving shortly before opening time. And in all there was a suppressed excitement and an anticipation of joys to come. They were having an "evening out" at the theatre and to them, those simple people of a simple age, that was something near heaven itself.

They knew, too, that there were pillars inside which might impede their view, if unlucky enough to be seated behind them. They knew that the gallery contained only backless benches of little comfort, but, strange as it may seem to a more pampered generation, they did not care. They had come, not in search of bodily comfort, but to see a play in a theatre, and whilst they watched it they would be oblivious of their surroundings. They would not be allowed to smoke and would not want to. That probably sounds incredible to the young people of today, but it is true. These people were not satiated with amusement. They had no palatial cinemas furnished with such affluence as they themselves could never achieve. They did not sit in armchairs watching television or listening to radio. The cinemas they knew had far less comfort than the theatres, far less splendour too, and no atmosphere at all. They were wooed there by free cups of tea and biscuits. Their concert halls had hardly more comfort. They went to the theatre for illusion and, hail, rain and shine, they waited happily.

As the advertised time of opening drew near, they put away their books, magazines, knitting, what you will, and closed their ranks. Now, indeed, the real flush of excitement gripped them. Soon they would be in a theatre—in this case the St. James's Theatre—and wished nothing better. Those near the doors could now hear noises inside. Voices spoke, chains rattled, and the doors shook as the firemen unbarred them. There would be a surge forward, but the time was not yet. Now the impatience of excitement gripped them and their faces became tense. Their hands gripped their admittance money—2/6 the pit, 1/- the gallery. Almost all had the right amount, for they knew the horror of being held up while some thoughtless person wanted change. They were like thoroughbreds at the starting post, or those greyhounds in the slips, of which Henry V reminded his men at Harfleur.

Then from inside would come the jingle of cash: the money-taker was in his cubby-hole sorting his change. Again muffled shouts, voices inside approaching nearer, another rattle on those doors. Maybe those first in the queue would hear from inside the trill of a whistle . . . and then those portals to illusion were thrown open and the eager crowd surged towards joy.

The doors being open, let us too pass inside into the St. James's Theatre . . .

CHAPTER I

East Comes West

ST. JAMES'S THEATRE lay in the very heart of the West End of London, close neighbour to Royal palaces and to what were once the homes of great nobles, statesmen, the gentry, and the most exclusive and oldest established clubs in the world. Of all theatres it most merited the title "West End", geographically speaking; except for the Westminster Theatre, it was the most westerly of all. By its existence it rebutted that celebrated dictum: "East is East and West is West, and never the twain shall meet", because its own origin lay in the East End of London and indeed in basically oriental stock.

In the year 1774 a boy was born to poor but respectable Jewish parents in Goodman's Fields, Whitechapel. Their name was Abraham and they have been described as of Portuguese stock, but there is little doubt their origin was German. Like all their race they were hard-working and industrious, but otherwise undistinguished. The father was short and stout, with a hooked nose, far more pronounced than usual in his race. Indeed, he was called "Abey Punch" on account of it. Beyond that, however, little is known of them. And there was nothing to suggest that their little son, whom they called John, would be different.

Maybe there is something formative in natal environment. Anyway, near where the Abrahams lived stood the famous Goodman's Fields Theatre—where David Garrick had burst into fame overnight—and probably a smaller, far less distinguished theatre, of which the records are scant and confused. As the Jewish people have always supported the theatre—and still do—so the Whitechapel playhouses flourished. It may well be that "Abey Punch" and his wife (whose name is unknown) were regular playgoers. Even so, they could have had no idea of the eminence their son John was to attain, for they both died while he was still a boy. Though relatives came to the orphan's help, he had little or no education. His life was hard, as was usual for his kind in those days, but he had his wits about him. When only a little lad he went into business: he sold pencils about the streets to assist the family budget of those who helped him. Finding he could sing, he secured employment at the local synagogue, where he attracted the attention of a Mr. Goldsmid, a wealthy man who was keen on music. He introduced young John to Leoni Lee, known professionally as Leoni, a celebrated singer and even more famous teacher of music and singing. Impressed by the boy's superb soprano voice, he gave him tuition and launched him on his career.

Where this actually took place is not quite clear. One record says it was at the Garrick Theatre, Leman Street, but that playhouse was not then in existence, although the début may well have taken place at the odd little theatre previously mentioned. But he undoubtedly appeared at the ill-fated Royalty Theatre, in Wellclose Square, E., in 1787, billed as "Master Abram, pupil of Leoni", and described as an infant prodigy. He was then thirteen. Such was his initial success that on 21st April of the same year, Leoni presented him at Covent Garden in *The Duenna*. Between the acts he sang two special songs, "The Soldier Tired" and "Ma Chère Amie". This time his billing was: "Master Braham, His first Appearance on Any Stage."

The critic of the *Morning Post*, ignoring the billing, said these songs had been "given with great success by a little boy, Master Abram, a young pupil of Signor Leoni, who promises to attain perfection, possessing every requisite to form a capital singer". That critic's judgment was sound, although the young singer had a long and often uphill road to travel before the forecast was confirmed.

There is no list of his early appearances, but he certainly sang at Sadler's Wells in 1788, billed as "Master Abraham". There he did his master credit, and probably made a little money for himself and those who sponsored him. And then . . . his voice broke. But Master Braham did not despair. Keen and tenacious, he turned to instrumental music and soon became a first-class violoncellist. Nor did he let his voice go rusty: he kept it in trim, thus ensuring that when it settled he would be able to sing again. His tutor had already said he had little more to teach him, and in any case business took Leoni to Jamaica. Consequently, when Braham was able to use his voice again he had no mentor to guide him. For some time he arranged his own bookings, and when singing at a concert he met Ashe, the celebrated flautist, who advised him to taken an engagement at Bath for a series of concerts.

Bath was then the most fashionable place in England and all the great artistes went there to perform before the "smart set". Leading the stars that season was Rauzzini, the greatest tenor of his day and a man of benevolent disposition. He heard Braham and was so delighted that he gave him further expert tuition and became his patron. When he had become famous Braham always attributed his good fortune to the help given him by Rauzzini. Bath acclaimed Braham and his fame spread. Rauzzini recommended him to everyone likely to be of use. And no less a person than Stephen Storace, master of music and resident composer at Theatre Royal, Drury Lane, hastened down to Bath to hear and see for himself. The result was an offer to appear in a number of performances at Drury Lane. This was a tremendous lift for the young man, who was then twenty-two.

Braham first appeared at Drury Lane in 1796, with immediate success. Not only was his voice remarkable but he sang with such éclat that the management resolved to have a new opera composed especially for him. This was of course entrusted to Storace, who, however, died before it was completed, and his sister, the equally gifted Signora Storace, took over. The opera *Mahmoud* was staged and Braham, in the title role, achieved his first really outstanding success. He was a *tenore robusto* in the finest meaning of the phrase and his voice, despite its great strength, was capable of infinite tenderness and pathos. After enthralling his audiences with delicate and intimate passages, he would produce a crescendo of sound like the booming of a great bell and never wanting in sweetness. It was said that his voice had the softness of velvet and the lusciousness of honey.

After his Drury Lane success Braham went to Italy and there studied again, and sang as well. Even in that land of tenors he excelled. Tacchinardi, who had never recognised the possibility of a rival, exclaimed after hearing him: "There are now two tenors in the world; I and this Englishman." A similar tribute, but not quite so gracious, came from Davide, another claimant to the championship of tenors. He heard Braham in Venice, where the young man was acclaimed with an enthusiasm approaching frenzy. Someone asked Davide who he thought was the greatest singer in the world and he replied: "*Dopo di mè, l'Inglese.*" (After me, the Englishman.)

Braham toured the Continent and had not only Italy but all Europe raving about him. Sometimes he appeared with Mrs. Billington, the leading English soprano of her day: sometimes he was alone. The result was always the same. With his Hebrew determination and intense industry, he never ceased learning. He took lessons from Isola, at that time the finest tutor in the world, and in the process learned to speak Italian fluently.

In Venice, Cimarosa went to hear him, having travelled specially from Naples. Seconding the Venetian enthusiasm, he declared he would write an opera for Braham, something to do *il bel canto* real justice. He was actually working on it when he was poisoned by a rival. In Paris, Braham engaged to sing with Signora Storace for three weeks, an engagement that was prolonged into eight months. He must have had a really miraculous voice. Grove said it had a compass of nineteen notes from D to A in alt., and that his falsetto was perfection, as was his way of managing it. His skill lay in completely masking the transition from natural voice to falsetto. Another celebrated tenor, Johnstone, whose real voice most closely rivalled Braham's, could never quite manage the transition. His failure to accomplish the change smoothly earned him the nickname of "Bubble and Squeak". But of Braham, Grove wrote: "So complete was his command of his means that he could execute with incredible rapidity and unfailing accuracy the most complicated passages, in which the shrewdest listener could not have detected when or how the one voice glided into the other." Braham was the first English singer to accomplish it.

Absent on the Continent since 1796, Braham returned to London in 1801. He was now on top of the world. He appeared at Covent Garden, and London went as wild about him as the Continent had done. That same year he married a Miss Bolton of Ardwick, of whom little is known except that she died young. He never stopped working. In 1803 he composed an opera, for which he was paid £1,000—an incredible sum then. It was called *The English Fleet in 1342*—as bad a title as could be imagined—but it gave him an opportunity of singing the sea songs in which he had begun to specialise and which were so beloved by the British public. The highlight of that opera was the song "All's Well", maybe forgotten now but popular for many years. He threw tremendous spirit into it and, employing the great flexibility of his voice, always repeated the call as if from varying distances. It held the house spellbound and at the end evoked a thunder of applause.

Every musician has a favourite piece of music, and every singer a song which he must sing before an audience allows him to depart. Braham's song was "The Death of Nelson". He never could make an end to any concert without it, just as Patti always had to sing "Home, Sweet Home". He wrote the song himself, as part of an opera called *The Americans*, and it soared into fame. Never a performance passed without the gallery joining in the concluding lines of the chorus:

> "For honour, home and beauty,
> England expects that every man
> This day will do his duty."

Lady Hamilton made a point of being present if possible when Braham sang that song, and more than once created a sensation by being carried out fainting. Braham did not mind: it was good publicity. He excelled in oratorio. His singing of Jephtha's "Lamentation" always moved his audience to tears. Sacred music was his forte. His voice rang out like a silver trumpet when he sang Handel.

Like everyone else, Braham had his faults. He would sing oratorio in great churches and cathedrals, his voice like an angel's ringing down from heaven, and a few nights later sing the same music at a popular concert and so overlay it with vocal fireworks as to make it almost unrecognisable to purists. It brought down the house all the same. Weber said, after hearing him sing in *Der Freischütz* for the first time, "This is the greatest singer in Europe." But he was extremely annoyed when Braham took liberties with his *Oberon*. Braham, nevertheless, made a big success in it, from which it may be inferred that he was a good showman. He excelled in ballads and naval songs, his repertoire including many of Dibdin's masterpieces. At that time, when England was at war with France and the English fleet was the hope and stay of the populace, they could never hear enough of its glories.

A shrewd observer, Charles Lamb, wrote of Braham: "There is a fine scorn in his face, which nature meant to be of Christians. The Hebrew spirit is strong in him despite his proselytism. He cannot conquer the Shibboleth: how it breaks out when he sings 'The children of Israel passed through the Red Sea'. The auditors of the moment are as Egyptians to him, and he rides over our necks in triumph. The foundation of his vocal excellence is sense." Yet Braham embraced Christianity. As a Jew he would hardly, in those days, have been permitted to sing in the churches, minsters and cathedrals, especially *Messiah,* in which he was unrivalled. There is little doubt, however, that at heart he remained a Jew. Lamb, it must be agreed, showed excellent judgment as regards Braham's vocal abilities, for if ever there was a scientific singer, it was he.

Despite his glorious voice, it is almost a pity that Braham would insist on appearing in opera. Not that music lovers objected, but he had no physical qualifications for it. A little man, he lacked the necessary physique. All the same, he insisted he was born to be an actor. On the platform he was always at it. His audiences never demurred, for as long as he kept on singing they were happy. The degree of drama he put into "Bay of Biscay" by voice alone always moved them to frenzy, and he should have been content. Even after his voice had become old and tired his dramatic use of it outshone all others. But he simply could not resist the urge to act. Once, at a provincial festival, it led to trouble. He was performing on a rather high-fronted platform and, being a little fellow, hardly the half of him was visible. He was piling the action into "Biscay" and, coming to "A sail, a sail!" in the last verse, he sank down on one knee as though in thankfulness—and promptly disappeared altogether! The audience, thinking he had struck an unexpected trap-door, simply roared. Eventually his round face, topped by the brown wig he always wore, reappeared above the rail—but they could not stop laughing.

Braham made a deal of money. He had married well and was in good standing with the social leaders of his day. A fine *raconteur* and much travelled, he was a welcome guest in many of the stately homes, and if after lunch he could be induced to sing, well, that more than paid for the hospitality; but, quite rightly, it was difficult to get him to sing without a fee. He had a country seat at Dee Bank, Cheshire, and a town house, "The Grange", at Brompton, where he entertained lavishly. His one great weakness was his desire to be an actor first and a vocalist second. Maybe friends who should have known better flattered him in this futile fancy. Had they listened to Sir Walter Scott they might have seen the folly of it. For the wizard of "Waverley" refuted them succinctly: "He is a beast of an actor, though an angel of a singer," he said.

It was undoubtedly this urge to act and to be his own master that led Braham into theatrical speculation. Not content with taking money out of the theatre—and that in a big way—he started to put money into it. He wanted to be an actor-manager—the dream of all actors. Unlike most of them, Braham had the money to sponsor his dream. He concerned himself first with the Colosseum, near Regent's Park, and lost a lot of money there. Possessed of plenty more, he decided to build a theatre which should really be his: not one in the northern outskirts but right in the West End, of which he himself was undoubtedly part. And when a performer wants to own or build a theatre and has the means at his disposal, it is quite impossible to stop him.

So John Braham, in his sixty-first year, looked around for a suitable site. His choice fell on one in King Street, St. James's, upon which at the time was a very old hostelry named Nerot's, which had stood there since the days of Charles II. He acquired it and engaged as architect the eminent Samuel Beazley, who had built the Lyceum. The site alone cost £8,000. It is recorded that Braham's total investment was £26,000, which represented at that moment his entire savings. But research shows that the building when completed—the interior was decorated by Crace—cost no less than £50,000. Perhaps Braham had friends in the deal, but that is not likely. He probably relied on mortgages and loans. There can be little doubt that prudent friends who knew something about the hazards of theatrical speculation warned him what might be his fate. But he would not listen. None of them in similar circumstances ever do.

One of the arguments with which they tried to deter him undoubtedly was that the site lay outside Theatreland and was off the beaten track—that it was too far "West", and the public would not come. To which Braham would certainly have replied that King Street, St. James's, was in the wealthiest district in London, amongst the very best people. It was an old-established and famous thoroughfare, practically a Royal street, for the faithful cohorts of Charles I had given it its name when Charles II was restored to the throne. It was not one of the mushroom growths which were then springing up all around London, but a street famous in its own right. One end ran into St. James's Square, and surely the best people lived there. Was not the Duke of Cleveland living in Cleveland House? Let them just take a look round and see who would be his neighbours—dukes, marquesses, earls, statesmen—was not that good enough? And how about Pall Mall, which ran parallel with King Street? Was that a slum? And perhaps they would not overlook St. James's Street itself—it only led to the Palace, the Court of St. James's!

Outside Theatreland, indeed? The Haymarket Theatre was only a stone's throw away, and so was the King's Theatre, which was expanded into the Royal Italian Opera House. Braham had recorded huge successes there. Did anyone suppose people would hesitate to come a few hundred yards farther to hear him sing, and see him act? And if it came to entertainment, well, had they never heard of Almack's? Was that not the venue of the most exciting functions and brilliant balls, routs and ridottos? Why, it was so rigorously exclusive that the great Duke of Wellington had once been refused admission because he was in trousers, whereas full evening dress called for knee-breeches. Maybe his friends murmured that Almack's was becoming a little *démodé*, not quite so smart as it was. We may be sure that Braham did not agree. He could only see that the district teemed with the best people, which was true. His idea was to take the theatre to them and save them the trouble of coming to it. They were the patrons of the boxes and the most expensive seats. It was, according to him, the ideal site. Of course, no one could stop him. Remember that the theatre is a crazy world and those connected with it usually see only what they want—until they get a rude awakening.

Like many more before and since, Braham overlooked much more than he saw. Situation means a tremendous amount to a theatre, an amount hardly credible to a layman. That few hundred yards from the Haymarket might seem nothing to the novice, but to the experienced impresario it means a great deal. Theatres standing on their own, away from their fellows, often have a thin time. They do best in close proximity to one another. And they are extremely sensitive to so many small and often impalpable things. There are two theatres in London which stand side by side and even share the same party wall at their stages. One of them has always enjoyed much more success than the other, chiefly because it faces the normal stream of traffic, while the other faces the opposite way. That may sound crazy but it is true.

Two other things Braham overlooked. One was that the grand people who lived in and around King Street were not essentially theatre-goers. They patronised the Opera chiefly because it was a Society function, and in doing so they went to an opera-house, not to a theatre. The distinction is subtle, but there are many such subtleties in the theatre world. Besides, in the London of 1835 there was plenty of opera. It was the rule at the King's Theatre and was frequent both at Drury Lane and Covent Garden. But, despite all arguments, Braham went ahead with his plans.

Inevitably, his project caused a considerable stir. Maybe the residents of the aristocratic quarter were not too pleased at the prospect of a theatre coming among them. For play-actors (as distinct from opera singers) were not at all respectable people then. You simply did not mix with them. You might, on rare occasions, invite the greatest of them to your house—as a "lion"—and he or she would of course be expected to perform. You would be most polite and gracious to them in your capacity of host or hostess, but you never allowed them to presume on that. It is certain that the St. James's was not altogether a welcome neighbour.

But so far as Braham was concerned, this was his theatre, the veritable embodiment of his dream. Here he was master, and the public, he felt certain, were his friends. For years their applause had crackled in his ears, and there was no reason why he should not now take for himself the profits which others had previously made on his triumphs. Like all real public performers he was a vain man. All such people have to be. Vanity is one of the basic urges impelling them to a theatre career. But it is not the same kind of vanity sometimes manifest in a beautiful woman or a handsome man, or that is prompted by great wealth or fine clothes. It is not to be confused with pompous conceit or inflated pride. It is rather an expression of supreme self-confidence, an attitude summed up in the self-assured phrase: "I know I can do it, I've got it in me." If that sort of vanity ever dies out, then the theatre will indeed expire. But the theatre is not in any great danger on that score.

So Braham went ahead with his plans. King William IV, the Sailor King, sat on the throne. He was perhaps an omen, for as the Duke of Clarence he had loved the theatre and there discovered a certain Mrs. Jordan who had presented him with no fewer than ten little tokens of her love and esteem. He might, therefore, be regarded as a patron of the dramatic arts. Moreover, the country was prosperous, industry was expanding, and there were no more wars in sight. Surely this was the appropriate time? So the little man from the East End opened his princely playhouse in the West End. East and West had assuredly met.

CHAPTER 2

The Doors Open

THOSE living in that distinguished neighbourhood which Mr. Braham had decided should be graced by a theatre received, somewhere about the end of November, an announcement that read as follows: "St. James's Theatre.—Mr. Braham has the honour to inform the nobility, gentry and the public that his new theatre, in King Street, St. James's, will open on Monday, 14th December, 1835, when, and during the week, an opening address will be spoken by Mrs. Selby; after which will be presented for the first time, a new and original burletta, which has been some time in preparation, *Agnes Sorel*, written by Gilbert A'Beckett. The overture and the whole of the music composed by Mrs. G. A'Beckett."

Alas, neither the nobility nor the gentry—nor even "the public"—responded, except, perhaps, on the first night. Yet the theatre was an attractive edifice, its exterior not out of keeping with its locality, and its interior a cosy combination of taste and charm. The prices were most reasonable—boxes, 5/-; pit, 3/-; gallery, 2/-; and half-price to all at half-time. There was nothing vulgar, bizarre or undignified about Braham's theatre: in fact, it did the street much credit.

Braham had gone to enormous trouble to provide a brilliant opening. In this he committed another mistake. He might have won a bigger public by a gradual wooing. It is always a most difficult task to put a new theatre on the map of London. For some recondite reason, the public never rushes to fill it. They go instead to the playhouses they know. There is little curiosity to see the new place. The play it offers is of greater importance—a truth as trenchant today as it was yesterday. The safest plan, if it can be managed, is to open with a success transferred from elsewhere, which has already attained a certain momentum. Another procedure is to put up a leading player in a part which the public always flock to see. Often, of course, the name of a theatre gives little indication as to where it stands, managements unwisely assuming that because *they* know the public must also know. But in this case the name of the theatre left no doubt of its location, and Braham had the sense to advertise the actual street in which it stood. He opened the doors punctually on the advertised date, and no doubt he had seen to it that the house would be full. He probably invited his numerous friends and hoped they would go away and sing its praises. In any case, he offered them the best fare he could muster.

The main attraction was the burletta, *Agnes Sorel*, by Gilbert A'Beckett, renowned then as a comic writer and extremely popular. Just six years afterwards he became one of the founders of *Punch*, and later a London police magistrate as well. Born in 1811, he was already celebrated by 1835. He died in 1856, aged only forty-five, after an active and eventful life. His work did not sparkle at the St. James's. Maybe he had, in deference to the district, restrained his comic gift, for despite the description "burletta" (which the law then demanded in compliance with the Charter rights of Drury Lane and Covent Garden) it was a very serious little operetta indeed.

Braham, eager to do his best, gave it a fine cast. He himself sang the principal role and had with him Morris Barnett, a popular performer, Miss Priscilla Horton, a charming vocalist and most accomplished actress, and a Miss Glossop, who played the heroine and was making her first appearance on the stage. She was Braham's star pupil at the time. There were two other items in the programme, an original interlude called *A Clear Case*, and an original farce entitled *A French Company*. It was evidently "novelty night": a new theatre, a new actress, and three new plays. There was also the Address spoken by Mrs. Selby, who does not appear to have left any footmarks on the sands of dramatic time.

But novelty was not enough. None of the plays pleased. After this opening night, there was no precipitate rush: they stayed away in hundreds. It must have been a severe shock to Braham, so confident of his own drawing-power and so proud of his handsome theatre. He had to take off *Agnes Sorel* after a month. It was followed by a musical piece called *Monsieur Jacques*, by Morris Barnett. When this too failed to pull them in, he put up some short revivals—operas like *Fra Diavolo* and Dibdin's *The Waterman*, in which he was a known draw. He was a famous "Tom Tug", and "Did You Not Hear of a Jolly

Young Waterman?" always fetched the cheers. But still they stayed away.

With the approach of Lent—then a very difficult time theatrically—Braham played for safety. He put on two well-tried pieces. Mrs. Honey, a very popular singer, was engaged to play Captain Macheath in *The Beggars' Opera*, in which she had never failed, and also another favourite part, Kate O'Brien, in *Perfection*. But the public still would not come in.

After a season lasting only three months Braham closed down. For a period he let the theatre to Madame Jenny Vertpré, who presented a short run of French plays in which Mlle. Plessis appeared. This may have sown a seed, for later there was to be much French spoken on the stage of the St. James's. The Vertpré season opened in April and lasted but a few weeks. Then Braham closed down again. He must have wondered what was wrong. No doubt he and his friends went through the list of alibis, and perhaps found a reason for the failure.

But Braham was not beaten. It takes more than an initial setback to defeat a resolute man. He had, too, discovered what he considered some defects in his theatre and he went to work on them during the summer. Out then went another announcement: "The Theatre having during the recess been perfected in all its departments, and being now admitted to be the most splendid Theatre in Europe, will open for the season on Thursday, 29th September, 1836." Once again Braham, to the delight and profit of the playwrights, pinned his faith to novelty. Indeed, amid his short span in command of his own theatre, Braham was a liberal patron of dramatists, for the great proportion of his productions were completely new.

For his first play on the opening night Braham had gone to a leading comic writer, who had given him a rather doleful operetta. Now he turned to a writer destined for immortality, and whose character studies had already made him a household word under the pseudonym of "Boz": he went to Charles Dickens. Perhaps it is more correct to say that Dickens went to him, via John Hullah, a composer of some merit, whose "The Sands of Dee" and "Three Fishers" had attained great vogue. The writer of "Sketches by Boz" was in himself a most dramatic person, and he yearned to write for the stage. A creator of the best kind of illusion, he wanted to identify himself with the true world of illusion. He had already arranged to write a libretto for music by Hullah, and the composer had proposed something with a Venetian setting and suggested as a title *The Gondoliers*, but this association was not destined to forestall Gilbert and Sullivan, for finally they decided on an English setting, in which Dickens was more at home. The delighted Dickens was soon to learn more about theatre people and their ways. He rattled off the libretto at express speed—and then failed to get the music out of Hullah! He begged, he stormed, he pleaded, but to no avail. Weary at last of waiting, he wrote another piece, which Braham decided to produce at once. This was a two-act burletta entitled *The Strange Gentleman*—really a stage version of one of the "Sketches by Boz" called "The Great Winglebury Duel". There is no trace of how much Dickens received as an author.

Already famous for his "Sketches", Dickens was then writing "Pickwick Papers" in weekly parts. His introduction of Sam Weller had sent the sales soaring, and Sam took his place on the literary stage just before *The Strange Gentleman* took the theatrical boards. Dickens enjoyed his association with the theatre, especially during rehearsals. He loved being backstage, despite his penchant for burlesquing actors in his books. But he came to understand them, and it is not unlikely that he often had a fleeting fancy to be one himself, for he did plenty of amateur acting.

Braham gave his play a good cast, with Harley, who was his stage manager and a fine actor, as chief comedian, and Mrs. Sala (mother of the celebrated George Augustus Sala) also in a leading role. The result was encouraging and raised Braham's hopes. He *could* get the public to come to his beautiful theatre, for they came, though maybe not in great crowds, to see *The Strange Gentleman*. The opening night was 29th September, 1836. There is no real proof of the length of the run, for nobody troubled about theatrical statistics in those days, nor were long runs the rule. Some records speak of fifty nights, some of seventy. Either figure was pretty good, and it looked as though Dickens had brought luck to the St. James's. For Dickens had also provided a lesser piece, called *Is She His Wife?*, an amusing item, and this, together with *The Strange Gentleman*, formed the evening bill. Dickens was then twenty-five years old and an established author, and now saw himself as a successful dramatist. And teeming in his brain was "Oliver Twist"!

By this time Hullah had completed the score of their first idea, which, however, had ceased to be *The Gondoliers* and become *The*

Village Coquettes. Braham was enchanted with it and predicted a vast success. Dickens does not appear to have been so sure. He wrote a preface dedicated to Harley in which he said: "This drama may have a plot, or it may not; and the songs may be poetry, or they may not; and the whole affair, from beginning to end, may be great nonsense, or it may not; just as the honourable gentleman or lady who reads it, may happen to think. So retaining his own private and particular opinion upon the subject (an opinion which he formed upwards of a year ago, when he wrote the piece) the author leaves every such gentleman or lady to form his or hers as he or she may think proper, without saying one word to conciliate them. It is needless to add that the libretto of an opera must be, to a certain extent, a mere vehicle for the music, and that it is scarcely fair or reasonable to judge it by those strict rules of criticism which would be justly applicable to a five-act tragedy or a finished comedy."

Though non-commital, Dickens was probably hopeful. Braham was highly confident. He declared it the best thing of its kind since Sheridan's *The Duenna*, and he could claim to know about that as it had formed one of his early successes. But the gentlemen and ladies who came to St. James's applied their own criticism as invited by the author, and definitely turned it down. *The Village Coquettes* had a run of twenty nights to poor business.

His optimism dampened but his tenacity untouched, Braham refused to renounce the musical motif. He appeared himself in that famous ballad opera *Love in a Village*, in *Guy Mannering*, and *The Waterman*. Time was when Braham, in any one of these, could draw the town. But whether he was getting too old, or had lost his attraction, he could not draw them into the St. James's. He closed his second season with a heavy loss.

Nor did fortune turn his way during the third. He now deserted musical productions and fell back on the drama, though this was hardly likely to help in his very select district; for among its residents the legitimate theatre occupied a very lowly position in the 1830s. Nevertheless, he experienced a flash of success when he produced *The Spitalfields Weaver* in 1838. His cast included Alfred Wigan, an outstanding actor (eventually to be first leading man for Hollingshead at the Gaiety), E. Wright, J. Webster and Miss Allison—all first-class names. This play, afterwards one of J. L. Toole's most popular vehicles, stopped the rot. But its success seems to have been only comparative. It is reported that during its run Braham went into the green room one night and said, "I feel quite proud tonight. I have just counted the pit and there are seventeen people in it." Whatever he meant by that, *The Spitalfields Weaver* was as near a success as Braham had.

Poor Braham! He must have been almost in despair. Was this to be the culmination of those long years of success? Was it for this that he had progressed from peddling lead pencils to being the most renowned singer of his day, possessed of popularity, wealth, and a town and a country house? His ascent of the ladder of fame had been swift and apparently secure. Was he now, in his advanced years, to crash to the bottom? It is a risk any man takes who builds and runs a playhouse. But he had nothing with which to reproach himself. His theatre was an excellent place, and he had spared no pains to make it so.

By way of keeping the record complete, it should be noted that Braham had produced a number of items besides those already mentioned. These included *The Sham Prince*, by John Barnett, *The Tradesmen's Ball* (both original burlettas); Arne's opera, *Artaxerxes*, with himself as Artabanes, and Miss Rainforth, a notable singer, as Mandane. He always mounted them in polished style and invariably found good casts. His production of *The Village Coquettes* was widely remarked and it embraced the aforesaid Miss Rainforth, himself, Morris Barnett, Harley, and John Parry, the latter a real top-liner. Yet it scored only twenty performances. Maybe the plot was wrong, and if so the fault was Dickens's. It concerns a village maiden who nearly falls victim to the wiles of the wicked squire; a rustic hero, given to moralising in a strong "Mummerset" dialect; and a comedian who came on when a laugh was considered due. It was all very conventional, but that was the sort of thing popular in those days.

When Braham turned to drama he also dealt in big names. He had the great Mrs. Stirling, who had won real fame at the Adelphi, and also Mrs. Honey, fresh from her triumphs at the old Strand. He also had Edward Wright, a really fine actor. Braham always did his best. But money was flowing out like a flood, and only the poorest trickle coming in.

By the close of the 1838 season, the end had come. Braham was at last beaten. His resources were exhausted. He must admit defeat and close down. The St. James's had been his Waterloo. It must have been a bitter moment for the ageing man, now in his sixty-fifth year—quite an advanced age in his time.

Resolved now to face realities, he started settling his accounts. He would leave no debts. He realised everything he had, sold his country house, sold his town house, all his furniture and *objets d'art*, of which he had a fine collection. His creditors were paid, right up to the last farthing. He would not bring disaster or disgrace on anyone.

Braham's wife had died some years before his crash, and his sister-in-law helped him to bring up his family. His eldest daughter had already become Frances, Lady Waldegrave (this was her second marriage, and a gipsy foretold she would marry four times—a prophecy that came true). His sons—Charles, the eldest, Spencer (in Holy Orders), Hamilton and Augustus, who had a magnificent bass voice, and another married daughter, had all grown up. Braham took the small sum left after squaring accounts, and faced the world anew. With his son Charles, in whose future as a singer he believed, he went on a concert tour in America. Although Charles's voice was but the faintest echo of his father's (in fact, Charles never made much mark), the tour succeeded and Braham returned home no longer penniless but with a modest competence. His fame and reputation and his still fine voice had captivated Americans wherever he went.

Now Braham settled down in a boarding house in Westbourne Terrace with his sister-in-law. But still the St. James's called him. He made one more appearance at a concert there, the only names on the bill being those of his son and himself. He wanted to establish Charles in London. And London had great sympathy for Braham, and great admiration for the way he had met his debts. The tickets sold like wildfire. Every seat was taken, and they were standing in the aisles and even in the lobby. And everyone, even the connoisseurs and critics, agreed that never in his whole career had Braham sung so beautifully as on this occasion. He announced that there would be no encores, but after he had concluded with "Scots Wha Hae", the enthusiasm was such that he was forced to repeat it.

This time the nobility and gentry had come to his theatre and they were swept off their feet by his artistry. The Duke of Wellington stood in his box, leaning forward and applauding rapturously. Braham bowed again and again, and went through all the motions of pleasure and gratitude. Still they shouted and yelled "Bravo!" At length, with tears streaming down his face, he turned and made for the wings, facing them just before he vanished, with a last wave of the hand. This, at last, was his moment of triumph. His dream had come true. He had seen his theatre packed with the best people, and they were applauding him to the echo. Maybe all his hardships fell away as he savoured this great artistic triumph. It was his final appearance at the theatre he had created. He sang again elsewhere, finally retiring in 1852. He was then seventy-nine, but no reference was made to his age. Probably few people realised he had sung to three generations. He died in Westbourne Terrace on Sunday, 17th February, 1856, at the age of eighty-three.

Braham had run the whole gamut of life, from poverty to riches, from obscurity to fame, from the East End to the West. He had lost all and regained some, and everything had been done by his own efforts. He had put his money and his faith in the St. James's Theatre and it had failed him. But he never failed it. And it stands until now (or until recently)—the memorial to a great artiste and a good man.

After the passing of Braham the St. James's smelt more than ever of failure. That, however, did not deter a manager named Hooper. Hooper had a flair for showmanship and, like Braham, believed in giving the best. He also tried to give the public what he believed they wanted. He employed the best talent the profession could offer. There was Dowton, a veteran then but immensely popular. An accomplished fellow, Dowton had one strange peculiarity—he refused to be starred. He always declined to have his name billed larger than anyone else's. On one occasion Elliston—the Great Lessee, as he called himself—gave him what was then star billing at Drury Lane. He plastered Dowton's name all over the town. And in the morning a furious Dowton raged into his office and demanded the removal of the bills, telling Elliston the sight of them made him feel like a runaway slave or an escaped convict with a price on his head. Elliston, staggered and amazed, had to comply and old Dowton, who came from Devon, had his way. At the St. James's also were Walter Lacy; Wrench, the leading light comedian and the Charles Mathews of his day; Mrs. Glover, the acknowledged queen of the stage; Mr. and Mrs. Frank Matthews, a most popular couple; James Bland, the best burlesque comedian at that time; Alfred Wigan, a young man playing small parts but already making his mark; Miss Turpin, with a splendid voice; and Mrs. Honey, a beautiful woman who sang, it is reported, like a nightingale.

It was a company that would have packed any other theatre. Yet it failed to fill the St. James's. But Hooper was not defeated. He had another trick up his sleeve: he called in the animals—and, of course, nobody could resist them. Hooper engaged Van Ambergh, the supreme animal trainer, a Dutchman, to see whose show Queen Victoria had visited Drury Lane no fewer than four times in one month, a quite unprecedented event. Naturally, that made the animal show fashionable. Announced as "A Forest of Wild Animals", it included lions, tigers, leopards, panthers and jaguars. The box-office never closed, and the humans played second fiddle to the menagerie. After Van Ambergh, Hooper brought over from Paris a troupe of performing dogs, monkeys and goats, and dispensed with human actors altogether. They did the trick, too, whilst the novelty lasted. And at the end of his one season, in May 1839, Hooper withdrew, whilst the going was good. It is an interesting fact that when George Alexander took over the theatre in 1890 he discovered, in the cellars, several large iron cages, the "dressing-rooms" of the animal actors.

CHAPTER 3

From Bunn to Braddon

IN view of the current outcry about the declining state of the theatre, and the demolition of the St. James's Theatre in particular, it may be of interest to look at conditions in the year 1839, when Hooper had been indulging in zoological attractions. No less an authority than Theodore Hook felt obliged to comment upon it in the course of a long essay. He said:

"Perhaps as great an alteration as any which has occurred during the present generation is to be found in the present theatrical taste of the people—not to go back to the theatrical reign of Garrick, which terminated in 1811, during which the acceptance or rejection of a comedy formed the subject of general conversation. Then there were but two theatres, the seasons of which were limited from 15th September to 15th May. Then each theatre had its destined company of actors, a change in which, even in an individual instance, created a sensation in society. Theatrical representations had a strong hold upon the public up to a much later period—in fact, until that which modern liberality denounced as a gross monopoly was abolished, and theatres sprang up in almost every street of the metropolis. The argument in favour of this extension was that the population of London and its suburbs had so much increased, that the demand for playhouses was greater than the supply and that 'more theatres' were wanted."

And Hook proceeded:

"We have the theatres, but where are the authors and the actors to make them attractive? Monkeys, dogs, goats, horses, giants, lions, tigers, and gentlemen who walk upon the ceiling with their heads downwards, are all very attractive in their way, and they will sometimes, not always, fill the playhouses. But as to the genuine drama, the public taste has been weaned from it, first by the multitude of trashy diversions scattered all over the town, and, secondly, by the consequent scattering of the theatrical talent which really does exist. At each of these minor theatres you find some three or four excellent actors, worked off their legs, night after night, who if collected into two good companies, as of old, would give us the legitimate drama well and satisfactorily."

Mr. Hook's dates are a little confused, for Garrick had retired from the stage in 1776 and died in 1779, but presumably he means that his methods still dominated the theatre. Anyway, by and large, his picture was true. Mr. Hook believed in concentration of artistic effort, or centralisation of talent, and he was in all probability right. It seems certain today that the number of West End theatres will continue to decline until the few that remain will represent only the very pick of the best and thereby succeed. Be that as it may, it is clear from Hook's lamentation that the cry of the decline of the theatre is no new thing. It is, in fact, as old as the theatre itself.

But to return to the St. James's. After Hooper's departure, a French company took it for a few weeks; then it remained closed from the end of July until the 5th November, 1839. Few theatres opened in the summer in those days. On Guy Fawkes night it reopened, this time with a blaze of vocal fireworks exploded by that ebullient Guy Fawkes of the theatre, Alfred Bunn himself. Mr. Bunn could always be relied upon for sensation. He was for ever dealing in theatrical explosions. He was a focal point for uproar, dissension and excitement of all kinds. And he was, with it all, a remarkable man.

Actor, stage-manager, impresario and poet (which last he prized most and deserved the least), he was perhaps the most derided man of his day. At one period he controlled both Drury Lane and Covent Garden and had no compunction about making his players run from one place to the other on a joint contract at the lowest possible terms. Always in the public eye and exulting in it, he was a stern taskmaster and a tough personality. He coped with the fiery Edmund Kean, fell to fisticuffs with the great Macready, and, among many other dubious achievements, reduced both his famous theatres to the status of booths. Yet, as though in mitigation of his vulgarity, he brought Malibran to this country, he engaged the inimitable Taglioni to dance on the nights when Malibran was not singing, and he inspired Balfe, the composer, to his greatest heights. He also wrote the libretto to *The Bohemian Girl*, to the score of that same Balfe, a feat in which, it must be said to his credit, he took more pride than in all his other exploits.

Under the name of "Dolphin", Thackeray immortalised Bunn in *Pendennis*, where he is described as "a tall, portly gentleman with hooked nose and a profusion of curling brown hair and whiskers. His coat was covered with the richest frog-braiding and velvet. He had under-waistcoats, many splendid rings, and jewelled pins and neck-chains." Bunn was the typical theatrical manager, a supreme optimist and a supreme opportunist. He was in and out of the bankruptcy courts but never unable to raise money. He was always being assailed, and always able to return better than he received. His numerous wars and vendettas—often against the Press—kept his name unfailingly in the news. He was game for any venture, and though often almost submerged in failure always bobbed up again.

To a fellow of such unlimited vigour the unlucky St. James's presented no problem at all. He was absolutely certain that he—the sole transcendent genius of the theatrical world—could make it go. So he took it over, and by way of announcement no doubt issued one of those grandiloquent manifestos he so loved to write, calling upon the world to witness the marvels he was about to release. As opera lay nearer to his heart than anything else, he gathered together an impeccable company of prodigious singers, and in quick succession presented *Guy Mannering*, *Masaniello*, *The Waterman*, and *The Beggars' Opera*. Alas, he was to learn that if the world had declined to come and hear Braham, who had often scintillated in some of those pieces himself, it would not inconvenience itself to support Bunn. After six weeks of disastrous business he retreated. But Bunn was neither defeated nor dejected. He calmly closed his theatre and waited for a golden moment to arrive. Within six months a gleam of hope appeared. The gleam grew, and finally compounded itself in the marriage of Albert and Victoria, the most jubilant royal occasion of the century.

London was packed, gaiety reigned, and all things German were the vogue. Bunn, inveterate opportunist, cashed in. In compliment to the Crown, he rechristened the theatre The Prince's, putting on a series of German plays and operas with German players and singers. He placed Herr Schumann, director of grand opera at Mayence, in titular command, but doubtless ruled the roost himself. Bunn could at no time stomach any divided authority. For a time he basked in a blaze of success. But this had little to do with the imported talent, for contemporary criticism condemned it well and truly, saying it was beneath contempt, except in one or two isolated cases. Still, the Teutonic craze brought the people in, and Bunn thought he had done the trick. His path was not all roses, for at Drury Lane, which he also controlled, he got stuck in a tangle of weeds. As a result he was again made bankrupt and his failure compelled him to close the St. James's (or, as he called it, The Prince's). But he had kept the place going to good business for some months at least. Herr Schumann, on his departure for Germany, said he was confident that he had laid the foundation of a permanent German opera in England, and that he would return the following year, this, his experimental season, having proved it would be worth his while to bring over the élite of German singers.

Those who had taken part in the experiment were certainly not élite. *The Era* said of their performance in *Euryanthe*:

> "Herr Poeck sang with great spirit and power, Schmerzer was good in some parts; but the ladies, whom out of gallantry we ought to praise, can only claim it on that head. If they had but tolerable execution, and could but sing tolerably in tune, we would willingly excuse their badness of school, for we should at least hear the composer without being offended; but really (and the ladies must pardon us for saying so) such singers as Madame Fischer Schwarzbock and Madame Michaeleis are sufficient to destroy the effect of any opera, however fine it may be."

So Herr Schumann's hope was never realised.

Despite these frequent and costly disasters, even more opera was offered, this time by Morris Barnett, whose effort was short-lived. He staged a new opera by Frank Romer, called *Fridolin*, in November 1840 and closed before Christmas. Now an Englishman came to the rescue. His name was Mitchell and he was the king of the ticket agencies. His firm, as Ashton and Mitchell, flourished for years and always looked after the theatre-going of the Royal Family. It is now part of the famous agency called Theatre Tickets and Messengers Ltd., with Lord Gifford in command, and still retains its royal prerogative.

Excitement over the royal wedding having now abated, Mr.

Mitchell wisely jettisoned the temporary title, The Prince's, and resumed the original name. He believed it possible to establish a French Theatre in London, and thought the St. James's eminently suitable, as a number of French companies had already appeared there. He began his experiment in 1841 and remained in possession for twelve years. Mitchell presented the best that France could offer, both in opera and plays. There London saw Mlles Plessis, Déjazet, Messieurs Perlet, Lemaître, Clarisse, Bouffé and Leroy, our own Vestris, and Mlle Judith too. There also Rachel the Great sparkled and thrilled in such plays as *Phèdre*, *Roxane*, *Polyeucte*, *Adrienne Lecouvreur*, *Andromaque*, *Marie Stuart* and *Mademoiselle de Belle Isle*.

Rachel is one of the outstanding names in the St. James's story, despite the fact that when she came there she was, from the Society point of view, under a cloud. Certain details of her private life had come to light and she was immediately ostracised. The strict respectability of the Victorian way of life, of which the Queen herself was the pattern, had already replaced the looseness of Regency times and the easiness of William IV's reign. So, except in the eyes of ordinary playgoers, Rachel's sun had set when she appeared at the St. James's. Yet, on her first appearance at Her Majesty's—the old theatre, not the present one on the same site—the aristocracy had almost worshipped her. The Duchess of Kent, mother of Queen Victoria, even went backstage to see her, and when the actress complained of feeling cold while standing in the wings, Her Royal Highness wrapped her own beautiful shawl around her. The Queen herself, enchanted by her performance, presented her with a diamond bracelet inscribed "Victoria R à Rachel." When the actress fell ill and bulletins were issued at frequent intervals, her condition occasioned anxiety, and on her return to the stage the Queen and her mother attended to see her perform. All that had gone by now, but still the public—the "great unwashed"—supported her.

The frequent French invasions, which appear to have pleased the ordinary playgoers (few of whom could speak French, and who probably went because it was the thing) aroused the ire of the theatrical profession who regarded these cross-Channel folk as poachers. When a distinguished company from the Théâtre Historique, Paris, came to Drury Lane, the leading London actors started a campaign against them. Charles Kean, Benjamin Webster, Charles Mathews, Harley, Buckstone and other top-liners led the protest, and only Macready championed the visitors. The public sided with their own and demanded protection from foreign competition—except at such times as Rachel played.

At Drury Lane the French company was hissed off the stage while endeavouring to perform *Monte Cristo*. Pamphlets demanding that the rights of British actors to the British stage should be upheld were showered on the audience and there was a pretty riot. This boded no good for the St. James's, where the "upper ten thousand" supported the French company and the common people stayed away. When Rachel performed, however, the position was reversed.

Mitchell struggled on bravely. He even brought over some German companies, despite Bunn's dismal experience, and they played Goethe's *Faust* in the original language, and even Shakespeare in German.

But the popularity of the Germans had long passed its peak. It was now 1852 and at last, after twelve years, which had witnessed a few purple patches but more failures, Mitchell gave up. He had lost a good deal of money and the theatre was no more popular than when he started. During his tenancy Mitchell had done a bit of sub-letting, and in 1851 the great Barnum had brought in a couple of juvenile prodigies from America, Kate and Ellen Bateman, aged six and eight respectively. Their scenes from *Richard III* amazed the critics. George Henry Lewes, one of the most prominent of the time, offered his meed of praise but predicted that their talent would perish with their youth. He was wrong, for Kate Bateman became a magnificent actress.

In 1854 Mrs. Seymour, in whose powers Charles Reade had great faith, became St. James's actress-manageress. She produced a play called *The King's Rival*, in which he collaborated with Tom Taylor. In the cast were George Vanderhoff and a young comedian, J. L. Toole. Toole was already known in the provinces but had made only one fleeting appearance in London, at the Haymarket. This was now his real London début. He put himself over to great applause, and in the next production, a burlesque-burletta entitled *The Spanish Dancers*, he consolidated the good opinion. Lydia Thompson, who appeared with him, danced her way into London's heart in a little piece called *Magic Toys*. But the bad luck continued. A bright but vain experiment—at that time—was the production of *Alcestis*, adapted by Henry Spicer from a French version by Hippolyte Lucas. This brought before the London public Miss Vanderhoff and an actor named Barry Sullivan, who had already made a big hit at the Haymarket. Already in the front rank, he was destined for real greatness. But not even this magnificent combination could bring support to the St. James's. Despite two lighter afterpieces—*Abou Hassan* and *The Miller and his Men*, the *Alcestis* perished after a few nights.

For four years the theatre languished, opened only for odd periods with scratch companies, and at times by amateurs. In June 1858 came Ristori, the wonderful Italian actress, who took the place for a short season and no doubt got it cheaply. She played in *Phèdre*, *La Locandiera*, *Maria Stuarda*, *Adrienne Lecouvreur*, and *Elizabetta*, a repertoire almost exactly similar to that of Rachel, and also to Sarah Bernhardt, who was to come later.

Then came a real man of the theatre, in the person of F. B. Chatterton, as good a manager and as honest a man as ever staged a play. In his time he ran the Adelphi and many other theatres, and in the end also Drury Lane, which, however, defeated him despite his splendid record. On giving up management there he pronounced his famous dictum: "Shakespeare spells ruin and Byron, bankruptcy." Really, it was pantomime which defeated him, due to the almost complete domination of the cast by the Vokes family—clever enough, but the public had tired of them—and poor Chatterton had to close down in the middle of a week because the treasury was empty. On taking over the St. James's he tried to make it a popular house, with boxes (i.e. seats in boxes) at 3/- and 2/-; pit, 1/-; gallery, 6d. He opened on 1st October, 1858, with a fairy spectacle called *The Swan and Edgar*—a title with a very different significance today. In it he had Lydia Thompson, who made a big success as Cygnetta, and the spectacle more than paid its way. But not even Chatterton's verve and experience could really do the trick.

In June, 1859, an attempt was made to connect the name of Braham once again with the theatre by means of an English opera entitled *Raymond and Agnes*, by Edward Loder, staged under the management of Augustus Braham, son of John, the founder, and having in the cast Hamilton Braham, another son. But the young Brahams were not more fortunate than their father. The opera expired ingloriously on its sixth performance. The critics praised the music but no more was ever heard of it. Chatterton carried gallantly on, but lost money steadily. In 1860 he gave up, much lighter in pocket.

The hoodoo seemed unbreakable. But, incredible as it may seem, there were still men ready to take a chance. One such was Alfred Wigan, who has already entered the story. He was now an established favourite and a really grand actor. He ventured into management on 29th October, 1860, with a play called *Up at the Hills*, by Tom Taylor, an experienced and popular playwright. The cast included Kate Terry, Miss Herbert, and Wigan himself. It was a near-flop. Then Wigan put on *A Scrap of Paper* (an adaptation of Sardou's *Pattes des Mouches*, by Palgrave Simpson), combined with a farce, *Done on Both Sides*, starring G. Vining, J. Robins and Mr. and Mrs. F. Matthews, and it really proved a winner. At this point Wigan, like a wise man, got out, and George Vining, who had been in that farce, took over. He opened on Boxing Night, 1861, with *A Wonderful Woman*, by Charles Dance. She did not seem so wonderful at the St. James's. But *Self Made*, which Vining wrote himself, did better. He filled the bill again in March, 1862, with *Friends or Foes*, adapted from Sardou's *Nos Intimes*, by Horace Wigan. Vining himself was in the cast, and with him were Miss Herbert, Mrs. Frank Matthews and W. H. Stephens.

If, so far, the St. James's had not itself been a success, it was a place in which actors had climbed the ladder of fame. Wigan, during his early appearances there, had received favourable notice and, during his own brief tenancy, had set the seal upon his reputation by his splendid performances in *The Isle of St. Tropez* and *The Poor Nobleman*. Toole had made a hit there, as had Lydia Thompson. So did another young lady: her name was Kate Terry, elder sister of Ellen. Kate stepped into the lead in *Friends or Foes* at a moment's notice when Miss Herbert was suddenly taken ill, and so magnificently did she perform that Tom Taylor, who was present, immediately engaged her as his leading lady at the Olympic Theatre. *Friends or Foes* was Vining's final production. He had done pretty well and was taking no further risks. He moved on to a brilliant career elsewhere, notably at the old Princess's, in Oxford Street.

Frank Matthews, who had been playing for Vining, next took over the helm. He was in his day the best of performers in old men's parts and was well known at the St. James's. Louisa Herbert remained in the company with him and became one of the great names in the St. James's. Matthews produced to indifferent business for some months, but was soon to present his public with a dazzling draw. His production of *Faint Heart Never Won Fair Lady*, by Planché, and *Golden Hair the*

Good, by H. J. Byron, occasioned no excitement. Nor was there any frenzy over F. C. Burnand's *La Carte de Visite*, although the company was first rate, including Pattie Josephs, Arthur Stirling, Miss Herbert, and Frank Matthews himself. *The Dark Cloud*—an ominous title—run in conjunction with a play prophetically called *The Merry Widow*, brought a fair meed of financial approval. Then Matthews threw them a bombshell. He announced that on 28th February, 1863, he would present a stage version of *Lady Audley's Secret*, Miss Braddon's amazing best-seller.

That really set the town agog, for this was the most talked-of novel of its day, perhaps of any day up to that time. It was a "must". Not to be familiar with *Lady Audley's Secret* was to invite social ostracism as a person gravely lacking in culture. Now George Roberts had dramatised it and Frank Matthews was to play Luke Marks. All London looked forward to a stupendous thrill. Arthur Stirling was to be Robert Audley—a part which Irving played afterwards—and Miss Herbert would play Lady Audley.

The first night was an event. Circle and stalls were packed with celebrities and the humbler people thronged the pit and gallery, all wildly excited. Would the play live up to the success of the book? As the grim story unfolded none was left in doubt. The cast was on top of its form and Miss Herbert made an enormous hit. Even the critics raved. Said *The Times*, among a lot more: "There is no doubt that a great success has been achieved and that it has been fairly earned by all persons concerned in both the production and performance of the work." Henry Morley wrote:

> "It is only in two acts; and the putting of the superfluous husband into the well follows so closely on the bigamy, the glow of arson, again, so closely on the stain of murder, and the interesting heroine goes mad so immediately, with the glow of the house she has burnt yet on her face, and the man she has burnt in it dying on a stretcher by her side, that the audience has a pudding all plums."

It was just the kind of gory stuff Victorian playgoers wanted. They relished every spark of villainy, gasped at every spot of blood. All classes flocked to see the book they loved brought to life on the stage. At last someone had picked a certain winner. It ran for 105 nights, did *Lady Audley's Secret*, a long run then and a record for the St. James's Theatre.

CHAPTER 4

Bright Intervals and Deep Depressions

IT may surprise some young people to learn that the Victorians were so completely captivated by that lurid melodrama, *Lady Audley's Secret,* both in novel and book form. But the Victorians were not the stuffy, sentimental, narrow-minded folk they are often said to have been. While they insisted on a certain standard of refinement they did not turn up their noses at a spot of highly-coloured sensation, virile and venturesome, and one in which all the arts found generous patronage. Living in a spacious era they employed their leisure in the dissemination of learning and the cultivation of good taste. Their choice of literature and pictures may nowadays be derided, but they would—and with good reason—have laughed uproariously at much of what now passes for great painting, sculpture and literature. They were industrious people with orderly minds and they laid great store on discipline. They may have been conventional, but those conventions were really the formal expression of good behaviour. Essentially honest in their dealings, they expected value for their money, and money was plentiful with the middle and upper classes. Their preference in art was for things which looked like what they represented. They had little use for the devious and the super-subtle. Straightforward folk, they prided themselves on being the subjects of the greatest country in the world, as, indeed, they were.

In the theatre, they did not look for naturalism. What they wanted was to be taken out of the everyday world. They did not mind coincidences so long as the story thrilled. They regarded the theatre as an unreal place, a place where they could chase illusion. When the theatre deals in illusion, it succeeds. When it deals in realities, it fails. *Lady Audley's Secret* had all the elements of illusion, and yet retained sufficient reality to glorify the conventions and ethics in which the people believed. The Victorians loved a lord and were always titillated by a title, and Miss Braddon knew it. That is why she made her murderous, adulterous "heroine" a titled lady: "Lady Audley". Miss Braddon exploited to its full the dramatic law of contrast. Had her central figure been a woman of the middle class, she would have attracted little attention. Had she been of the lower class, she would have attracted none. But as "Lady Audley" she compelled attention.

It is probable that few people today have either read *Lady Audley's Secret* or seen it on the stage, although it was revived not long since. In either case, they would find it very "old-fashioned". The stage conventions of the Victorian era are far removed from those of today. But the story is there all the same, and it moves forward with a relentless sweep. In those days people wrote books and plays which relied on the plot or story. They did not delve into the often very shallow depths of minds and feelings. They wanted action, and the state of mind could be excitingly expressed that way. They had no sympathy with the modern "crazy, mixed-up kid". They had their own way of dealing with that sort of thing, and it rarely failed to work.

One of the stage conventions then completely accepted was the "aside". That is nowadays discarded—the telephone takes its place. Often the Victorian—and Edwardian—plays opened with a conversation between a couple of servants—frequently the butler and the parlourmaid—who put the audience in possession of the plot and the qualities of the characters. Nowadays a psychiatrist is used—but the result is the same. No Victorian minded the "aside": it was expected. And the players knew how to deliver it. Some of the best of Shakespeare is found in his "asides", in fact, the soliloquies are nothing else.

As an example of the "aside", take one from *Lady Audley's Secret.* It would embarrass a modern actress, she would feel archaic and out of place in speaking it, and at once become imbued with the spirit of burlesque. But Miss Herbert found no difficulty at all. Lady Audley had been a poor governess, but she had married the father of her pupil, a baronet of great wealth who lived in a stately home. She had omitted to mention that she was already the wife of George Talboys, who, she hoped, believed her dead, and whom she intensely hoped was dead. But of course he was not, and so her initial crime of bigamy led to all sorts of complications. And here is an "aside" which led into a big scene.

LADY AUDLEY (*throwing off her levity and reflecting*): It must be my aim to stand well with this young man; he is my husband's favourite, I know. I manage Sir Michael as I like, and if his nephew gains too firm a hold upon him, he may prove a dangerous rival in my path. I live now for ambition and interest, to mould the world and its votaries to my own end. Once I was fool enough to wed for love. Now I have married for wealth. What a change from the wife of George Talboys to the wife of Sir Michael Audley! My fool of a first husband thinks me dead. Oh, excellent scheme, oh cunning device, how well you have served me. (GEORGE TALBOYS *enters at back and comes down silently to her side.*) Where can he be now? Still in India, no doubt. He is mourning my death perhaps—ha, ha! Why, I have only just begun to live, to taste the sweets of wealth and power. If I am dead to George Talboys, he is dead to me. Yes, I am well rid of him, and on this earth we meet no more.

GEORGE (*touching her on the shoulder*): Yes—we do!

Now, that scene and that "aside" held the Victorian playgoers spellbound. When they saw that first husband enter they were almost giddy with suspense and with bated breath they waited for him to reveal himself. And when he said: "Yes, we do!" they gasped in excitement. One can almost hear them gasping: "Ah, now what?" And a scene that does that is real theatre, no matter what the means employed. The absolute "theatricality" of the situation did not disturb them. They came to the theatre to be "theatricated", and they were! They asked for strong, unrepressed acting, with every word audible, and no obvious "throwing away of lines" (although those old actors knew all about that, too, and exactly where to throw them). They got that also, and in full measure, in *Lady Audley's Secret*. It did indeed "pull them out of the plush".

The Victorians were not so concerned with scenery and what is now called décor. But these things were evidently right up to the standard they expected in *Lady Audley's Secret*, for *The Times* critic mentions them: "People liked the play, liked the acting, liked the scenery and were most anxious to demonstrate their feelings," he said. Calls were taken in those days at the end of each act and players gained thunderous applause for strongly played scenes when they made their exits. Today there are no "act calls"—applause is kept until the end.

DAME MADGE KENDAL

FAMOUS TRIPLE PARTNERSHIP

W. H. KENDAL

SIR JOHN HARE
As Sir John Vesey in *Money*, at the Royal Command Performance, Drury Lane, 1911

LADY ALEXANDER

MARION TERRY

ADA CAVENDISH

Yet a popular actor or actress who did not get a "reception" on his or her first entrance would be most upset. That seems just as great an anomaly as an actor taking a "call" straight after playing a good death scene. But, after all, he is there at the final curtain. Still, other times, other manners. The only person who got no call or even mention was what would now be called the producer or director. Nowadays he overshadows the players, who are all too often his puppets.

So important is *Lady Audley's Secret*, not only in the story of the St. James's but the history of the drama in general, that the full programme may not come amiss:

Sir Michael Audley ....Mr. Simpson.
Robert Audley ....Mr. Arthur Stirling.
George Talboys......................Mr. Gaston Murray.
Luke Marks ....Mr. Frank Matthews.
Slip ....Miss Lavenu.
Servants............................Mr. Norman and Mr. Wilson.
First Countryman ....Mr. Bush.
Second Countryman ....Mr. Taylor.
Lady Audley.........................Miss Herbert.
Alice Audley.........................Miss Adeline Cottrell.
Phoebe ....Miss Ada Dyas.
(Servants, Countrymen, Countrywomen, etc.)

It was practically an all-star cast. Frank Matthews always did things well. Henry Morley, the critic, wrote *à propos* of the success of *Lady Audley's Secret*:

"Mr. Matthews produced the best plays he could get of a creditable sort, and though they were not bad and were acted well, I saw one evening his curtain rise to an audience of five in the stalls, seven in the dress circle and thirty in the pit. He is now acting, to crowded houses, *Lady Audley's Secret* and a burlesque of Mr. Boucicault's *Effie Deans*."

So much for business at the St. James's until what the Victorians considered "the goods" came along.

When the autumn of 1863 arrived Matthews presented, amongst other plays, *Great Sensation Trial*, by William Brough, *Turning the*

Tables, The Little Sentinel, Perdita, or the Royal Milkmaid. But he also put on *Lady Audley* as often as possible—nearly always followed by the burlesque of *Effie Deans*, both by way of contrast and for good measure.

Despite his triumph with *Lady Audley*, due to the indifferent attraction of other plays, Frank Matthews did not find the St. James's profitable. At the end of the season he relinquished the management and Benjamin Webster stepped in. Webster had done wonders at the Haymarket and the Adelphi, but the St. James's beat him, too. Yet he did a very good best. In his company were Mr. and Mrs. Charles Mathews, Frank Matthews and his wife, Mrs. Stirling—a star of first rank, Fanny Josephs—another star, Henry J. Ashley—a popular actor who had made his début in *Up at the Hills* at the St. James's under Wigan and had never looked back, H. J. Montague—a first-class player, and also Miss Herbert. A better company could have been found nowhere in London. Yet no good came of it.

Plays in which Charles Mathews had won fame were revived but there was no response. On 11th May, 1864, Webster staged *The Fox Chase*, a most amusing play by Dion Boucicault. It failed and was followed on 9th July by a burlesque of *Faust*, by F. C. Burnand, with Charles Mathews and his wife playing the leading roles. That was no good either. Webster tried frequent changes of the bill, but drew blank every time. Yet he had never failed elsewhere. As a last throw he presented a new comedy called *Sybilla, or Step by Step*, by Palgrave Simpson. He had Mr. and Mrs. Charles Mathews and Mr. and Mrs. Frank Matthews—with only a "t's" difference between them in art and popularity—in the leading parts. He failed again, then gave up the unequal battle.

This time, there was no waiting for a new manager—only it happened to be, for the third time, a manageress. Miss Herbert herself took command. Now, one of the drawbacks to the position of the St. James's Theatre which John Braham had overlooked was that it lay in the heart of an essentially masculine district. True, it was residential and many ladies lived there, but the whole atmosphere of the locality was male. It was the centre of Clubland, and in those days no woman was ever allowed in a man's club. Nor were there any shops likely to attract ladies to King Street, and the passers-by were nearly all men. And men are not the mainstay of the theatre—it's the ladies who take the men along. Now here, in 1866, a woman took charge. Two others had preceded her in that role some years earlier, Mrs. Seymour and Madame Ristori—the first unsuccessful, the latter succeeding with a few special performances. Miss Herbert hoped to be a resident of long tenancy. Women go to see women, she mused, if only to exercise their critical faculties. London had flocked, male and female alike, to see her in *Lady Audley's Secret*. She concluded, with good reason, that she had more than a fighting chance.

Louisa Herbert was not only a first-rate actress but a very beautiful woman, and the glory of the pre-Raphaelite group. She had made her stage début at the Royal Strand Theatre (the Aldwych tube station stands on its site today) in September, 1854, as Maria Darling in a farce called *A Roland for an Oliver*, when she was twenty-two years old. She had done a lot of useful work but her reputation rested on her numerous successes at the St. James's. As has already been chronicled, she was there with Wigan and with Frank Matthews, and there she made her first big hit, as leading lady in *The Merry Widow*. There, too, she had added to her laurels in *Lady Audley's Secret*. What more reasonable than to assume she could bring success to the house that had brought success to her?

She surrounded herself with a good company, which included Walter Lacy and her old friends and managers Mr. and Mrs. Frank Matthews, and Miss Dyas. There was also a newcomer—a man who had made only one appearance in London before, and that at the Princess's Theatre in Oxford Street. His reputation lay in the provinces, especially in Edinburgh and Manchester, and it was from the latter city that he came to the St. James's, where he was to endear himself to London audiences. So, once again, the unlucky theatre showered luck upon its players. That man's name was Henry Irving.

On Saturday, 6th October, when Miss Herbert opened, Irving played Doricourt in *The Belle's Stratagem*, opposite her. He scored an instant success. *The Athenaeum* declared: "His mad scenes were truthfully conceived and most subtly executed." He had arrived. It had taken him ten years of hard, uphill work, but he had done it. Today, of course, success is expected at once, without long experience, and sometimes even without a modest apprenticeship. But although a beginner may once in a while score an initial success, without the real foundation of experience and knowledge, that is easily where it may stop. It was by means of his hard-won knowledge of his craft that Irving succeeded as Doricourt at the St. James's. He had been engaged not only as actor but as stage-manager too, though his salary was modest enough.

Miss Herbert had intended to open her season with a production of *The Two Lives of Mary Leigh*, under the title *Hunted Down*. Irving was to play Rawdon Scudamore, a gambler and villain. He had created this part in Manchester, which was the reason Boucicault, the author, had recommended him to Miss Herbert. But Doricourt was new to him. He had scant time to learn and study it, especially with his stage-managerial duties thrown in. Running his mind over the distinguished actors who had played it before, he felt distinctly nervous of trying it. The author had conceived this character as a polished man of the late eighteenth-century world, who returns home to this country and finds the women insipid compared with the coy charmers of the Continent. The part called for a really exquisite light comedian. But Irving always brought something entirely his own to the delineation of a character. He decided that the man he had to portray was not really alive until the scene in which he feigns madness. Only then did his real character appear.

Irving has recorded his feelings anent his first performance:

> "I had never played the part before and I felt it did not suit me: I felt that this was the opinion of the audience soon after the play began. The house appeared to be indifferent, and I believed that failure was conclusively stamped upon my work, when, suddenly, upon my exit after the mad scene, I was startled by a burst of applause, and so great was the enthusiasm of the audience, that I was compelled to reappear upon the scene, a somewhat unusual thing except upon the operatic stage."

As contemporary records show, Irving understates his impact on the audience. They were wild with enthusiasm and even demanded an encore—to which, wisely, Irving did not accede. Had he done so, he would not have lacked precedent, for Quin, the great tragedian, and Alexander Pope, another distinguished tragedian, both had similar ovations, and both obliged with the demanded encore. But that was considerably before Irving's time. What he had thought was indifference was really the contrast between the provincial audiences to which he was accustomed and the less demonstrative West End houses. But even they could at times be demonstrative, as they proved that evening.

The Press were eulogistic. *The Morning Post* said: "In the difficult scene in the third act, in which he affects insanity, he almost tempted the audience to the genuine lunacy of encoring his freak of mock madness." *The Athenaeum* declared: "Mr. H. Irving was the 'fine gentleman' in Doricourt; but he was more, for his mad scenes were truthfully conceived and most subtly executed."

Miss Herbert registered a big success as Letitia Hardy. Others in the cast were Walter Lacy, Mr. and Mrs. Frank Matthews, Mr. Gaston Murray and Miss Carlotta Addison, who that night made her début and lived to delight audiences almost until the First World War.

Playing Doricourt at night, Irving had by day to rehearse *Hunted Down*, and also to produce the one-act plays which always formed part of the bill and were frequently changed. One of these minor items was *Dulcamara, or A Little Duck with a Big Quack*, written by a stage-struck officer in the Highland Militia. A barrister as well, he made up for his lack of briefs by contributing comic poems to *Fun*, a very lively rival of *Punch*, and illustrating them himself. His name was W. S. Gilbert. Laurence Irving, in his splendid work on his famous grandfather, chronicles the fact that Gilbert was grateful for the hints he received on stage-management from Irving, and tells how they would talk things over in Gilbert's chambers after rehearsals.

Miss Herbert was now ready to put on *Hunted Down*. In Manchester it had been called *The Two Lives of Mary Leigh*, but Boucicault had wisely altered the title. It was produced on 5th November, 1866, before a distinguished audience, art and literature being strongly represented and the theatre full. It looked as though Miss Herbert had solved the problem of the St. James's.

The Manchester press had not been enthusiastic about this play. It now remained to see what London thought of it. Irving had few qualms. He knew all about this part—Rawdon Scudamore—and had succeeded in it. Now he triumphed again. He received a curtain call after the first act, and at the end the walls rang with an ovation seldom, if ever, heard there before, except perhaps for *Lady Audley* and Braham's solitary concert.

As she left her box George Eliot said to G. H. Lewes: "What do you think of him?" Replied Lewes: "In twenty years he will be at the head of the English stage." "He is there already, I think," said the great novelist.

After the performance, W. S. Gilbert took Irving, his new-found friend, to the Arundel Club in Salisbury Street, a meeting-place for the lions of art and letters. Hearty congratulations greeted him all round. He was introduced to Schérer, the leading French critic, who was fulsome in his praise. He said to Irving: "You may call yourself a son of Somerset, but your temperament and genius, like other things about you, are those of a Celt. You will yet introduce to the stage a churchman such as your Glastonbury reared." Those words are recorded by Laurence Irving. And Sir Henry did as foretold when, many years later, he played Becket to rapturous applause.

A correspondent of the present writer, Mrs. Katherine Cross, told him that she was present in the dressing-room of Suzanne Avril, in Paris, when several critics were discussing actors and actresses from Salvini to Réjane. Oppenheim, the critic of *Figaro*, said: "The greatest I've ever seen in my life was Henry Irving. He was marvellous." There was at once an outcry in favour of Guitry, of Coquelin ainé, but Oppenheim said: "No, no! Admittedly, they were all great artistes, but they didn't hold a candle to Irving. What force, what magnetism, and at the same time what sympathy! He didn't hold the stage, he dominated it. Irving was not only a great actor but a great man, of the Napoleonic type."

The Press raved about his performance as Scudamore. They also favoured the play, but with reservations. *The Athenaeum* said:

> "We have but four persons, and of these one lady has two husbands and one husband two wives. Of this perplexity the plot is woven, and it rises to an obvious state of distress and emotion in which the two wives share in equal proportions, thus dividing the interest between them . . . The piece is so delicately written and otherwise so elegantly constructed, that for finish and effect it must take rank with the best of Mr. Boucicault's dramas. The four persons who bear the weight of the action are John Leigh, a Royal Academician (Mr. Walter Lacy); Mary Leigh, his wife (Miss Herbert); Rawdon Scudamore, a gambler (Mr. Henry Irving); and Clara, his lawful wife (Miss Ada Dyas)."

Even John Oxenford praised Irving this time—he had been critical of his Doricourt—saying that the part: "completely serves the purpose of displaying the talent of Mr. Irving, whose ability of depicting the prevalence of the most malignant feelings merely by dint of facial expression, is very remarkable." Another critic, William A'Beckett, said, many years afterwards, that although he had forgotten most of the play: "I can see them standing before me even now—Henry Irving as the most admirable stage villain, cool, calm and implacable—and Ada Dyas as his suffering wife." Charles Dickens was enthusiastic, emphasising the singular power of the performance. Miss Herbert and the whole cast scored heavily. Yet the play came off on 9th February, although that was a pretty good run then.

Miss Herbert next revived *The Road to Ruin*, but did not play in it as she was ill. Irving scored as Harry Dornton. And in March came *A Rapid Thaw*, by T. W. Robertson, adapted from the French. It lived up to its name and disappeared quickly. Irving played a very stagey Irishman. Miss Herbert then played Lady Teazle in a revival of *The School for Scandal*. Irving was cast for Joseph Surface and, of course, had his own ideas. Instead of an obvious and lurking villain, he made Joseph the polished, plausible hypocrite the stage knows today. Some sections of the Press attacked him for this, but Henry Morley upheld him and also Miss Herbert's somewhat unconventional Lady Teazle. A revival of *Robert Macaire* followed, with Irving romping home in the name part.

Then Miss Herbert produced one of her major pieces, a play called *Idalia*, adapted by George Roberts from Ouida's novel of the same name. Much care was lavished on the production and a tank of real water was introduced—which overflowed on the opening night, to the despair of the actors and the unbounded delight of the audience. The play achieved a fair success and Miss Herbert was much acclaimed. Irving, as a villainous Italian count, got good notices; so did a new young actor, who had just joined the company and who shared Irving's dressing-room. His name was Charles Wyndham. Miss Herbert also revived *Lady Audley*, with Irving as Robert Audley, but by now the strain was beginning to tell.

During her chequered tenancy, Miss Herbert occasionally sub-let the theatre while she went on tour. One such let was to an American comedian, John S. Clarke. Born in Baltimore, Maryland, in 1834, he was of English blood on his mother's side and spoke with no American accent. He had been very successful in the land of his birth and now repeated his success in the land of his ancestors. He staged a lively little play called *The Widow Hunt*, which drew quite creditable houses. Originally produced here as *Everybody's Friend*, J. B. Buckstone had made a big success in it as Major Wellington de Boots. This success John S. Clarke duplicated, playing it in his own much broader way. That was in October, 1867.

In April, 1868, Miss Herbert relinquished the management. She had done nobly and had earned widespread praise. She had kept the theatre open and had brought at least two young people, both destined for greatness, to the notice of the London playgoers—Henry Irving and Charles Wyndham. But the St. James's had lost her a lot of money.

CHAPTER 5

No Luck About the House

AFTER Miss Herbert's final departure the St. James's languished for some months. Then it reopened, on 22nd July, 1868, with Offenbach's *La Grande Duchesse de Gérolstein*, sung in French with no less a star than Madame Hortense Schneider playing the title part. This really fabulous woman was the talk of the world. A beautiful redhead, she counted amongst her victims men of every rank and position, right up to the apex of Royalty. The opera had been produced at the Variétés in Paris in 1867 at the height of the Great Exhibition there. Schneider was the idol of the piece and of Paris. She had dignity and she had impudence. One day an elegant lady drove in the smartest of carriages drawn by a pair of perfectly matched horses up to the gates of the Exhibition and wanted to drive in. The officials at the entrance, barring the way, explained with real French politeness that only Royalty had the privilege of driving round the Exhibition. "Make way, make way!" commanded the lovely lady, "I am the Grand Duchess of Gérolstein." The officials hastily let her through and Hortense Schneider drove round the Exhibition.

All the world went to that Exhibition, certainly all the élite and all the royalties, major and minor. It was a splendid excuse for a few days in Paris. They went not only to the Exhibition but to the Variétés as well, to see *La Grande Duchesse*—and Hortense Schneider. The Emperor of France, Napoleon III, was among the first to attend, and gave it his blessing.

Towards the end of May, a perfectly dressed young man arrived in Paris. He wanted to see the show but it was sold out. So, being a resourceful youth, he sent a note to Schneider herself—whom he had never met—asking if she could secure him a box. This threw the lady into what is now called a "flap", for that young man was none other than His Royal Highness the Prince of Wales (afterwards King Edward VII). Hortense dashed frantically from agency to agency, and at last found him a box, although not one of the best. His Royal Highness was delighted and duly appeared in the company of the Duke and Duchess of Manchester and the Marquis and Marquise de Gallifret. After the second act he went round to Hortense's dressing-room to pay his respects, accompanied by the Duke and the Marquis, but *not* by the ladies. He found a state of fine confusion. There was Hortense's dresser fussing about, her hairdresser performing his office, the leading comedian Couder—who played General Boum—a well-known journalist named Wolff, a couple of officers and the librettist Ludovic Halévy. And, of course, Hortense herself, who, almost bursting with pride, insisted on introducing the prince to everyone. H.R.H. was captivated and charmed. He did not want to return to his box but decorum insisted he must. However, he saw a great deal of Grand Duchess Hortense during his stay, and after returning to London with a pile of her photographs he displayed them to everyone on the slightest pretext.

Czar Alexander of Russia also attended the Exhibition. He too wanted to savour *La Grande Duchesse*, not to mention the bewitching lady. Taking no chances about a box, he telegraphed his Ambassador to secure one, and within three hours of arrival in Paris was comfortably ensconced watching the opera. It is said he fully expected to encounter some uncomplimentary references to himself and his country, but forgot all about that under the seductive influence of Hortense Schneider. His son Vladimir was likewise an instant captive. Their visit led to a quite spicy scandal in the Paris press. King William of Prussia turned up in Paris, too, and with him his son, the Crown Prince Frederick, and also a man named Bismarck and another called General von Moltke. But there is no record of any back-stage visits.

Hortense Schneider soon grew accustomed to royal homage. To her pink-papered dressing-room came the kings of Portugal, Bavaria and Sweden, and notabilities and eminences and high-and-mighties beyond reckoning. The success of the opera and of Schneider was colossal. And then *Gérolstein* came to London, and its Grand Duchess with it—to the St. James's Theatre, where so many French companies had come before.

Clubland was vastly excited. The ladies were not so pleased, yet anxious and eager to see this amazing woman. The opera opened to a glittering house, and H.R.H. the Prince of Wales led the applause. But something went wrong. The Lord Chamberlain, who controlled London's theatres then as he does now, began to make difficulties. He was, of course, most courteous and polite, but still, he made difficulties. The opera was closed and so was the theatre, after a very short run indeed. There were those who said they knew the reason. There had been considerable gossip about the Prince's interest in the prima donna, and perhaps the Lord Chamberlain had heard the salacious Paris chatter concerning the Czar and his son. The Royal families of Great Britain and Russia were related, on the distaff side. It was said that Queen Victoria had not been amused at the prospect of having the "Grand Duchess" as a near neighbour in the locality of St. James's, and that her lack of amusement had been shared by the Czarina . . . her near relation. The Lord Chamberlain was of course, and is, a Court official. Anyway, the "Grand Duchess" went away and the St. James's closed again.

It remained shut until Boxing Night, 1868, when Mlle de la Ferté from Paris opened it with a new comedy by Arthur A'Beckett, son of the author of the original production there, called *Glitter*. All that glittered was the cast, which included, as well as the French actress, Charles Coghlan, Arthur Williams—a ripe comedian, and Gaston Murray.

The St. James's was "dark" again until October, 1869. Then another actress-manageress made a bid. She was Mrs. John Wood, and hers was a name that almost commanded good fortune. Mrs. John Wood was a daughter of the theatre. Her mother, Mrs. Henry Vining, had been a well-known actress, especially at the old Surrey Theatre. Her father, too, was a celebrated actor and manager. She herself first appeared at Southampton and then went to America where she achieved both fame and fortune. Back in England, she played Miss Miggs in Watts Phillips's version of *Barnaby Rudge* at the old Princess's in Oxford Street. Then, having decided to go into management, on 16th October she reopened the St. James's with a revival of *She Stoops to Conquer*. She mounted the production beautifully. In the cast were Lionel Brough, William Farren, John Clayton, Henry Marston, Mrs. Herman Vezin, Lydia Foote and herself. None could wish for better. Goldsmith's classic pleased the public and ran for well over 100 performances. During the run she added a further attraction —a burlesque entitled *La Belle Sauvage*, in which she played Pocahontas.

She had previously tried it out at the Princess's. The two plays really packed the St. James's and once again it looked as if the luck had turned. As she occasionally took leave to play at other London theatres, it is to be assumed she needed the fees to assist the St. James's exchequer. On Monday, 20th June, 1870, she revived *Paul Pry*, playing Phoebe, and lifted the funds a little with that too.

One of Mrs. Wood's most important productions was *Fernande*, adapted by Sutherland Edwards from Sardou's play. In this Fanny Brough made her London début in the title role. One of the cleverest of a highly talented family, she will be remembered by many as a magnificent actress. She was a wonderful comedienne, and, with the exception of her uncle Lionel, the most brilliant of that remarkable family, making an abiding impression on all who saw her. A complete mistress of her art, she found no difficulty in playing in large theatres—as some players seem to do today. One of her outstanding successes was in *The Whip*, at Drury Lane. She was clear-cut and incisive, her diction a joy, her voice properly controlled and her timing perfect. Fanny Brough could really create a part. Give her comedy and she gave you delight. Large theatre or small, it made no difference—she knew how to expand and contract. She stood high in her profession, even among the giants of her time.

She appeared at the St. James's on 15th October, 1870. In the play were W. Farren, Gaston Murray, Lionel Brough—a superb performer in straight plays or light opera and one of the finest of all Shakespearean clowns, Mrs. Herman Vezin—who made a real hit as Clotilde, and Mrs. John Wood. Fanny Brough, in a sentimental part, played exceptionally well. But soon afterwards she took to comedy, to her own lasting benefit and the regalement of her public. One of Mrs. John Wood's missions in life, too, was to make audiences laugh, and she always did. *Fernande* was a real success.

In January, 1871, *War*, by T. W. Robertson, was produced, lasting only three weeks. Mrs. John Wood was not in it, but she came back to play Jenny Leatherlungs in a burlesque called *Jenny Lind at Last*. That helped matters along. She initiated many improvements at the St. James's, introducing, among other things, a programme in something like its modern form. It was useful, too, containing not only details of the evening's play but also theatrical gossip, news about forthcoming productions, and even short stories. Following *Jenny*, she put on *Poll and Partner Joe*, a burlesque by F. C. Burnand, and in the same bill, Planché's adaptation of *Michel Perrin*, in which William Farren and Fanny Brough played the leads. And in April, 1871, Mrs. John Wood staged *Anne Bracegirdle*, an English version of Fournier's play *Tiridate*, now called *An Actress by Daylight*.

Mrs. John Wood appeared to be doing so well that everyone thought she had broken the hoodoo, as she deserved to do. But the truth was that the hoodoo had nearly broken her. She left the luckless place and went to America to make some more money. She had nothing with which to reproach herself, for all her productions had been first class. London had taken her to its heart, and she also had launched two new people—Fanny Brough, and an actor called John Clayton, who was before long to do fine service to the stage.

After Mrs. Wood's departure, the St. James's stood empty for three years. Nobody wanted it. Money had been poured into it and had vanished like water spilled on the sands of the Sahara. People now began to call it, not the St. James's Theatre but Braham's Folly.

Then, in 1875, another woman had the pluck to try. She, too, was an actress of note. Her name was Marie Litton. Only four years before, she had taken over a derelict theatre which had been badly converted from a Nonconformist chapel and called first the New Chelsea and then The Belgravia. Miss Litton had further reconstructed it, made it into a charming theatre and named it the Royal Court. It had opened with a play by W. S. Gilbert called *Randal's Thumb*, with a company including Herman Vezin, Mrs. Stephens and our old St. James's friends, Mr. and Mrs. Frank Matthews. Gilbert had also contributed a big success there called *The Wedding March*, adapted from the French, in which the very large and corpulent actor, William Hill, made a success worthy of his size. It became almost a Gilbertian house, for his burlesque, *The Happy Land*, drew all London. It was a biting satire on the Government of the day, and eventually the Lord Chamberlain had to intervene, ordering the actors to "make up" a little less like the statesmen they burlesqued, which was of course magnificent publicity.

So when Miss Litton came to the St. James's she knew everything about management. She went in for farce, reviving a popular one, *Brighton*, which she had done profitably at the Court with Charles Wyndham (who, it will be remembered, had started at the St. James's). Also in the cast were W. J. Hill and Edgar Bruce. With *Brighton* was played *Conrad and Medora*, in which Henrietta Hodson, Rose Egan, W. J. Hill and Miss Litton herself appeared. Another new production was W. S. Gilbert's *Tom Cobb, or Fortune's Toy*, and in the same bill were *A Small Frock* and *Trying It On*, with Wyndham playing Walsingham Potts. Triple bills were popular then. Later, two other plays joined *Tom Cobb*. These were *The Dancing Barber* and *The Zoo*, with music by Arthur Sullivan. So already Gilbert and Sullivan had their names billed together, though not actually connected in the plays.

Miss Litton, a shrewd woman, had had enough by 1876 and made way for an old St. James's hand, Alfred Wigan, eager to try his luck again. He probably had a soft corner for the playhouse in which he had scored some personal successes, and, besides, he had a play in which he firmly believed. This was an adaptation by Herman Merivale and Palgrave Simpson of Dickens's *A Tale of Two Cities*, entitled *All for Her*. These two experienced authors had not attempted to dramatise the novel in the true sense of the word: they had simply condensed the story and altered the names of the characters. William Archer gave it a good notice: "An excellent play, the least faulty if not the best of all Mr. Merivale's works, romantic, without bombast." And he gave full marks to the young actor, John Clayton, who played the Sidney Carton part (called in this version Hugh Trevor). Clayton's forte was really light and farcical comedy, but such was his versatility that he made Trevor a lovable and intensely sympathetic character. The play had originally been produced at the Mirror Theatre in Holborn, long since vanished. Wigan ran it to good business, and then he too moved on—going while the going was good—and Mrs. John Wood, her coffers replenished, returned for another try.

Now she did rather a daring thing. She presented a play called *The Danischeffs* which, less than a year before, had been staged in London with Mme Fargueil and M. Marais in the leading roles. They played it in the original French and were pronounced perfect. But Mrs. Wood did not hesitate to challenge them. She had with her John Clayton, Charles Warner, Herman Vezin, Lydia Foote, and Fanny Addison, and all gained eulogistic notices. The play hit up more than 300 performances.

Charles Warner was one of the finest actors the English stage ever possessed. He played right on into modern times, and many will remember seeing him in *Leah Kleshna* at the New Theatre in 1905. His great claim to immortality was his performance of Coupeau in *Drink*. This was a masterpiece of acting, in which his evocation of horror terrified his audiences and held them enthralled. He also had a one-act sketch called *On the Telephone*, which he played alone, with just a telephone (a novelty then). His conversation revealed that his beloved wife at the other end was in mortal danger, and he powerless to help. It is hardly possible to describe his grip on his audiences. Warner was a charming and dignified man, beloved by all who knew him. An incident at his club indicates the esteem he enjoyed in his profession. It was a very exclusive club in the West End, membership of which was mostly theatrical, and which met under "old time" conditions—with a sanded or sawdust-covered floor, good old English fare, beer in tankards, and churchwarden pipes. Warner was, by popular acclaim, president of this club, and when he appeared there after his first *Drink* performance, meticulously dressed and in a velvet smoking-jacket, all the members rose as he entered and did not sit until he bade them do so. It was a personal tribute and he appreciated it deeply. He died in 1909 at the age of sixty-two, leaving a gap that has never been filled.

Herman Vezin also was a remarkable actor. Born in Philadelphia in 1829, he graduated at the University of Pennsylvania in 1847, and three years later took his M.A. Charles Kean persuaded him to become an actor. He made his first appearance in England at York and eventually gained high commendation with Kean's company at the Princess's Theatre. He had very great gifts. After gaining further acclaim with Samuel Phelps at Sadler's Wells, he married the widowed Mrs. Charles Young, a fine actress, who has already entered this story. His first outstanding success was at the Princess's under his own management, when he produced *The Man o' Airlie*, dramatised by W. G. Wills, and played James Harebell. He did this dialect tragedy at a time when burlesque held most of the London stages. It was played, as it should be, in broad Scots, yet working-class folk who flocked to see it and hardly understood one word wept bitterly at the anguish Vezin portrayed. Only Irving, apart from Vezin, had the tremendous gift of making the audience visualise what was in his own mind. It is not surprising, therefore, that when Irving fell ill within a few nights of his triumph in *King Lear*, it was Vezin whom he desired to carry on. But the latter was playing elsewhere and could not do it. However, the tribute of the greatest actor our stage ever produced was something to remember.

After Vezin's performance of *Œdipus* at the Crystal Palace in 1876, *The Times* said: "As a declaimer of English, Mr. Vezin has no equal on our stage." And in the following year he scored his resounding success as De Paldi in *The Danischeffs*. The play, as already recorded, ran for more than 300 nights, which was a marvel for the St. James's. But Mrs. Wood, having achieved that, did not stay. She had things to do elsewhere.

She was succeeded by Samuel Hayes. He sought favour by presenting as his leading lady Miss Ada Cavendish, an actress of the very front rank, but only for a short season, prior to her departure for America. She appeared in *The School for Scandal*, in Palgrave Simpson's thriller *The Scar on the Wrist*, and as Desdemona in *Othello*. Forrester played the Moor, G. S. Titheradge Iago, and Mrs. Bernard Beers was Emilia. It was a delightful cast.

Yet at the end of the season the lights went out again at the St. James's. The bird of good fortune alighted there, it seemed, only for short periods, and the house had now such a thoroughly bad name that it was regarded as a place to be avoided. The very darkest hour had arrived. And then, as usual, and as the old silent films so often captioned, then "Came the dawn"...

SIR HENRY IRVING

LILY HANBURY

LILY LANGTRY

H. B. IRVING

THREE ALEXANDER ROLES

BEN WEBSTER, A. VANE TEMPEST, NUTCOMBE GOULD, H. M. VINCENT and GEORGE ALEXANDER in *Lady Windermere's Fan*

With MARION TERRY in *Sunlight and Shadow*

With HERBERT WARING in *The Masqueraders*

CHAPTER 6

Success at Last

DAWN came to the St. James's in a way that might have delighted a civil servant. It came in triplicate—in the persons of John Hare and Mr. and Mrs. Kendal, all three of whom were actor-managers. Perhaps Hare should be dealt with first, for he originated the partnership among the trio. And in tracing his early career it will be necessary to say a word about the Bancrofts also.

John Hare first appeared on the London stage at the old Prince of Wales's Theatre on 25th September, 1865, in *Naval Engagements*, in which he played Short. There also on 11th November of the same year he made his first outstanding success in a play by T. W. Robertson who, with Mr. and Mrs. (afterwards Sir Squire and Lady) Bancroft, revolutionised the English stage. Robertson broke away from the haphazard form of construction and abandoned the long arm of coincidence. He brought to the drama a semblance of naturalness hitherto lacking. True, he is often accused of founding the "drawing-room play"—the "cup and saucer comedy"—but in the main his plays were extremely good. Moreover, the Bancrofts mounted and dressed them properly. The old-fashioned conventions, and the idea that almost anything would do, went overboard. Also, the plays were perfectly cast and performed. Consequently, the Prince of Wales's became the smartest and most popular theatre in town.

One of Robertson's characteristics was his preference for a single-word title, and on that 11th November the one produced was *Society*, always an attractive subject in those distant days when there was still a Society with a capital S. The play, after a try-out in Manchester, was now brought to London. In it young Mr. John Hare, who was then twenty-one, played Lord Ptarmigan. *The Times* said of him:

"Next in importance is Lord Ptarmigan, a remarkably thin nobleman of unmistakably aristocratic appearance, who, less from weakness than from indolence, allows his wife to tyrannise over him till he finds that he has to defend a righteous cause, and then surprises the audience by a sudden display of authority. This 'bit of character' is made up to the life by Mr. Hare."

The Daily News was even more complimentary:

"The acting throughout was admirable. Mr. Sydney (Squire) Bancroft who performed the hero, Mr. Hare, who played the part of a listless middle-aged lord, and Mr. Clarke, who represented the vulgar-minded, self-sufficient young man of property, were most artistic . . . It is a real pleasure to welcome such an actor as Mr. Hare to the London stage."

Any actor would be grateful for such a notice. (Mr. Clarke, by the way, is not to be confused with John S. Clarke, the American mentioned in the previous chapter.)

John Hare continued to attract attention, scoring heavily in Robertson's next play, *Ours*, in the part of Prince Perovsky. Then came a really outstanding success for everyone—dramatist, management, players, and John Hare. It was *Caste*, the best of all Robertson's comedies. The leading character, of course, is Eccles, the drunken old reprobate whose charming daughter marries the marquis-designate George d'Alroy, and in this capacity George Honey made a specially resounding success. It is a gem of a part and many famous actors have played it, notably Cyril Maude who was wonderful.

John Hare played Sam Gerridge, in love with the daughter, Polly Eccles, and his success fell very little short of George Honey's. Produced on Saturday, 6th April, 1867 (the Bancrofts liked Saturday as an opening night, just as George Edwardes did later), it won general acclaim. *The Daily News* declared:

"Mr. Hare is so refined and perfect an actor, so true an observer of life that we were not surprised to find him made up as a sharp, wiry, veritable working man who might have stepped out of any carpenter's shop in England . . . The scene in which he reads to his 'intended' the trade circular he has just composed is the most exquisite and unforced bit of comedy we have seen for years."

That circular, by the way, bore a striking resemblance to the one issued by Braham when he opened the St. James's, only Braham did not mean his to be funny.

Though himself quite young, Hare was always at his best when playing old men. This was specially noted when, in *M.P.* he portrayed Dunscombe Dunscombe. *The Times* commented:

> "Mr. Hare is the most finished actor of old men that our stage has had since the late W. Farren, if we except Mr. Alfred Wigan, who might, and no doubt will, be pre-eminent in this line of business whenever he takes to it. As it is, Mr. Hare has no rival in our theatres at this moment."

Hare went from success to success at the Prince of Wales's: in *Money*, in *Man and Wife*, and especially in 1874 as Sir Peter Teazle. This performance might well be studied as an example by young actors today. He had the courage to throw off many of the old conventions attached to the part down the years—it was then ninety-seven years old and there had been hundreds of Sir Peters; that of William Farren, to whom Hare had been compared, being one of the greatest.

For the proper understanding of John Hare's art, as for an appreciation of one part of the new force which had come to the St. James's, a notice from the *Daily Telegraph* may be helpful:

> "How loyally and well Mr. Hare would assist such a performance we all know, and how the performance was in itself brought into relief by Mr. Hare's good taste we must all be convinced. Without such a 'Sir Peter' who refines everything to a nicety, who remembers the tone and character of the old English gentleman and studiously forgets the coarseness and, we may add, the grossness which has been attached to the character by tradition, how much less expression would have been obtained in the great scene with Lady Teazle! Surely a young actor can play Sir Peter Teazle without being obstinately compared with such geniuses as are identified with the character, and we may well congratulate Mr. Hare in successfully passing through a most harassing and almost overwhelming ordeal. It is difficult to shake the conviction of anyone, and with old playgoers old memories are necessarily dear; but it will be gratefully remembered that in Sir Peter Teazle Mr. Hare, true to his art,

discarded those coarse effects which are so telling, and, remembering his own standard and outlook of the character, played it with evenness and finished like a refined and well-bred gentleman."

Actually, he had returned to the original rendering, as given by King when the play was first produced. Beerbohm Tree played it the same way in that notable revival at His Majesty's in 1909, when old Herman Vezin came back to the stage and played old "Rowley" with a touch of perfection.

Hare had been with the Bancrofts since 1865 and it was now 1874—nine years of steady advancement in status and art. Having saved some money he now contemplated management on his own account and informed his employers of his intention. Bancroft, in his book *Mr. and Mrs. Bancroft On and Off the Stage*, makes mention of it. He says:

> "It was at this time that our company suffered a great loss in the departure of its oldest and most valued member, John Hare. Wisely enough, for there was ample room for two such theatres as the Prince of Wales's, he had for some time entertained ideas of commencing management on his own account; how wisely has been proved by the splendid record of his work in that direction. When *The School for Scandal* was withdrawn, Hare left us, Sir Peter Teazle being the last part he played under our management; but time has not weakened our remembrance of his valued services and the great aid he gave to the Robertson comedies—with which his name must always be associated—or, I rejoice to add, altered our friendship. He and I had dressed in the same room together for years, those years being, at least on my part, the happiest of life, for they began when I was twenty-four and ended when I was thirty-three."

Hare had his eye on the Royal Court Theatre. His savings amounted to £2,000, which he knew was not enough. So, casting around for a partner, he suggested to Mr. W. H. Kendal that he should put up a similar sum and between them they should take over the remainder of its lease, which had almost two years to run. Hare was a wise man, for in Kendal and his wife he had selected two people who had a considerable box-office draw. He discussed the matter with Kendal at the Garrick Club. Mr. Kendal said he must consult his wife, who was very much the dominant partner. In her autobiography Mrs. Kendal says that her husband told her of the proposition and remarked "Your brother Tom believes in him and brought him to London." This was T. W. Robertson, in whose plays the Bancrofts and Hare had achieved such enormous credit.

Mrs. Kendal was cautious. This was their own money, not that of a syndicate or put up by friends. "Two thousand pounds is all we have in the world," she said to her husband: "Don't part with it yet. Tell Mr. Hare you will send it later." Kendal laughed. "My dear," he said, "whatever else you may be, you are not a good business woman. I'm afraid Mr. Hare will not agree to that. Not only must I pay this money into our joint account at once, but as a business man I have to see that my partner does the same." He had evidently made up his mind to take the risk. Each of them was to draw twenty-five pounds a week salary and to appear in every play, no matter what sort of a part there was for them. Mrs. Kendal, in her book *Dame Madge Kendal, by Herself*, says that Hare violated this agreement by failing to act in the third production—a charge to which Hare has entered no known defence.

They opened the Court Theatre on Saturday, 13th March, 1875—evidently the number thirteen did not appal them, although theatrical folk as a rule are decidedly superstitious. In the company, besides the Kendals and Hare, were Amy Fawsitt, John Clayton (who had made a big success at the St. James's, it will be recalled), and Henry Kemble. They pulled in good houses, thus confirming Bancroft's forecast that there was room in London for two theatres devoted to the best kind of comedy. Not every play, of course, made the grade, but by far the greater proportion did. In the first season they produced four: *Lady Flora*, which was a failure, *A Nine Days Wonder*, *Broken Hearts*, and *A Scrap of Paper*, this last becoming a standby for the Kendals for the rest of their lives. In *A Nine Days Wonder*, Hare took the part of a young man, just to show that he could do it, and succeeded very well. He played the young lover to Mrs. Kendal, whose name in the play was Amabel, and he called her that to the end of their days.

Amongst the plays produced in successive seasons was *A Quiet Rubber*, which became Hare's standby and in which he had the honour of a Royal Command Performance. Their management of the Court placed that theatre in the front rank and everything was done in the best of style. In 1878, Hare produced *Olivia*, a version of *The Vicar of Wakefield*, with Herman Vezin as Dr. Primrose and Ellen Terry in the title role. Fascinating though the story of that venture at the Court may be, its only purpose here is to prepare the ground for what was to follow at the St. James's. For Hare and the Kendals decided to continue their partnership and, not a whit afraid, took over the theatre with the hoodoo.

Now a word about those wonderful people, Mr. and Mrs. Kendal, who, with Hare, were to bring the dawn to the St. James's. Mrs. Kendal was born on 15th March, 1848, in a small hostelry in Grimsby (the author had the honour of unveiling a memorial plaque there a few years ago) and her name was Margaret Robertson, always reduced to Madge. She was practically born into the theatre, and at the age of four appeared at the Marylebone Theatre as the Blind Child in *The Seven Poor Travellers*. In 1855, when she was seven, she played Little Eva in *Uncle Tom's Cabin* at the Prince's, Bristol, and there she remained for a long time, under the watchful care and tuition of its manager, J. H. Chute, a great man of the theatre.

She came to London in 1865, to the Haymarket Theatre, as Ophelia, with Walter Montgomery as Hamlet, and made a deep impression. In the same year she played Desdemona at the Haymarket to the Othello of the negro actor, Ira Q. Aldridge. There was no outcry about a white woman appearing with a black man and Madge Robertson took it in her stride, even when this dusky Othello dragged her round the stage by the hair of her head. The audience hissed the brutality of the scene but the actress did not mind at all.

She went on tour, then in 1867 to Drury Lane, as Edith, heroine of *The Great City*. Returning to the Haymarket, she played a large round of parts, her talent making her a great favourite.

Madge must have been highly delighted when, at twenty, she was chosen as leading lady in one of the plays with which the Gaiety opened on 21st December, 1868 (though Nellie Farren was on the programme with her). She played opposite Alfred Wigan in *On the Cards*, part of a triple bill. She was also there in a play by her brother, called *Dreams*. Then, back at the Haymarket again, she made a big hit in a revival of *New Men and Old Acres*. This was a creaky old compost, but young Madge Robertson lifted it to triumph. She was splendid as Lydia Languish in *The Rivals*, and magnificent in W. S. Gilbert's *The Palace of Truth*; and then, as Galatea, in the same author's *Pygmalion and Galatea*, she created what many people regarded as her masterpiece, although some preferred her in *The Wicked World*. Opposite her in the former play was a young man named Grimston. He was a tall, well-set-up fellow, good-looking according to Victorian ideas, and as an actor he was sound, competent and dependable without being brilliant. His stage name was W. H. Kendal. Now, Madge Robertson had already gained a reputation for tremendous respectability in a calling not renowned for that quality at the time (but really far more respectable than most people wanted to believe), and W. H. Kendal's rectitude matched hers. It is said he wooed her with far more impetuosity than he ever showed on the stage. After an engagement which lasted two years, they were married in Manchester in 1869.

They made a model partnership, both on the stage and off. Going into management, they played in the West End, in the provinces and in America, and were everywhere greeted with approval and applause. Their respectability was such that people often went to see Mr. and Mrs. Kendal who would not in other circumstances have entered such a wicked place as a playhouse at all. Many young people went on tour with their companies, in which they were trained to their craft in the best possible way—on the stage itself. The Kendals were hard task-masters. Only the best would do, and they always gave that themselves. Mrs. Kendal was a stern lady in the theatre. She allowed no nonsense, on or off the stage. Hard work and decorous behaviour constituted the twin pillars of her philosophy, and she set the example herself. Her companies feared and respected her. Only one man ever defied her—the completely irrepressible Seymour Hicks—and even he was afraid of her.

Mrs. Kendal's technique was irreproachable. Maybe she lacked passion—on the stage and off—but she excelled in everything else. She had a gift of laughter and of tears. Nobody on the English stage could ever cry as could Mrs. Kendal, not even Dame Marie Tempest, who ran her a close second. For she cried quite naturally, and it was so real that the women in the audience cried with her—and thoroughly enjoyed it. She was a very splendid actress, indeed.

Always playing together, the Kendals became great public idols. Nobody ever called them by their Christian names. None would have dared to presume familiarity with them: they lived remote and supreme on their pedestal of public esteem. But their names were household words, and they were not only venerated but beloved by a large mass of the people. With John Hare, they took over the St. James's in the autumn of 1879.

CHAPTER 7

The Sun Shines

THE news that Hare and the Kendals were to open up the St. James's caused quite a flutter in theatrical circles, and indeed, beyond. The venturesome partners did not lack for pessimistic advice. Many reckoned it as something akin to madness to desert their glowing reputation at the Court for a speculative plunge in the gloomy jungle of King Street. But being practical people, Hare and his partners were making no blind bid. They were not unfamiliar with the doleful story of St. James's, nor had they forgotten to assess the obvious risks. Against the grim predictions of the Jeremiahs they were able to set their own sober estimates of what was happening and what was wanted in the theatrical world. And who better than they to judge the public trend? Between their sessions at the Court they had invariably gone on tour, Hare with one company and the Kendals with another. In so doing they had measured the taste of the provinces no less than that of the town. They had their finger on the public pulse.

One of the things that inspired their confidence was the belief that the new kind of construction, *à la* Robertson and some other playwrights, had evoked a new interest among the mass of theatre-goers, while the production technique evolved by the Bancrofts had re-awakened the attention of "the best people". These developments and their increasing appeal they had themselves witnessed at first hand; for the Kendals also had been with the Bancrofts, registering their greatest joint success to date in the latter's first and somewhat spectacular production of Sardou's *Diplomacy*, she as Dora and he as Beauclerc. Not improbably, it was Hare's aptitude in the new technique and his confidence in its future that prompted him into the realm of management. It will be remembered that Bancroft approved Hare's decision and foretold his success, a forecast in which he probably included the Kendals.

The venturing trio were doubtless moved by many other considerations, one of which, it is permissible to believe, was the unique eminence to which Mrs. Kendal had now attained. Not only was she voted the best all-round actress on the stage, but, perhaps more importantly, she was regarded as the epitome of public and private rectitude. If her playing appealed to many, her numerous public utterances on the sanctity of marriage and the sacredness of established ethics appealed to more. At this date, Queen Victoria had been eight years in retirement, almost completely cut off from the populace, following the death of her beloved Prince Albert. Mrs. Kendal was in large degree occupying the gap created by the withdrawal of the Royal Exemplar. And when it is remembered that Mr. Kendal held a corresponding position as the veritable essence of the upright English gentleman, it will be appreciated that the pedestaled pair had gained a new public which extended far beyond the range of the theatre.

In addition to these social assets the Kendals knew their business backwards, as did their colleague Hare. They knew how to stage a play with every appearance of splendour but at the minimum of expense, and they knew from experience that a successful performance could rarely be achieved without giving of their best. On this foundation they had gained encomiums at the Court. Now with their many added advantages they struck out on a new conquest and, despite the "knockers"—as active then as now—they moved into the St. James's and rang up the curtain for their first production on 6th October, 1879.

The play was *The Queen's Shilling*. Here the good sense of the management showed itself. This play had been a success at the Court and had not exhausted its popularity when withdrawn. There was a great demand to see it, not only for the first time, but again. In the character of Kate Greville, it contained a part in which Mrs. Kendal was at her brilliant best. The company included William Terriss, Albert Chevalier—who had no thought then of the music hall triumphs and Cockney songs to follow, William Mackintosh, Brandon Thomas, Cissie Graham, Kate Phillips, and Mrs. Gaston Murray.

These players were all well-known then and destined for fame afterwards. Kate Phillips was a daughter of Philip Goldney, of Bradleigh Hall, Essex, a fox-hunting squire, and her family dated back to Henry I. She had started with Irving and had gained repute for more than competence in many parts. Her husband was H. B. Conway.

Cissie Graham, who married W. E. Allen, head of a large printing establishment which owned a number of theatres, had a distinguished career on the stage and later took a most active part in the business of David Allen and Sons. William Terriss, as everyone knows, became the idol of the Adelphi. He had been a leading man with Henry Irving, and was the father of that lovely lady, Ellaline Terriss, who is still sometimes seen adding grace to the auditorium at a first night. Albert Chevalier was to become the topmost singer of Cockney songs and the author of *My Old Dutch*, while Brandon Thomas, a distinguished actor for many years, later wrote the immortal *Charley's Aunt*.

The new management were, it seemed, starting with all the talents. A brilliant throng gathered in the St. James's that opening night. The place had been redecorated and in part reconstructed, giving it a bright and cheerful countenance. A hum of anticipation tinged with a ground-bass of doubt hovered in front of the curtain, while behind raged the usual cacophony of suppressed excitement and jangling nerves. But there was no sign of depression. The whole company had complete confidence in its leaders, and all knew the play was right. And so, indeed, it proved.

The Queen's Shilling, written by G. W. Godfrey, was from a French play, *Le Fils de Famille*, which had been twice adapted before under the titles *The Lancers* and *The Discarded Son*. But neither of these versions did well, and it was left to Mr. Godfrey to give it the vital touch. The plot concerns a young man of good birth who enlists as a private soldier and while serving in the ranks falls in love with a Society lady who, for reasons of her own, is assuming the role of barmaid at an inn. While off duty and out of uniform (both entirely without permission), the young man (whose name is Esmonde Maitland) discovers that his Colonel is engaged to the girl. Maitland then puts on the manners of his assumed lowly rank and is extremely rude, making fun of his superior officer in public. He taunts the Colonel into a duel, and is run through the arm for his trouble. When it is discovered that he is a private in the regiment, he is at his opponent's mercy, for he cannot even buy himself out without the latter's consent. But the Colonel turns out, of course, to be a gentleman, and all ends happily.

It was a defect of the play that the young hero should be such a very bad-mannered cub, but as the predominant note was comedy, everyone was delighted. One satisfied customer wrote to Mrs. Kendal, when another adaptation from the French was announced, saying that people would much prefer a revival of that "purely English comedy", *The Queen's Shilling*!

A first-night report said:

> "Mr. Hare, as Colonel Daunt, gives an admirable study of the martinet officer who has a heart, though he does not wear it on his sleeve; and the marvellous art with which he simulates a face and figure familiar on parade or in Pall Mall is equalled by the finished force by which the inner nature of the man is depicted in voice, manner and personal bearing. By Mr. Kendal a distinct artistic advance is made in his sketch of Daunt's lighthearted young rival, whose impertinence he makes as little offensive as it well can be; and Mrs. Kendal, if occasionally too much inclined to take the audience into her confidence, misses no point of the character created by Rose Chéri and makes it thoroughly entertaining."

One point that keen-eyed critic missed was Mr. Kendal's trick of being able to turn pale when he wished. He used it in *The Queen's Shilling*, and when the Colonel grabbed him tightly by the "wounded" arm he went so pale that women in the audience used to faint! One presumes that for this scene he used no make-up. Thomas Betterton is the only other actor of whom this ability to assume pallor is recorded.

In addition to *The Queen's Shilling* there was a special one-act play that night called *Monsieur le Duc*. This amusing little item, written by Val Prinsep, A.R.A., served as an excellent vehicle for John Hare, and in it also were William Terriss and Albert Chevalier.

The programme of that opening performance was a small card, the size and shape of an ordinary piece of folded notepaper, grey in colour. It had the Royal Arms in gold on the front (with no justification at all) above the words "St. James's Theatre, Lessees and Managers, Mr. Hare and Mr. Kendal". On the back page was a representation of a shilling, also in gold, supported by two crossed lances. And printed prominently in red were the words "No Fees", for like most actor-managers Hare and the Kendals made no charge for programmes or cloakrooms.

As the Kendal-Hare début in joint management was such an important occasion, the cast of the main play is given in full.

The Queen's Shilling

A Comedy in Three Acts adapted from *Le Fils de Famille* by Mr. W. G. Godfrey.

Colonel Daunt (19th Lancers)		Mr. Hare.
Jack Gambier		Mr. Terriss.
Frank Maitland (enlisted under the name of *Esmonde*)		Mr. Kendal.
Sam	(19th Lancers)	Mr. Mackintosh.
Sergeant Sabretache	"	Mr. T. N. Wenman.
Mickey Dooland	"	Mr. R. Cathcart.
Sandy McPibroch	"	Mr. Brandon.
Frederick		Mr. Rowley.
Kate Greville		Mrs. Kendal.
Mrs. Major Ironsides		Mrs. Gaston Murray.
Jenny		Miss Kate Phillips.

Act 1 was "Exterior of The Chequers"; Act 2, "Dingley Grange"; Act 3, "The Colonel's Quarters". The scenery was painted by Messrs. Gordon and Harford, and the song, "The Queen's Shilling", sung in Act 1, was written and composed by Walter Maynard.

The St. James's, under its genuine actor-managers, was off to a flying start. The box-office was busy and the public not only talked of the great show at the St. James's, but went there to see it, impelled by the force of its leading personalities.

On 18th December, 1879, *Monsieur le Duc* was replaced by another one-act play of outstanding interest, for it was a staging of Tennyson's poetic drama, *The Falcon*. While rehearsing this play Mr. and Mrs. Kendal went down to Haslemere to see him about it. After lunch Tennyson was asked to read to them. He was smoking a long churchwarden pipe and he asked Mrs. Kendal what she would like to hear. She replied at once "The Northern Farmer" and quoted from it, much to the great man's joy. He said he would like to attend a rehearsal, and in fact he did pay a visit to the St. James's. He sat in the stalls with a screen round him, a rug over his knees and a hot-water bottle at his feet. Apparently he was delighted, for Mrs. Kendal says he was the most complimentary man she ever met. He must have been very pleased indeed, because he was not always in a complimentary mood. But he told Mrs. Kendal she was the image of a great friend of his and ordered Anna Lee Merritt, a well-known artist of the period, to paint her portrait. He was delighted, too, with the song which Mr. Kendal sang in *The Falcon*, a piece composed by Willert Beale.

For this scene a real falcon was imported from Germany. A most ferocious bird, it devoured pounds of raw beef, but Mr. Kendal, who fed it, trained it to open its wings at a cue, which was no meant feat. The poor bird had a sad end: it got entangled with its chain and hanged itself on the very evening H.R.H. the Prince of Wales came to the St. James's. A property bird, which was kept in reserve, served as substitute. But Kendal disliked the dummy and mourned his falcon. So another, and even fiercer, bird was obtained from a French sailor, who, however, appears to have been as fierce as the bird, for they both thoroughly alarmed Mrs. Kendal, which took a bit of doing.

The Falcon, beautifully staged and mounted, was a tremendous success, the live falcon being symbolic of the lengths to which the management went. William Archer said of Mrs. Kendal's performance: "She was a living poem in her gracious stateliness and queenly yet tender womanhood. Never, in England or elsewhere, have I seen a piece of acting more instinct with the truest poetry." Now, indeed, the sun shone at the St. James's. It had found what it always wanted—real people of the theatre, who are the only ones capable of bringing a theatre to life. Space will not permit a complete record of the Kendal's productions, among which were many revivals, but also a goodly number of new and important plays.

In 1880, they revived *The Ladies' Battle* and *Still Waters Run Deep*, the latter a favourite—ultra-theatrical, but of great appeal. These filled the bill while they worked on a new version of Douglas Jerrold's famous *Black Ey'd Susan*, which W. G. Wills had prepared for them. Wills was a man who could compile a play about anything, either writing an original story or remodelling an old one. He wrote an enormous number and many leading people played in them. Irving commissioned many pieces from him, of which, perhaps, *Charles I* is the best remembered. An ill-dressed, untidy, unkempt genius, Wills had no objection to writing to order—in fact, he liked it. As an Irishman, he had a true theatrical instinct. He also had an unstinted respect for accuracy. When writing *Charles I*, he wanted a lively ending on the field at Naseby. Perhaps he also wanted to satisfy his Irish dislike of Cromwell. But Colonel Bateman, then associated with Irving, would not have it that way. He preferred a quiet, domestic scene to add poignancy. At his suggestion Wills produced that last scene in which the King, on the morning of his execution, bids his children farewell and, when leaving, turns to them with that one word—"Remember!" It was, of course, a sensation.

The attempt to revive the time-worn *Black-Ey'd Susan*, with its transpontine associations, and which had been so often and so mercilessly burlesqued, was a bold one. But the present management never lacked for courage, and they saw in this vintage drama of sailors and the sea, good and evil, just the vehicle they wanted. Wills made a first-class job of it. No expense was spared over the production. The scene on board ship was the best thing of its kind ever staged up to that time. It has been seldom equalled since. So as to have everything shipshape, the management engaged six real Marines, who knew the drill necessary for the arrest of a sailor charged with striking a superior officer. That, of course, is a highlight of the play. But after six weeks the Marines had to leave, having been detailed for the force commanded by Sir Garnet Wolseley (afterwards Field Marshal Lord Wolseley) in his campaign on the Red River. There was much discussion among the public as to whether this play, re-titled *William and Susan*, was the right vehicle for Hare and the Kendals, but those astute people knew what they were about. Produced on 9th October, 1880, when they had been established just over a year, it was an instant success.

The well-known critic Bernard H. Becker was at the first performance. He remembered the original version and had seen T. P. Cooke, an ex-naval man, play William. Knowing the old play with its simple direct appeal and its avoidance of subtlety, he realised where Wills had differed from Jerrold. His main complaint was that Captain Crosstree, by the suppression of some other minor villains, had been made a bit too villainous, and that he did little credit to the traditions of the British Navy. He said he could see the habiliments of the wicked squire peeping through the naval uniform! Apart from that, he had nothing but praise. He said:

> "Probably few melodramas have been more effectively played than *William and Susan*. One might perhaps like a little more youthfulness and dash in William, who need hardly appear from the first overcome by a forecast of his terrible trial; but nothing could be

better than Mr. Kendal's rendering of the later scenes. Susan, rescued from comparative insignificance by Mr. Wills, is admirably natural as portrayed by Mrs. Kendal. Mr. Hare, after his manner, makes much of a small character, and Mr. Barnes is so good a Captain Crosstree that the burlesque associations of the part are completely forgotten."

Mr. Barnes—J. H. Barnes, and justly known as "handsome Jack Barnes"—became a popular actor and carried leading parts for many years.

A word from William Archer is of importance as regards this production. He said:

"Mrs. Kendal wished to play at her own theatre one of her most delightful parts, a perfect embodiment of healthy English womanhood, but was conscious that Jerrold's play was too antiquated in manner to suit the taste of her audiences. Mr. Wills consequently undertook the delicate task of transforming a transpontine nautical drama into what may be called a nautical idyll. He infused both the humour and pathos of the older play, and gave it a touch of delicate and faithful poetry. The honest sentiment and homeliness remained, with an added grace and charm. This is the style of work in which Mr. Wills excels and here he excelled himself."

William and Susan was, indeed, a notable success. The Kendals and Hare had every reason to congratulate themselves. The long luckless St. James's had emerged from the shadows into the sun.

And now, standing in the wings, waiting to make his début, is a young dramatist destined to weave a strand of gold into the tapestry of the St. James's history. His name is Arthur Wing Pinero.

CHAPTER 8

A Dramatist Comes Home

ARTHUR WING PINERO, who was to become one of the greatest of British dramatists, began as an apprentice to the law. Born in London on 24th May, 1855, son of the solicitor, John Daniel Pinero, and his wife (the former Emily Daines), on leaving school he went into his father's office, but the law made no appeal to him and he yearned for the stage. He first appeared as an actor at the Theatre Royal, Edinburgh, in June, 1874, and a year later was playing in Liverpool, at the Alexandra Theatre. On these occasions he was a member of a "stock" company. His first London appearance was at the old Globe, on 15th April, 1876, as Mr. Darch in a play called *Miss Gwilt*, now entirely forgotten.

His rise was speedy. In the September of that year he joined the Lyceum touring company, and had the tremendous experience of playing Claudius to Irving's Hamlet. He was learning his job in the right school and under the right master. He went to the Lyceum itself, first under Bateman's management and then under Irving's, with whom he remained from 1876 until 1881, playing a round of parts in all sorts of plays, from *The Bells* to *Hamlet*. In 1881 he had two of his own one-act plays produced—*Daisy's Escape* and *Bygones*—in which he also appeared. From the Lyceum he went to the Bancrofts at the Haymarket, where until 1884 he gained a full knowledge of comedy. From then on, except for a single appearance at the Bancrofts' farewell performance, he devoted all his time to play-writing.

He had already started in 1887, when R. C. Carton, another actor who became a distinguished dramatist, approved and produced his first one-act play, called *£200 a Year*. From then on he poured them out, and when he sold *The Money-Spinner* to the Kendals and Hare he had already five plays to his credit, most of them in one act. It was with *The Money-Spinner*, at the St. James's, that he first attracted attention

As his own double in *The Prisoner of Zenda*

GEORGE ALEXANDER
(*right*) JOHN THOROLD, his double for *John Chilcote, M.P.*

With IRENE VANBRUGH in *The Thief*

With MRS. PATRICK CAMPBELL in *The Second Mrs. Tanqueray*

With DAWSON MILWARD in *A Builder of Bridges*

GEORGE ALEXANDER IN FOUR ROLES

With IRENE VANBRUGH in *His House in Order*

as a dramatist. He knew the technique of the craft and that of the actor, and had the knack of dovetailing them neatly, building his plays with meticulous care, like a cabinet-maker creating a piece of furniture. He knew, too, how to tell a story so that every word uttered on the stage forwarded the plot. Never a very good actor himself, he knew how to extract good performances from others. As time went on, he became a veritable martinet at rehearsals, with perfection as his sole aim. He could be brusque, biting, and incisive. His sarcasm withered, but he could also praise. He had a sense of humour, too.

It is related how Henry Kemble, the last of the Siddons family, an excellent actor and a great character, once came under the lash of Pinero's tongue at rehearsal. The dramatist expressed the view that his performance would disgrace "a Brixton amateur". Kemble, whom everyone called Beetle, was stricken to the heart. He turned pale and trembled, and then his inherent dignity came to his aid. He vouchsafed no reply but simply put on his coat and hat and walked out of the theatre, like a procession of One.

The next morning, however, he was back again. Before the rehearsal began he went down to the footlights and with dignified politeness asked Pinero if he might address him. Permission was accorded at once. "Mr. Pinero," said Kemble, in that curious, high-pitched but penetrating voice of his, "yesterday you were good enough to address some very impolite remarks to me on the general subject of my performance in this piece now in rehearsal—I repeat, in rehearsal. You said, Sir, that my performance would disgrace 'a Brixton amateur'. This, Sir, cut me to the heart. I am a man of experience. I have performed many parts to which the Press and public have been pleased to accord praise and applause. I was dumbfounded and deeply insulted. I walked out, Sir, with the fixed intention of returning no more to this play, nor to any play which emanated from your pen. Such was my mental stress, Sir, that I did not close my eyes all night. I lay awake and ruminated. And in the small hours I saw a vision. I remembered, Sir, how I had seen you act upon the stage. I remembered seeing you as an actor. And I took heart, for I have the honour of saying, Sir, that never have I witnessed such dreadful performances as you gave. I may have disgraced a Brixton amateur, but you, Sir, disgraced the whole of our calling. Realising that you were no judge of acting, or you would never have performed yourself, I came back just to say these few words, and now if it is your pleasure, I will leave the theatre." Pinero roared with laughter and said he agreed with every word. Kemble resumed his part and the two men became great friends.

The Money-Spinner had a first production at the Prince's Theatre, Manchester, on 5th November, 1880, where it was a great success. Pinero was hailed as the herald of the rising school of dramatists who were to kill the "cup and saucer" style of acting and banish the "china set of modern plays". Already, you see, the Bancrofts were becoming old-fashioned, they who had reformed the stage and English comedy. So prone to change is public taste, so ephemeral the impact of an actor! Let a critic who was present at the now vanished Prince's Theatre on the night of 5th November speak for himself:

"It was my good fortune to be present at the first representation of this play at the Prince's Theatre in Manchester on Friday evening, and I have never seen so small an audience give such a hearty welcome to a piece. *The Money-Spinner* is an original drama in two acts, both of which take place in a drawing-room at Rouen, one single scene being all that is required for the entire play, the action of which embraces twelve hours—from ten o'clock in the morning, the time of the first act, until ten in the evening, the time of the second.

"Here," continued the critic, "is the plot of *The Money-Spinner*. The young lady who gives the name to the piece is the daughter of a notorious adventurer, who keeps a gambling house in Paris, and who, because of her proverbial 'luck' at cheating at cards, has been called 'The Money-Spinner'. She has married the manager of a cotton firm at Rouen, who, during his employer's absence, has embezzled two thousand francs. To save her husband from disgrace, 'The Money-Spinner' resolves to cheat her former lover, who is now going to marry her sister, out of the sum, and for this purpose invites him to a card party and is carrying out her plan successfully, when a detective, who has been employed to watch her husband, exposes her. For the moment, the audience feels perplexed, but, for the sake of the love that he once bore the woman who was going to rob him, the rich lord forgives her and pays the money, so that her husband is free from the shame of exposure at the sacrifice of his wife's disgrace and consequent misery.

"An improvement in this *Money-Spinner*," affirms the critic, "the latest and certainly one of the best of our modern plays, would be effected by making the dialogue more crisp and nervous. The abolition, too, of the oft-recurring phrase used by the rich lord when speaking of or addressing anybody—'There goes the name again'—would help to enchain the serious interest of the spectators. Compared to the work which Mr. Pinero has given us here, these are but slight blemishes and can be easily rubbed out or altered. That we have in England young authors who can give us a play of such power as *The Money-Spinner* without borrowing from our more inventive neighbours, is something upon which we may more than congratulate ourselves. All success to the provincial manager who had the courage to produce the untried play. *Nil desperandum* should be the motto of the unacted. There is ever a market for a good thing and 'dramatic rings' are creations of the fancy of the confirmed grumbler. No combination in the world ever smothered talent. The chance must come some day—and the chance is everything.

"It may at once be conceded that as the last act of this drama progressed an uneasiness was experienced as to how it would terminate. But with wonderful skill the dramatist has woven his materials, and the end comes quietly, without any attempts at sensation, but most impressively; and on the first night of the performance the audience testified their approval by hearty applause after each act, and by loud cries for the author at the end of the play, which were responded to by one of the company observing that Mr. Pinero was on the stage of the Lyceum Theatre, London, and that as the telegraph company were unable—owing, no doubt, to the weather—to summon the author to receive their applause, he would have much pleasure in telegraphing what he considered, and I consider, the news of a great success."

Thus came to public notice the first great success which was to make the name of a dramatist. It was produced and performed by a provincial touring company before a small audience on a Friday night, and judging by the little joke attempted in the speech of thanks, either a wet or a foggy one.

The Money-Spinner came to the St. James's on Saturday, 8th January, 1881. It had a magnificent cast. Kendal was the gullible but generous lord, John Clayton the erring husband (whose name in the play was "Boycott"), Mackintosh (always John Hare's understudy) was the Detective, Mrs. Kendal played Millicent Boycott (the Money-Spinner), Kate Phillips was Dorinda Croodle, a plain, downright if vulgar girl, Mrs. Gaston Murray was the Landlady, and Hare played Baron Croodle. The small part of a Porter was filled by de Verney.

The result was an overwhelming success. A critic said: "Indeed it would be difficult to quote a precedent for the spontaneity of the enthusiasm awakened by the play as acted by as excellent a company as London has ever seen." That critic was Clement Scott, and even de Verney got a good notice for his few lines. John Hare scored heavily. It was Austen Brereton who had seen the play in Manchester and it was noticed that his advice had been taken. Lord Kengussie's oft-repeated gag about the name "Boycott" had gone, and the plot was slightly altered, for now the Money-Spinner sat down to play a straight game but yielded to the temptation to use her old skill and save her husband. The play filled the St. James's for 105 nights, a very long run then. And Pinero took his place amongst the established dramatists.

It was followed by a revival of *The Lady of Lyons*, a great favourite with Mrs. Kendal, and then by a double bill composed of Robertson's *Home*, adapted from the French, and *The Cape Mail*, which Clement Scott had taken from another French play, *Jeanne Qui Pleure et Jeanne Qui Rit*. It tells of a wife who loves her blind mother-in-law, and, when her husband is reported killed at war, reads imaginary letters to the mother to keep the news from her. (This gave Mrs. Kendal a wonderful chance for her emotional acting.) Then, as she is pretending to read one letter, she sees her husband standing in the doorway, and has to improvise words to prevent the shock being too much for the infirm old lady (who was brilliantly played by Mrs. Gaston Murray). This play had just the right combination of surprise and sentiment to fill the house with tension. There was also *Coralie*, adapted by G. W. Godfrey from *Le Fils de Coralie*.

On 29th December, 1882, Pinero came back again with *The Squire*. This was one of the management's greatest triumphs, both from the point of view of acting and of staging. One critic said: "It wafted the scent of hay over the footlights." This play created tremendous controversy. Most people were quite sure they detected a marked resemblance between it and Thomas Hardy's famous novel *Far From the Madding Crowd*. And there is no doubt they were right. Names were altered, social status was different, but the essentials were the same even if the development varied. But what did it matter? It was a first-class play and gave the St. James's company acting opportunities of which they took full advantage. The critics were as unanimous in remarking the similarity as in giving praise to the dramatist. Clement Scott said: "Mr. Pinero, with his knowledge of stagecraft, has done more with the subject than Mr. Hardy could ever have done. He has given us persons, not sketches; his characters are flesh and blood, and his dialogue is, from first to last, admirable and the very thing that the stage requires."

The Kendals and Hare received immense praise, and so did Mackintosh for the character of old Gunnion. Frederic Clay supplied some charming incidental music. The play, which ran for 170 performances, gained much publicity from the charge of plagiarism, which Pinero hotly denied. He put up a splendid case, too. With Hardy's sanction, Comyns Carr, a noted dramatist, had made a stage version of *Far From the Madding Crowd*, which he had submitted to various managements including the Kendals. He claimed that Pinero must have seen it. This was also denied by Pinero. Dutton Cook, a famous writer on the theatre, said he did not believe him. Pinero, however, stuck to his guns. The battle raged for some time, and drew hosts of people to the play. No legal action was ever taken and *The Squire* was a stupendous success. Comyns Carr's version, produced later at the Globe, did not draw: it had been killed by *The Squire*.

Next, in December 1883, came *Impulse*, adapted by B. C. Stephenson, a practised playwright, from the French play *La Maison du Mari*. This, too, was a great success, and in it Kendal had a catchword, which always got roars of laughter: "Mrs. Beresford, you *are*, you really *are*!" Everybody repeated it. John Hare did not play in this production, rather to the annoyance of Mrs. Kendal; but it included that fine actor Herbert Waring, and also Linda Dietz as the erring wife. Mrs. Kendal's part of Mrs. Beresford was only about fifty lines, so that for the first time in years she had time for some social activity. Long afterwards she recorded her impressions of the social life followed by the people of the profession she adorned, saying that when she had an emotional part to play she found it impossible to attend a social function afterwards. She continues:

"Today I notice that most prominent actors and actresses, no matter what parts they have been playing, are constantly seen in society and in the night clubs which are a recognised part of the life of today. I may be quite wrong, but I am firmly of the opinion that if one is a really conscientious actor and plays for all one is worth when on the stage, it is impossible to go out even two or three times a week after the opera is over. Similarly, if one is to give one's best to the public—and the public pays its money for the express purpose of seeing an actor at his best—it is again, in my opinion, unfair to be out all day, playing golf or at the races, and go tired into the theatre just in time or with barely time to dress or put oneself in the mood . . . Of course, it is quite easy to walk through a part, making no effort to convey the emotion which animates it, but that is *not* acting and the people who do that sort of thing are not actors, they are merely on the stage."

Mrs. Kendal's idea was shared by her partners and those who played with her, which was one of the reasons why the St. James's broke its years of bad luck. Young people today may think it funny and take refuge in the "relaxed" methods now so fashionable. Mrs. Kendal would not have understood how playing in a relaxed state could hold an audience. But the old order changeth . . .

Impulse ran for nine months and was followed in October, 1883, by *Young Folks' Ways*, an adaptation of Mrs. Hodgson Burnett's *Esmeralda*. William Gillette, the famous American actor, was part-author. This play was really a milestone in the St. James's Story, for into that theatre, for the first time in a professional capacity, came a man who was to give it an abiding greatness. His name was George Alexander.

When he came for the first rehearsal, tall and thin, the stage manager said to Mrs. Kendal: "The new juvenile man has arrived." He went into the green room and was introduced to the company. One of the young members, a Miss Campbell, whispered: "Oh, Mrs. Kendal, isn't he good-looking?" George Alexander had made his first impression! Mrs. Kendal agreed. "But," she said, "you are not to take any notice of that. Just wait until you see him act."

The play read well but did not come to life on the stage. There was nothing wrong with the cast, which included Kendal, Hare (returning after an absence of almost a year), George Alexander, Herbert Waring, Mrs. Kendal, Linda Dietz and Mrs. Herman Vezin.

Clement Scott thought it a disappointing play: "It begins well, dawdles in the middle and ends badly. Founded on a good idea, the story is arranged with so little skill that the audience droops under its influence, instead of being animated by its interest," he said.

The plot concerned a family transported from the wilds of North Carolina into the gay life of Paris. Scott said it was padded with indifferent comedy but that admirable acting carried the thing through. He was frank about George Alexander—who played the faithful young hero—and said regarding the pivots of the love story:

> "To make matters worse for this play the young lovers were not so strong as they might have been. Miss Webster, the grandchild of Benjamin Webster of happy memory, has evident talent, but she is still a novice and under no circumstances should have been overweighted with the burden of the character of Esmeralda. It was not fair to the actress, nor the public. It is a charming character, but the beauty of it was lost on the audience. Mr. George Alexander again was strangely out of tune. Usually interesting, he here became commonplace. His heart did not appear to be in his work, and the brave backwoodsman of Carolina became a maudlin and sentimental lover."

It sounds like a thoroughly bad part.

Mrs. Kendal was delighted that Mrs. Herman Vezin, a very great actress, was in this play. She records that she cried with joy when Mrs. Vezin came into the theatre, for it was impossible to watch her without learning something. She saw to it that Mrs. Vezin had a dressing-room to herself—a rare thing then—and a special maid as a dresser. Which drives another nail in the modern belief that actor- and actress-managers hogged everything for themselves. Mrs. Kendal was an artiste and appreciated the talent of Mrs. Vezin. There was no jealousy, only deep respect.

Young Folks' Ways was followed by a round of revivals, and also Shakespeare's *As You Like It.* Mrs. Kendal's costume as Rosalind, dressed as a boy, was the very acme of Victorian decorum. The play had a bad Press, despite Herman Vezin as Jaques and John Hare as

Touchstone, one of the few parts in which this great actor failed completely. Nor was Kendal the best of Orlandos. One of the revivals was *The Ironmaster*, which Pinero made over from the French. This pulled in big houses and was thereafter kept in the Kendal repertory. Hare was not in it, but the company included George Alexander, Herbert Waring, Kendal, Mrs. Gaston Murray, Linda Dietz and Mrs. Kendal. This time Alexander got a good notice, and the general verdict was that it was a perfect Kendal play.

Pinero came back again to the St. James's—where he had now become part of the fabric—on 31st October, 1885, with a play called *Mayfair*, adapted from Sardou's *Maison Neuve*. This, however, was one of the pieces which failed to survive the Channel crossing. Yet after the dress rehearsal the company were certain they had a winner. It had been a wonderful performance—and should have been reserved for the first night. Mrs. Kendal, with her sure intuition, was aware of it. She was right. It was the old story of "good dress rehearsal, bad show". Despite a fine cast it soon petered out.

During the run Hare and Kendal went over to Paris to see a play which might suit them. Their understudies took over and Mrs. Kendal was in sole control. When business, which had been bad, took a leap upwards, she wired to Paris telling the good news—and the two men stayed for a whole week instead of just a day or two! She also bought herself a hat which she had long coveted. But the following week business dropped almost to zero. Kendal roared with laughter at his wife's surprise. "It was Cattle Show week," he told her. "You could not have kept the people out if you had tried." In the days prior to the First World War the Cattle Show, held at the Agricultural Hall, Islington, brought a tremendous influx of country visitors, and theatre business boomed as it does now during a Motor Show.

CHAPTER 9

The Sun Sets Again

NEXT came *The Wife's Sacrifice*, by Sydney Grundy and Sutherland Edwards, from the French *Martyre*. Though not a spectacular success, it held the stage from May until October, 1886, when Pinero returned with *The Hobby Horse*. He called it a comedy but it was really a farce. Pinero was now supplying farces to the Court Theatre, and they were perfect examples of their kind, such as *The Magistrate*, *Dandy Dick*, *The Schoolmistress*, and the like. *The Hobby Horse* was not quite so farcical or it would not have attracted the Kendals and Hare. It was produced on Saturday, 28th October, 1886, having in the cast Herbert Waring, John Hare, C. W. Somerset, Mackintosh, Ernest Hendrie, Fuller Mellish, Albert Sims, Mrs. Kendal, Mrs. Gaston Murray and Mrs. Beerbohm Tree.

It had a wonderful first night. Pinero's farces at the Court had set a fashion. But this was not in the same class. It hovered between farce and comedy and never quite made up its mind. There were moments of sympathetic high comedy, almost of drama, and then wild farcical outbursts. Characters introduced as if they were principals just petered out. Nobody quite believed in Mrs. Spencer Jermyn, who leaves her husband and home to work on philanthropic schemes, and with whom the hardworking East End curate falls in love. Nevertheless, Hare was so pleased with his own part of Mr. Spencer Jermyn that they kept it on for one hundred nights although it was unprofitable.

Mrs. Beerbohm Tree scored a success and Mackintosh and Hendrie made a big hit as two decayed jockeys. Albert Sims was to become one of the best stage butlers of all time. Mrs. Kendal, had an accident during the run. This was big news and was duly chronicled. She was away for six weeks. When the date of her return was announced no fewer than eleven very important people offered her the use of their carriage. She chose that of the Duke of Fife, husband of H.R.H. The

Princess Royal—both of them great theatre-goers and staunch supporters of the Kendals—and drove down in triumph to the theatre, to find her dressing-room a blaze of flowers, and a decorated bath-chair waiting to take her from the carriage down the alley to the stage door.

The Hobby Horse was the management's last new production at the St. James's. They followed it with some revivals, including *Clancarty*. When she first appeared in this play, following Ada Cavendish who had taken the town by storm, Mrs. Kendal received some bad notices, but she persevered and it became one of her most popular portrayals. Hare would not play William III, but gave it to that most efficient actor, Mackintosh. They also produced *The Witch*, which had been done previously at the Princess's; a rather grim play but important to this story inasmuch as it brought into the St. James's a man—then a very young actor—who was destined to play an important part in one of its most sensational productions. His name was Allan Aynesworth. George Alexander has made his appearance, and so has Herbert Waring. All three are important to the story.

The Kendals revived *A Scrap of Paper*—a certain success—but it had now become known that their partnership with Hare was drawing to a close. Clement Scott remarked:

> "The delight that was experienced by the audience on Monday, 16th January, 1888, at the most excellent performance of *A Scrap of Paper*, must have been tinged with a feeling of sorrow to many, in that it was the forerunner of a change in the management at the St. James's Theatre, and the probable absence, at no distant date, for some time from its boards of Mr. and Mrs. Kendal."

Those two, with John Hare as Dr. Penguin, Mrs. Gaston Murray, Mrs. Beerbohm Tree and Herbert Waring were all on top of their form in this play, which was for so many years one of the Kendals' most reliable standbys.

As their farewell performance the triumvirate presented a revival of Pinero's controversial piece, *The Squire*. It was 21st July, 1888, and the packed house hummed with emotion. London had taken these three people to its heart. Known and popular before they went to the St. James's, their work there had put them at the very head of their profession. When the final curtain fell there was tremendous applause and numerous curtain calls. There were special calls for the three partners, of course, and John Hare, responding first, said:

"Whilst fighting to live amidst a keen and vigorous competition, we have endeavoured not to forget the advancement of our art in the more sordid care of theatrical management. It has been argued to our prejudice that we have favoured too much the productions of foreign authors; but I would ask you to remember that, in the matter of plays, the demand has ever been greater than the supply, and that the history of the English stage for many years has proved it to be incapable of being entirely independent of foreign work. I can safely say, however, that to England we have always turned first for the dramatic fare we have placed before you. That we have not done so more has been our misfortune; I would like to think it not altogether our fault. I must also thank publicly the partner whose loyal aid and help I have enjoyed for so many years, Mrs. Kendal, whose talents have shed lustre and given vitality to so many of our productions."

Mr. Kendal said:

"It would be an affectation on my part were I to be restrained by any unworthy bashfulness from declaring that for our success we are principally indebted to Mrs. Kendal. Without her we could, indeed, have done little. No one, I am sure, will more sincerely endorse this avowal than my late partner to whose uninterrupted friendship, hearty loyalty and generous co-operation during our entire connection I now gladly bear testimony."

What those two men said was true. Mrs. Kendal was indeed the heart of it, though Hare had done well, too. Think what they had accomplished! The St. James's had been "Braham's Folly" when they went there. When they left, after nine years' partnership, it was a prosperous, vital theatre. They had effected this transformation because all three partners were professionals who knew their job. They worked in their theatre as in a workshop. They did not sit in distant offices and issue orders. Although their salaries were not immense, they made it a full-time job and did not go running after sidelines. They concentrated on giving satisfaction to their ever-widening public. But they knew better than to mix with their public. They confined themselves to the other side of the footlights, to their own land of illusion. Yet there was a great bond of friendship between them and their followers, and they had not to rely on the frail link of familiarity which might snap at any time. Their management of the St. James's is a landmark in the history of the English theatre.

Hare and his colleagues were friends as well as partners. They had their little tiffs on occasions, for Hare was rather a touchy man. At one time, he did not speak to Mrs. Kendal, except on stage, for six weeks because of a joke of hers he did not like. Mrs. Kendal was not too easy, either. But such squabbles were small affairs. There was never a real quarrel or a threat of severance, nor a major dispute on policy or choice of play. They even took their holidays together. And their families were always fast friends.

At the conclusion of their lengthy partnership, the Kendals went on their first American tour. She said she was tired of being a leading lady in the West End at £25 a week—all three of them had stuck to that original agreement. They had a send-off banquet at the Hotel Metropole on 16th July, 1889, the chairman being the Rt. Hon Joseph Chamberlain, M.P. The tour was a triumph. Home again, they graced the stage for many years. The older generation will remember that marvellous performance by Mrs. Kendal, with Ellen Terry, in *The Merry Wives of Windsor*, with Sir Herbert Tree as Falstaff. She became a Dame of the British Empire, and never was honour better bestowed. She died full of years and honour on 14th September, 1935, aged eighty-seven. Her husband had predeceased her at the age of seventy-three in 1917. Nothing is more typical of Dame Madge than her manner of acquainting her friends of her husband's death. They all received a telegram which said, simply, "I am now a widow." These telegrams, hundreds of them, were, at Mrs. Kendal's behest, written and dispatched by Marie Löhr, then a junior member of the Kendal company—now, of course, one of the best actresses on the British stage.

John Hare continued for many years as a leader of his profession. Constantly in management, he took over the Garrick Theatre, Charing Cross Road, built for him by W. S. Gilbert, in 1889, and ran it with distinction until 1895. He toured America and there added greatly to his laurels. In 1907 he was knighted. Born at Giggleswick, in Yorkshire, in 1884 and educated there, his real name was Fairs. He was the typical English gentleman of his period. His sharp, incisive style, his distinction of manner and appearance, were widely noticed, and also his complete grasp of character parts, in which he always sank his own identity. Yet when playing straight parts he was equally superb, his performance in *The Gay Lord Quex* being outstanding in theatrical annals. He was remarkable also, in an entirely different style, as Benjamin Goldfinch in *A Pair of Spectacles* and the old man in *A Quiet Rubber*, with both of which his name is so closely associated. He died on 28th September, 1921, aged seventy-seven.

After bidding farewell to the Hare-Kendal combination, the St. James's welcomed another actor-manager in the person of Rutland Barrington. He was an extremely popular singer and actor with a fine record, especially in the Gilbert and Sullivan operas. His aspiration to management caused D'Oyly Carte considerable heart-burnings, for he was most reluctant to lose this pillar of his Savoy Operas. Nevertheless he gave him many hints on the snags and tricks of the business and wished him luck. Having a large personal following, Barrington had no doubt he could keep the St. James's afloat. Not even the thought—if it ever occurred to him—that another singer, Braham, had built the theatre and been ruined by it could have restrained him. Had someone mentioned the coincidence he would probably have discounted it at once by reference to his reputation for seldom if ever singing in tune! Report mischievously asserted that he had once done so, while appearing under the banner of the late George Edwardes. But Edwardes told the company not to worry. "It's only first-night nerves," he said, "He'll never do it again!"

But it was not opera with which Barrington sought to inflame the St. James's. While performing in *Ruddigore* at the Savoy he had become possessed of a couple of plays in which he had enthusiastic confidence. This same confidence he extended to a friend, a financier who was said to be fabulously wealthy. Promising ample backing the friend encouraged Barrington's ambition. So Barrington took the plunge. While negotiations for the lease proceeded he prepared for his first production, a comedy-drama entitled *The Dean's Daughter*, written by Sydney Grundy and F. C. Phillips (the former a well-known playwright who never had the luck he deserved). No sooner was the lease signed and commitments entered into, than Barrington's backer withdrew, leaving him high and dry with only his modest savings as capital. It was a glum situation, and perhaps the old hoodoo of St. James's was beginning to assert itself again.

Fortunately—or unfortunately—Barrington obtained aid from a better friend, Colonel North, and carried on. He wanted his old stage associate, Mrs. John Wood, to appear with him. She was inclined to accept, but at the last moment received a quite irresistible offer from the Court Theatre. She urged Barrington to take himself and his play along to the Court as well, but he was committed.

So Barrington got together the best cast he could, and it was by no means a bad one either. Besides himself, it included Caroline Hill and a number of clever young people, among them Olga Nethersole, who became so justly famous and was now playing her first important part. Barrington later claimed it as her London début but it was not, for she had been in *The Union Jack* at the Adelphi earlier in the year; but this was certainly her first big part and marked the initial flowering of that tremendous art which showed itself subsequently in so many leading roles, including Sapho. There was also Allan Aynesworth, as to whom Barrington made a similar claim later, but again wrongly. Aynesworth had been at the St. James's in *The Witch* and had also played with Tree in *The Red Lamp* before joining Barrington. Another young man in this first cast was Lewis Waller, then on the threshold of his career and already attracting the critics' attention. There were also other rising young men like John Beauchamp and Edward Sass.

Barrington rang up the curtain on the night of 13th October, 1888, to a house that seemed ready to acclaim his offering an immediate success. Unfortunately—the old hoodoo again?—the atmosphere was soon shattered by less propitious portents. Clement Scott, the critic, had by some unknown word or deed provoked the ire of the pit and gallery, and when he took his seat in the stalls the hoots and boos from those quarters concentrated in a dreadful din. This demonstration, repeated during the interval, inevitably upset the new actor-manager and his company and negated any chance of them assuaging their usual first-night nerves. It distracted the audience, too, whose thoughts right from the start were intrigued more by the row than the happenings on stage. After all, they could watch a show at any time, but a rowdy show, if only because so rare, had its own special appeal and peculiar points of attraction. The commotion, simmering throughout, broke into fury again at the end. Barrington was trying to quell the disorder by dimming the lights when help came in the person of George Edwardes, known by common consent as "The Guv'nor". He addressed the malcontents in his own impressive style. "Boys," he bawled, "you're not giving Barrington a chance. Go home quietly and say what you like to Mr. Scott outside." As they cheered, George improved the occasion by adding: "Don't forget the first night at the Gaiety next week." They cheered again, and presently went on their way.

So far as could be estimated through the din, the play itself had a good reception. They all had a warm spot for Barrington, and he had to take a call at the end. So did his young leading lady, Olga Nethersole—another of St. James's lucky artistes—who, from that time on, never looked back. Discounting the anti-Scott riot, the chances of a reasonable run looked fairly bright. So much so that when D'Oyly Carte went round to see Barrington, who was in a dreadful state of nerves, he was able to reassure him. "Don't worry, B.," he said, "you've got a winner and you won't need any more money."

But Carte had misjudged. Next morning the notices were bad, although some of them gave full marks for the staging and acting. Olga Nethersole had a splendid Press, as did some of the other young players. Scott, who had been the occasion of so much damage, said: "Mr. Lewis Waller achieved another success as George Sabine. One of the best acted parts was that of Lord Ashwell, taken by a newcomer, Mr. Allan Aynesworth. In a most trying situation, he acquitted himself admirably and showed great promise." Both these young men justified Scott's judgment.

The trouble with the play was really the character played by Barrington himself—Rev. Augustus St. Aubyn. This clergyman, head over heels in debt, constantly dunned, a shocking hypocrite who interlarded his conversation with Scriptural texts and then persuaded tradesmen to supply him with immense amounts of food and drink to satisfy his gluttony, wants a well-paid Deanery. The price is his daughter. She is saved by her young lover, George Sabine, played by Lewis Waller. With Olga Nethersole as his daughter, Barrington played the clergyman for comedy. It is difficult to understand what he saw in the play. It was applauded by the few who came in; but far too many, for Barrington's liking, stayed away.

So he put on his second venture, *Brantinghame Hall*, the first straight play W. S. Gilbert had written since his association with Sullivan. With a very popular Savoyard in the lead, this seemed a certainty. Gilbert wrote the part of Ruth specially for a young actress, whose name was Julia Neilson. Barrington, who believed in youth, engaged her at £10 a week—a staggering sum then for an inexperienced player who had been barely a year on the stage. But Gilbert, too, believed in her and it was at his suggestion that she had abandoned singing for acting. In the cast were Mrs. Gaston Murray, an old favourite at the St. James's; Rose Norreys, a very charming actress; Nutcombe Gould, Norman Forbes, Lewis Waller, Julia Neilson and Rutland Barrington. These last five players all achieved fame, Julia herself becoming one of the great leading ladies of the St. James's.

A large and expectant audience gathered. A new play by Gilbert was an event, and all hoped Barrington's second venture would bring him luck. But Gilbert's Gilbertian sense had been too strong for him. He had contrived a series of impossible situations in which nobody could believe. Despite beautiful mounting and splendid action, it was a disaster. Rose Norreys and Lewis Waller were commended. Clement Scott, who also had faith in Julia Neilson, nevertheless found fault with her, saying: "Miss Julia Neilson gave me the impression of being over-schooled. She was mechanical, and it was only when she had apparently forgotten her lesson and was her natural self that this beautiful and sweet-voiced actress showed of what she is capable."

It sounds as though Gilbert, the martinet of what are now called directors, had done a bit too much "producing"—a sure way of killing spontaneous talent.

> "Mr. Nutcombe Gould played with dignity and feeling as the aristocratic but obstinate old peer and Mrs. Gaston Murray was a true and tender wife," continues the critic: "Mr. Norman Forbes drew a clever and original sketch of the missionary, the Rev. Noel Ross; he and Miss Neilson were excellent in their one special scene in the third act . . . Seldom has a young actor so completely satisfied every demand made upon him as did Mr. Lewis Waller. His was a vindictive, revengeful character as Ralph Crampton, but with the germs of good lying dormant, and most thoroughly did he convey this; his hatred and passion were never boisterous, but were none the less intense, and there was a touch of deep pathos when he 'repented him of the evil' he had done. Mr. Rutland Barrington had to fulfil the role of a good-natured, soft-hearted country gentleman and by

MAUDE MILLETT

EVA MOORE with H. V. ESMOND

E. S. WILLARD

FAY DAVIS

LEADING LADIES

EVELYN MILLARD

LILIAN BRAITHWA

JULIA NEILSON

Another study of EVELYN MILLARD

IRENE VANBRUGH

his ease and bonhomie brightened up some occasions which were inclined to be too sombre."

Brantinghame Hall was a flop. Gilbert waived his royalties but the other creditors pressed for their money and Rutland Barrington went straight from the St. James's Theatre to the Bankruptcy Courts . . . The old ill luck was back again. St. James's was about to languish once more. Mrs. Langtry tried her luck, as Rosalind to the Jaques of Arthur Bourchier, and thereafter kept the theatre open a little while with *Esther Sandraz*. Arthur Bourchier also tried a few plays but with no success.

Then came another managerial disaster. The St. James's had once been the French theatre of London: it might become so again. Louis Meyer took possession with that end in view. It was not a very long view, for in 1890 he retired, hurt in pride and pocket, and the theatre was dark again. The hoodoo reigned once more. The sun had set and night was blackest.

But, as so often happens, that dark hour brought forth another dawn. Waiting round the corner was the man in whose destiny the salvation of the St. James's truly lay. His name was George Alexander.

CHAPTER 10

St. George for the St James's

IF ever a man and a theatre were destined to form a perfect partnership, that theatre was the St. James's and that man George Alexander. They came together in 1891, and only death on the human side dissolved the partnership. Alexander was the St. James's, and the St. James's was Alexander. Only the case of Tree and His Majesty's transcended this perfect combination of art and personality (and Tree built his theatre to fit himself). Cyril Maude was the ideal actor-manager for the Haymarket and Irving for the vast spaces of the Lyceum. But in the Alexander-St. James's alliance there seemed to be something extremely personal. It was as though they had been waiting for each other, so perfect was the mating. From the moment of their coming together—their marriage, as it were—the St. James's entered into a period of glory such as it had never hitherto experienced and which continued for twenty-seven years until Alexander's demise in 1918.

Alexander came there when the era of the actor-manager was approaching its zenith. He himself helped to make that era more glorious than it might have been without him. He knew what he was about: he laid his plans and he followed them. The result was nearly three decades of theatre at its best and most brilliant. Whatever happens in the future, the story of George Alexander and the St. James's, together, will provide one of the brightest patches in theatrical history.

George Alexander Gibb Samson was born on 19th June, 1858, and it is believed the event occurred in a railway train as it approached Reading Station. So Berkshire and the Great Western Railway may claim him as their own peculiar indigene, although by blood and breeding he was a Scot.

His father was an agent in the soft goods trade, whose territory covered most of the western counties. He was always on the move and indeed the whole family seemed to be a bit nomadic, for young Master George sent his father a remarkably well-written letter, at the age of five, from Bath and another at the age of six from Carlisle. It is not known what he was doing there. There is also a letter to his mother in the family archives, addressed from Bradford-on-Avon. Evidently his entrance into the world on a train had some influence on his mode of living! He went to school first at Clifton, then at Ealing, finishing off at the High School, Stirling. Naturally, he was taught the classics, and he kept as a relic of his school days an essay on Ovid written at fourteen, and a rhymed translation, in the style of Pope, of an extract from Virgil's *Bucolics*. He apparently appreciated Ovid even at that early age, for he classed him as one of the ablest, even if not one of the cleanest, poets of his time. The Virgil translation was made when he was fifteen. One thing common to both compilations was the amazingly clear handwriting. His knowledge of the classics remained with him. The good handwriting did not.

Young George Samson seems to have had excellent manners even as a boy, for his schoolmaster was struck by the difference between him and the much rougher lads of his class. But George was a manly lad who could, and did, look after himself. His schoolmaster, Duncan MacDougal, reported well of him at Stirling, and Alexander in later years always kept in touch with that excellent man. Indeed, the actor-to-be early showed his tenacity of purpose and appreciated at least one of old Polonius's precepts:

> "The friends thou hast, and their adoption tried,
> Grapple them to thy soul with hoops of steel."

Although by no means open-handed, Alexander never forgot old friends and, as he rose in the social scale, took delight in seeing that they benefited in a way suitable to their own position. He had the reputation of being a bit "near" but that was not so. It was simply his Scottish caution and his excellent business ability. He hated waste of any kind, but he knew how to give wisely.

On leaving school at the age of fifteen, young Samson became clerk in the famous soft goods firm, Messrs Leaf, Son and Company, then of Old Change, London, probably through his father's influence. He had a fine business brain and doubtless those few years in the City served him in good stead afterwards. The only pointer to what he thought of City life is contained in a letter from his old schoolmaster, with whom he maintained a constant correspondence, who regretted hearing that the business hours were very long. And, by modern standards, they were. Work normally began at 8.30 or 9 a.m. and was supposed to finish about six. But it was often much later, and in his particular line there would be seasonal rushes which meant working overtime. But the old dominie was sure he would become what he calls, in his old-fashioned, full-phrased manner "one of the merchant princes". He also sent good advice: "Avoid, I entreat you, the pernicious habit of smoking, the prevalent vice of the day. As to beer-drinking to excess I need say nothing, as I know by experience you are too much of a gentleman and have been trained too well ever to be guilty of so odious a crime." What the old Stirling schoolmaster—who opens for us that little window into 1873—would have thought of the smoking habit of today is something to muse upon.

There is no real evidence as to when young Samson began to feel the lure of the stage. Undoubtedly, however, while he was a clerk at Leaf, Son and Co. he went to theatres as often as he could—in all probability to the pit and gallery. But the urge was there already, because the young man soon joined an amateur dramatic society run in connection with the firm. It seems that fate then struck the first note on the lyre of his life. For the society gave a performance in aid of the Royal Hospital for Consumption, and it took place at—the St. James's Theatre. George Alexander Gibb Samson played in it. So, for the first time, he acquainted himself with the place which was to become so completely his. One wonders if he felt some premonition at the time, some thrill and quickening of the spirit, for in the world of the theatre such things are not unknown.

The young amateur must have had a fairly good part and probably made a success, because he wrote an account of it to his old schoolmaster and although that gentleman had a strong objection to tobacco he does not appear to have been averse to the stage, for he replied that he was glad George's superior dramatic talent had been devoted to so good a cause. If the part had not been good and the success considerable—as described by the young man—he would hardly have used that phrase. Those dramatic performances were annual events, and it would appear that Alexander was in them all.

The battle between business and the theatre came to an end for young George in 1879, with a victory for the theatre. But his period in the soft goods trade was never forgotten by his detractors, and like all successful men and especially successful actors, he had them. They would describe him as a "shopwalker"—a gent that no longer exists but who once loomed large in the drapery world.

Samson chose the stage with a perfectly clear knowledge of all the risks he ran. But as he knew the risks he also knew how to avoid them. His orderly mind and shrewd common sense enabled him to plot his way ahead. He knew what he wanted and he went straight towards his goal. He was now twenty-one, and had doubtless waited until he was free from parental control before he took the plunge. His birthday was in June and it was in the autumn that he entered the profession which he was so greatly to adorn. There was, indeed, a family row. His father was furious. He severed relations and for a considerable time they neither met nor wrote to each other. But the young man's resolution was not shaken. Instinctively he knew he had made the right decision. Indeed, it is highly probable that he regarded the choice as his duty, for he had a motto, a concept which he kept constantly before him:

"Do thy duty, that is best,
Leave unto thy God the rest."

It must be said that he always lived up to it.

The stage was alive with great players and the theatre was booming. In the provinces also it was flourishing, and it was there that young Samson made his entry. He was more than content to tour and gain the experience without which no London management would engage him. Many of the provincial theatres still played "stock", and there were on the road real repertory companies which carried a selection of pieces and changed the bill nightly. Such a one was run by Ada Swanborough and W. H. Vernon, who had trained many stars, including Kate and Ellen Terry, Mrs. Kendal, Mrs. Bancroft, Henrietta Hodson and Arthur Stirling. At Bristol, Vernon had played everything from Hamlet to farce. In 1879 he had scored a resounding success in *The Snowball*, adapted from the French by Sydney Grundy, and it was in this play that the young beginner, who now took the name he was to make so famous, George Alexander, first appeared when the company opened at the Theatre Royal, Nottingham. With this repertory company he played a variety of parts and always acquitted himself well. He was perhaps a "natural" actor, as David Garrick had been, though not as great a one as he—not at least at this point of his career. But he had the same natural aptitude, the same superb capacity for learning, remembering and putting it over.

When that tour ended, Alexander was engaged by William Foulis, another touring manager, to play George d'Alroy in *Caste*, on a run of the smaller English towns. His salary was £2 10*s*. a week. The tour opened on Boxing Night, 1880. His success did not go unnoticed, for Tom Robertson, Junior, who toured his father's plays and had a more ambitious company, offered him £3 10*s*. a week. Naturally, Alexander accepted. He was re-engaged for the autumn season at £5 and for the winter season at £6. These were fine salaries at that time: George Alexander was going up! The incipient knight who was to slay the dragon of bad luck which the Kendals had already shaken at the St. James's soon won his spurs in the provinces. Approaching the venue of his conquest somewhat deviously, he made his first professional appearance in the metropolis at The Standard, Shoreditch, rather far to the east, on 4th April, 1881. It was in a farcical comedy called *The Guv'nor*, adapted from the German by S. G. Lankester (pen-name of Robert Reece), which had been seen at the Vaudeville the previous year. In this piece, probably much to his relief, he confirmed the repute which had preceded him to the capital, and as a result found himself very much a topic of conversation in theatrical circles.

An early upshot of the talk was an invitation which simultaneously thrilled and alarmed him. It came from no less a luminary than the great Henry Irving, and offered him the part of Caleb Deecie in a revival of *The Two Roses* at the Lyceum, at a salary of seven guineas a week of six performances. Alexander's calm Scots caution made him pause. With Irving at the Lyceum, he would come face to face with the real London public and with the critics, and he was sensible enough to realise that one precipitate move might set him back severely. In a dither of doubt he called on Irving and expressed his misgivings. Irving, however, insisted he considered him fit for the part or would not otherwise have offered it to him. He no doubt admired the young man's diffidence. Anyway, he dispelled his doubts and on 26th November, 1881, a pigmy among giants in experience, Alexander played the part.

He had to follow the great original of Thomas Thorne who had created the role at the Vaudeville in 1870, played it in the subsequent revival of 1874, and was still fresh in the memories of those who would watch Alexander. In some slight degree his fears were confirmed, for inevitably the critics did compare him with Thorne. But he made the grade all right, for Clement Scott remarked that "though it may be confessed that Mr. Thorne seemed an ideal Caleb Deecie, no one can deny that Mr. George Alexander is a very promising young actor. In fact, he did more than promise, he fulfilled. His good looks, his quiet manner and his manly dignity won the entire house." In the cast with him were, besides Irving, William Terriss, David James (as "Our Mr. Jenkins"), Mr. Howe—an excellent actor, Winifred Emery, Helen Mathews, Claire Pauncefort and C. Ewell. So he made his mark in most distinguished company. How deep that mark was is shown by the fact that during the run he received (as already noted) an invitation to join the Kendals and Hare at the St. James's, where he undertook to play second parts to Mr. Kendal, at a salary of ten guineas. His value was steadily mounting and he had now reached what was affluence in those golden and elegant days.

His arrival at the St. James's has been chronicled. He played there in *Impulse*, *Young Folks' Ways*, and later in *The Ironmaster*, and his salary rose to twelve guineas. He was indeed getting on. In 1884 he returned to the Lyceum, for a season run by the beautiful Mary Anderson who put on *Comedy and Tragedy*, the author of which, W. S. Gilbert, personally picked George Alexander for the part of d'Aulnay. The play opened on 26th January, 1884, but, disappointingly perhaps, he received no rave notices. He was said, in company with J. H. Barnes, to be "adequate but not extraordinary".

Still, that was good enough for Irving, who was in need of a competent player. William Terriss had left the Lyceum and he wanted a successor in the roles that fine actor had played. He decided on Alexander, who during the next six years added polish to every aspect of his art. It was July, 1884, when he rejoined Irving, and in September he accompanied him on his second tour of America. In the same company was another young actor marked for greatness, but then only making himself generally useful. His name was Martin Harvey.

Meanwhile, Alexander had married Florence Theleur, who aided him so greatly in his career and was to be the unseen but all-pervading hostess at the St. James's. Irving refers to the couple in a letter home from Quebec, on 30th September, 1884, from which Laurence Irving quotes: "You will remember Alexander. He has succeeded Terriss as the leading young man of the company and is one of the most gentlemanly and unaffected fellows I've ever met. His wife is a perfect lady and their society alone would make the tour a pleasant one." Those qualities were exactly right for their subsequent administration at the St. James's.

Gordon Craig, who was with his mother, Ellen Terry, on this trip, also mentioned Alexander in a letter commenting on the egoism of actors:

> "You would be amused," he said, "by the petty jealousies of this expedition. This contemptible littleness seems to be fostered by the theatrical atmosphere and Alexander is the only actor I have ever met who is absolutely free from it. And because he has a finer nature than any of the men with whom he is associated, he is made to suffer things which are very hard to bear."

During the tour Alexander went on for Irving in certain parts. Gordon Craig reported that, except for a few slips, he did it very well and at very short notice. Mrs. Alexander in her nervousness bit to pieces the fan she was carrying and tried to prompt her husband from a stage box. Alexander was by no means word perfect but he managed to improvise and to give cues. Once only did he dry up completely. He turned to an actor nearby and asked: "What is it?" When given the line, he smiled sweetly and continued, and the audience responded with sympathetic laughter and applause.

Home again in 1885, he remained at the Lyceum for the seventh of Irving's seasons there. It is not in the scope of this story to give a life of Alexander or to record all the parts he played with Irving. Suffice it to remark how that expert schooling paved the path of his ambition—which he already nurtured—to become an actor-manager. In this season he did well in *The Amber Heart*, and here again came in for comparison, this time with Tree. Marie de Mensiaux, a capable critic, said: "Mr. Alexander is excellent in the first act, showing an earnestness that was wanting in Mr. Beerbohm Tree, but he does not equal him in the weary but courteous indifference in the second act; in the last, he is very good." Tree had scored because he was essentially a character actor, which Act 2 called for; Alexander scored in the others as a fine straight actor.

Those years, formative and valuable as they were, often almost drove Alexander to distraction. Irving was a hard master. He rehearsed furiously, ceaselessly and often mercilessly. He had a fine vein of sarcastic venom, quiet but deadly, in which he loved to indulge. It was always to the point and doubtless more valuable than any amount of raving and cursing would have been. Alexander met it himself when rehearsing as Macduff, a part he played eventually with great success. It was Irving's habit to give the players their heads for a few rehearsals, to see how far they had grasped their roles. Now Alexander was the quintessence of courtliness and gentility, and was always faultlessly dressed. Somehow these qualities had "come through" the character of Macduff, or so Irving thought. He called Alexander and said: "I see what you are driving at, my boy. But Macduff, you know, is a Highland chieftain, a rough soldier, man of blood and battle, living by the sword, used to keeping his own head with his own hands and to killing his man as part of the day's work. Stark, strong, violent—hardly anything of Piccadilly." He surveyed Alexander pointedly. The result was a subjugation of the actor and a really excellent Macduff.

Often, when returning home weary and exasperated from hours of slave-driven rehearsal, he told his wife that he thought he had made a dreadful mistake in going on the stage at all. He said also that if and when he had a company of his own he would let them down pretty easily. He had, in fact, made no mistake in his vocation and his wife would tell him so, always adding her approval as to the way he would treat his actors when his turn came. He got some consolation from the knowledge that he was pleasing Irving, for his salary rose steadily. He had begun his regular engagement to replace Terriss at £20 a week of six performances, all matinees one-sixth extra; at the end he was earning £45, with the same matinee percentage.

Along with his triumphs he had, of course, his disappointments. The worst of these came when Irving produced *Faust* on 19th December, 1885. Alexander had counted on the title role, but it was given to H. B. Conway, another very popular player. Only an actor can understand the heartbreak he felt. But he took control of himself. Allotted Valentine, a showy but small part, he swallowed his pride and decided to do his best, which he evidently did. Godfrey Turner wrote: "The honest and legitimate success of Mr. George Alexander as Valentine is fair ground for such congratulation as, considering the smallness of the part, would appear impertinent if carried to the bounds of high praise." Soon afterwards came his reward. Conway, who had been in bad health, broke down. On the fourth night he retired and never played again. Alexander stepped into the coveted part and played it to great applause for the remainder of the 384 performances—a run almost unprecedented then.

By this time he had firmly set his heart on management and a theatre of his own, which remained unattainable while he stayed with Irving. But those years had taught him much: he had seen the immense care with which Irving prepared his productions, and how he mounted magnificent spectacles without dwarfing the acting; and he saw what appeared to his cautious Scots business mind tremendous waste, for Irving would pour out money like water to obtain what he desired. He had watched, listened, suffered, triumphed and learned. And he was always grateful for the opportunity. He understood Irving's greatness and held him in the highest respect. It was this supreme regard that induced him to give H. B. Irving an engagement at the St. James's which did that young actor much good, and also to his leading a deputation to the Dean of St. Paul's to ask that Sir Henry might be buried there. Indeed, on being refused he went to the Dean of Westminster to ask for an Abbey burial, and after a battle—for there was still a prejudice against actors—gained his point.

In 1889, after he had been with Irving for five years, there was no part for him in the next production. His last was Macduff and he made a big impression in it. That celebrated critic and theatrical scholar, Percy Fitzgerald, said: "Mr. Alexander was a valiant, solid Macduff without anything of the declamation (and often ranting) associated with this character." Evidently nothing of Piccadilly, either!

Alexander left the Lyceum and went farther up the Strand into a melodrama called *London Day by Day* at the Adelphi. This was by those two experts in that line of drama, George R. Sims and Henry Pettitt. It was a good title, for most newspapers carried features under that heading. Both authors knew their London well, and they incorporated many of the "sights". They staged a Jewish money-lender's office, a night club, Leicester Square, and the old Alhambra music hall by night (with scuffles between revellers and the police), together with a murder in perpetration, a trial in a metropolitan police court, and St. Katherine's Wharf with the dark Thames slowly gliding by at night. Produced on Saturday, 14th September, 1889, it was just the stuff for the Adelphi. William Terriss had made melodrama the staple fare there for some time. Now he was away for a while and Alexander followed him in, just as he had followed him with Irving.

The staging of *London Day by Day* got an excellent Press and so did the company, which was pretty well an all-star cast. The critics acclaimed George Alexander, and foresaw him soon a great favourite. Those Adelphi days must have been extremely busy ones for Alexander. However, he had now taken his decision—he would go into management. He had been on the stage for only ten years and a great part of that time had been spent in the provinces. Nevertheless, he felt secure in his confidence and had courage enough to try.

Though he had saved money he had not a lot of capital; but he considered it enough. He discussed the matter with his wife, a graceful and clever woman, and they decided on the enterprise. He had already acquired a play with that end in view before he left the Lyceum. It was a farce by Hamilton Aidé called *Dr. Bill.* He visualised himself in it and foresaw success. While playing in *London Day by Day* he had also acquired a theatre—the Avenue (on the site of the Playhouse, now a B.B.C. studio). He had the money, the play and the theatre, but when he was ready to start, the Gattis, who ran the Adelphi, refused to release him from his contract. Bitterly disappointed but undaunted, he sought another actor to play the part until he was free. So he engaged no less a person than Fred Terry, on the understanding that he would relinquish the part when Alexander was ready to take over.

Dr. Bill opened at the Avenue on Saturday, 1st February, 1890. In the cast were Fred Terry, playing Dr. William Brown, Albert Chevalier, Benjamin Webster, Henry Grattan, Fanny Brough, Elizabeth Robins, Carlotta Leclerq and Marie Linden. The play was an adaptation from a risqué French original. The Doctor, who is the central figure, is respectably married and settled down. In younger days he had been the favourite doctor of ballerinas, burlesque actresses and the like, and was *persona grata* with them all. He wants to conduct a quiet steady practice, but his father-in-law is determined to push him along, and although doctors are not allowed to advertise, this gentleman gives him some stunt publicity, and his old colourful patients begin to descend on him. This results in all sorts of complications peculiar to French farce. Not the least is a dance, called "The Kangaroo Dance", which Miss Fauntleroy, a former patient, insists on introducing into the surgery and making him take part. The whole thing caused hurricanes of laughter and storms of applause. The entire company had to take calls after every act and there was an ovation for the adapter at the end. Thanks largely to that dance, Alexander was off to a flying start. The music for it was composed by a young man who himself became famous—Herman Finck, immortalised by "In the Shadows". Finck was first violin in the Avenue Theatre orchestra, under the baton of John Crook (who, amongst many other things, composed the music for *The Lady Slavey* and *Peter Pan*) when he wrote that lovely tune.

In due course Alexander joined the cast and *Dr. Bill* ran on merrily. Unfortunately, the manager bolted with the cash. That, however, did not daunt Alexander. When *Dr. Bill* was withdrawn, he staged *The Struggle for Life*, which was a failure. Now, when Alexander had told Irving of his venture into management, the Master had smiled cryptically and told him that if at the end of six months he wanted to come back to the Lyceum, he would be welcome. But Alexander had plenty of pluck and tenacity. He doubtless recalled the conversation but he had no intention of going back. He put on another play by R. C. Carton called *Sunlight and Shadow*, which was only a moderate success. Then, in November, 1890, Alexander took his next step forward. He signed the lease of the St. James's Theatre.

CHAPTER II

Light and Shade

ONE play, *Sunlight and Shadow*, with which Alexander saw fit to make his managerial début at the St. James's, is worthy of more than passing attention, for it marked the beginning of a period of distinction almost unrivalled in the British theatre. First produced at the Avenue on Saturday, 1st November, 1890, it was by R. C. Carton, a most successful playwright. It took the stage at St. James's on 31st January, 1891, with the following cast:

Dr. Latimer	Mr. Nutcombe Gould.
Mark Denzil	Mr. Yorke Stephens.
Mr. Bamfie	Mr. Ben Webster.
George Addis (Choirmaster, a cripple)	Mr. George Alexander.
Scollick (a Gardener)	Mr. Alfred Holles.
Helen (the Doctor's daughters)	Miss Marion Terry.
Maud (the Doctor's daughters)	Miss Maude Millett.
Janet Pelton	Miss Ada Neilson.

Of its original Avenue production, a distinguished critic had said:

> "This is one of the most delightful plays that has been seen for a long time. There was sufficient incident to keep the interest thoroughly alive, the dialogue was crisp, epigrammatic, and infinitely above the average, and in it were two types of English womanhood specially true to life."

The story concerns Helen Latimer, daughter of a hardworking country doctor, who has few pleasures but finds happiness in being a comfort to those around her. Her young sister Maud, the beauty of the family, is rather a tyrant but Helen is her willing slave. Miss Maud is being courted by young Bamfie, a pleasant but empty-headed young man. To Helen comes Mark Denzil, no longer young but a man of the world. He has married beneath him and his wife has led him a distressing life. He now believes her dead and comes to offer himself to Helen. They are just about to become engaged, when the wife, who has taken the name of Janet Felton, turns up and the dream of happiness is dashed.

Four months elapse: Helen becomes resigned and then discovers that George Addis, the poor, plain, crippled choirmaster of the place has loved her all his life. His fortunes have improved and now he proposes to her. As she cannot marry the man she loves and has a great compassion and some affection for Addis, she is inclined to accept but defers decision. Then Addis discovers that Denzil's wife is really dead. What shall he do? He believes that Helen will now marry Denzil. Shall he suppress his news and gain his own happiness? He is tortured almost beyond endurance. Denzil comes to say good-bye to Helen and Addis heroically tells him the truth and sacrifices his own hopes.

It was thus a play with a sad ending, and very much risk for any rising actor-manager. Alexander, however, had the courage to take the chance, and, furthermore, to play the part of a cripple devoid of any attraction save nobility of soul. By so doing he threw to the winds his charm and good looks, which were his stock-in-trade, and relied solely on his acting. He took a big chance and it paid off. A critic said: "I cannot say which played the better—Miss Marion Terry, in her pure, unselfish, graceful womanhood or Mr. George Alexander in his noble, long-suffering and self-denial. Both afforded an artistic treat."

But for the unhappy ending the play would have been a huge success, but it did well enough and fully justified Alexander's "hunch" in opening the St. James's with a revival rather than take the double risk of a new play. The Kendals had done the same sort of thing.

The supporting cast was splendid. Nutcombe Gould was a fine, virile actor, and Yorke Stephens one of the best who ever trod the stage. Ben Webster became famous and later married Dame May Whitty. He was a handsome man—if not a great actor a very well-graced one. Alfred Holles, a fine character-man, provided the low comedy, and Maude Millett abounded with charm and talent. Ada Neilson had power and dramatic strength.

On the first night this was preceded by a curtain-raiser, *Man Proposes*; but later in the run they played as an afterpiece a light, powder-and-patch comedy. *The Gay Lothario*. Alexander gave good measure, as he always did. He used to provide a curtain-raiser if the play was short, thus giving an opportunity to little-known dramatists and young actors. Nor did he disdain to play in them himself. He did so on this occasion, and his handsome appearance in the powder and silk made a fine contrast to his pale, suffering, twisted figure in *Sunlight and Shadow*.

Other details in the programme showed that the play began at 8.15 p.m. and carriages were called at 10.50. The prices were: boxes, £4 4*s* to £1 1*s*; stalls, 10/6; dress circle, 7/- and 5/-; upper boxes (numbered and reserved and bonnets allowed), 3/-; pit, 2/-; gallery, 1/-. Programmes were free. The box-office opened daily from 10 a.m. till 5 p.m. Seats could be booked by letter, telegram or telephone. It is interesting to note that telephones were so few that no exchange was specified—just the number, in this case No. 3903. Alexander's musical director was Walter Slaughter, Robert V. Shone was the stage-manager and Alwyn Lewis the business manager. It is also noteworthy that the dresses for the afterpiece were designed by Percy Anderson, one of the very best stage designers.

For once, the two leading critics of the period agreed with each other. William Archer declared: "I said, and I will maintain to the last drop in my inkstand, that it is a genial, sunny and gentlemanlike piece of work; one of those plays (to adapt Emerson) 'which always find us young, and tend to keep us so.' " Clement Scott's verdict was: "The play charms, it does not startle. Its motive is simple, not exaggerated or improbable. Its characters are not cranks but flesh and blood, men and women."

The audience that night found themselves in a rejuvenated St. James's, for Alexander had had a spring-clean before entering into occupation. The dingy old theatre, so long untouched by the decorator, had blossomed like the rose. The new paint was of a warm and friendly tint, the new upholstered seats were attractive and comfortable, and electric light had replaced the fitful glimmer of the old gaslights. The St. James's had renewed its youth. It was starting afresh—and on the right road.

Sunlight and Shadow served its purpose by playing Alexander into his theatre and giving him time to prepare his first new piece. This was *The Idler*, by C. Haddon Chambers. Born in Sydney in 1860, Chambers had been in Government service and had then worked on a "station" as a stock rider. He first came to England on a six months' visit in 1880, and returned here in 1882. He started with short stories, became a journalist, and then wrote *Captain Swift* for Tree at the Haymarket in 1888. It was a big success. *The Idler* was his second important play.

R. C. Carton, author of *Sunlight and Shadow*, was a Londoner with a background of medicine. His father was Dr. D. Critchett, an eminent oculist, and his uncle, Sir Anderson Critchett, the well-known specialist. Carton, however, decided to become an actor but left the stage to write plays. In collaboration with Cecil Raleigh, one of the finest writers of big melodramas, he wrote, among other things, *The Great Pink Pearl*, *The Pointsman*, and *The Treasure*. His first original play written on his own was *Sunlight and Shadow*.

Haddon Chambers excelled in what was called "drawing-room melodrama", the type of play which—like *Captain Swift* in Tree's sure hands—had become quite a vogue. Alexander wisely followed popular taste. He made no pretence of educating the public: he just gave them what they wanted. And, young himself, he patronised young dramatists, while leavening their work by favouring experience in his players.

Alexander produced *The Idler* on 26th February, 1891. In it were Herbert Waring, Nutcombe Gould, Marion Terry, Gertrude Kingston, Maude Millett, and, of course, Alexander himself—an all-star cast. It was in three acts and covered four days. The acts were set at "Sir John Harding's" in Kensington Palace Gardens (Herbert Waring played Sir John); at "Mrs. Cross's" (Lady Monckton played that part); and at "Mark Cross's Rooms in Piccadilly" (this was Alexander's role).

Previously, it had been a success in New York. It was drawing-room drama all right. Mark Cross, a rich young man, makes an unhappy marriage and leaves his unfaithful wife. Although still married he falls in love with a young girl. He has the decency to go to America and there leads a wild life among the miners, making a great friend of one of them, "Gentleman Jack". News of his wife's death brings him home. He goes to the girl he had loved, only to find she has married Sir John Harding, M.P. . . . no other than his old acquaintance "Gentleman Jack"! Sir John has not told his wife about his past, which includes killing a man in a drunken bout and fleeing the consequences. The dead man's brother is in England seeking revenge on the killer, and Cross warns Harding about this. In due course the brother, Simeon Strong (played by an American, John Mason), calls on both men and lays his plans. Seeing a chance to win the girl he loved (played by Marion Terry), Cross plans to get her to his chambers and possess her, in return for saving her husband. Lady Harding, who loves her husband, sees no way out. Cross obtains a written promise from Strong that he will let Sir John alone. When Lady Harding visits him and he attempts to seduce her, her appeal to his better nature brings out the latent good in him, and he is allowing her to depart when her husband arrives and puts the worst construction on the situation. He demands a duel between Cross and himself with no witnesses. Strong turns up and stops this. Lady Harding convinces her husband of her innocence and they go away together. Cross decides to commit suicide—a worthless idler only causes trouble in the world. But his mother, whom he dearly loves, comes to see him. He puts away his revolver and orders his servant to pack for a long journey. Whither will he travel? "God knows!" he says, as the curtain falls.

A contemporary critic wrote:

> "The author was most fortunate in securing an actor of Mr. Alexander's ability, who could so ably depict the inner nature of a complex character like Cross, and even more so in having in Miss Marion Terry an actress who was so pure, and feminine and true, that the beauty of Lady Harding's devotion to her husband, and her pity for the man who so madly loved her, were admirably displayed. Mr. Herbert Waring supported the cast admirably with his firm grasp of character, and in Mr. John Mason, an American actor who made his first appearance in London, we had a gentleman who at once established himself as a leading spirit from his breadth of style and easy yet earnest manliness. His scene with Mr. Alexander was as finely rendered by both as could possibly be done." There were good notices for all, and the critic noted that "the dresses were marvels of beauty and taste. The luxury of the mounting of *The Idler* was only equalled by the exquisite taste displayed by all the ladies' costumes."

The Idler had a pleasing and profitable run of 176 performances.

Further comment on dress and décor came from A. W. Bean, a well-known journalist, who said:

"The action on the part of our managers in placing the furnishing of their stage interiors in the hands of competent men, proves that they are making an effort, and with success, to enable us to escape from the opprobrium of being a people without artistic taste. Some of us, especially the ladies, dress better than we used to do—often the result of seeing a model costume on the stage. The next step in the same direction is to furnish better—to better dress our dwellings. Hence the appreciation of art furniture and its accompanying decorations. For instance, who can visit *The Idler* at the St. James's Theatre and come away without their artistic perceptions receiving improvement? The charming set in the second scene, arranged in the Louis Seize style, shows a strong contrast to the sumptuous chambers of Mark Cross in the last act, so artistically arranged by the firm of Messrs F. Giles and Co., whose setting of this scene in antique oak furniture will be much appreciated by those who see the play, and especially by those persons whose financial positions will enable them to carry out in their homes such elegant designs."

All this goes to show how taste was improving and marks a new trend in theatrical history. It shows that Alexander, having absorbed Irving's example, was setting a standard of production at the St. James's. It reveals also his business acumen, for doubtless that firm of furnishers either lent the goods for the advertisement or let him have them at a very low price or on weekly rental. His own taste, and that of his wife, who supervised so much of this side of his work, would see to it that the furniture was displayed not as in a show-room but as part of a home that could be lived in. The article in question gives two other examples—a room in *L'Enfant Prodigue* and a scene in *A Million of Money* at Drury Lane, in which Gus Harris had given *carte blanche* to a well-known antiquarian named Litchfield. In décor the St. James's was leading the field. And Alexander was in his rightful place as its actor-manager.

A glance at his cast, some of whom were to be with him time and again, is instructive, as showing that he had the sense to attach players to theatres, and that if he did not have a definite stock company he did at least keep the nucleus of one, which is good theatre policy.

Marion Terry had been his leading lady in *Sunlight and Shadow*, as well as in *The Idler*. This splendid actress was the younger sister of

Ellen Terry (Kate being the elder, and Florence the youngest of all). Marion had all the Terry charm and talent. She was born in London on 16th October, 1856, and educated at Kingston-on-Thames. It is said that her stage début was at the Theatre Royal, Manchester, in 1873, but she had probably made small appearances before that, for the Terrys believed in doing things by degrees. Her acknowledged début was in the onerous part of Ophelia, and her family would have made sure she was fit for it.

In 1874 she was in London with Henry Neville at the Olympic, playing all kinds of parts. She made her first big success in *Weak Women*, by H. J. Byron, at the old Strand Theatre, and quickly followed it by an even more outstanding success in Gilbert's *Dan'l Druce, Blacksmith* at the Haymarket in 1876, where her quiet charm and unforced methods won her warm acclamation. It was the beginning of a career as distinguished as it was long. She had the knack of stealing a play without any effort, for she compelled attention. If she had to be epitomised in one word, that word would be "serene". Already an established actress when she joined Alexander, she added to her laurels at the St. James's. Her only imperfection was the Terry failing of forgetting her lines . . . but the public never knew it!

Fresh in the memories of many will be her delightful performance as the elder sister in *Quality Street*. She is finely summed up by Clement Scott, who said:

> "She is one of the very few actresses I have known who has never gone back from her gentle career of continued success . . . With her gifted sisters, some characters have suited her better than others; but from the old Olympic days down to the present time I never remember to have been disappointed with Marion Terry or wished she had not appeared in such-and-such a character."

Succeeding historians of the stage echo those words. She died on the 21st August, 1930, in her seventy-seventh year, regretted by all. She was as fine an actress as our stage ever held and a pillar of the St. James's.

Herbert Waring was also one of Alexander's pillars. He was born (was it prophetic?) at St. James's Place, S.W., in 1857, and his real name was Herbert Waring Rutty. Educated first at Dulwich College and then at Merchant Taylors, he became a schoolmaster, and something of his scholastic preciseness never left him. But he did not like his profession and abandoned it for the stage. He walked on as one of the Oxford crew in Dion Boucicault's drama *Formosa* at the Adelphi in 1877. After playing at the ill-fated Park Theatre, Camden Town, he returned to the Adelphi in *Proof*, followed by a considerable round of parts. Then he joined Tom Robertson to play Captain Hawtree in the No. 2 tour of *Caste*. In that same company, as D'Alroy, was George Alexander and a connection began which was to last, with intervals, for years. The Kendals saw him in this play and engaged him for *Impulse* at the St. James's. There, as the Curate in *The Hobby Horse*, he got his first big break. He played at practically every theatre in town, toured America, and essayed actor-managership at the Imperial. But at the St. James's, where he felt most at home, he was always right in the picture.

Herbert Waring had a clear-cut, incisive manner and knew how to hold a scene. He could when necessary impart tremendous intensity. As the years went on, he began to lose his sight but continued acting. Few who saw him give a polished performance and move about the stage with perfect ease realised that he could hardly see at all but had memorised the position of each exit, each piece of furniture, and how many paces were needed. He died on 31st January, 1932, aged seventy-four. Though not regarded as a star he was one of the best of that amazing array of "second" actors in which the Edwardian stage was so very rich.

Gertrude Kingston had a long and distinguished career before her when she played in *The Idler*. Born in London, of mixed German and Italian origin, she studied art but elected to go on the stage. She was with Sarah Thorne at the Theatre Royal, Margate—a magnificent apprenticeship—and first appeared in London with Tree at the Haymarket in 1888 in *Partners*. During the South African War she was mentioned in dispatches for her services with the Actors' and Actresses' Hospital Hut. She became an actress-manageress in 1910 when she opened the Little Theatre in John Street, Adelphi, with *Lysistrata*. Distinguished both as actress and woman she died in 1937 at the age of seventy-one.

Maude Millett, born at Rajanpur, India, in 1867, daughter of Colonel Ley Millett, made her début at the old Novelty Theatre in

1884 and was promptly engaged by Charles Hawtrey for his production of *The Private Secretary* at the Globe. She was the ideal "juvenile girl", pretty, graceful, sweet-voiced, and with a nice taste in comedy. She died in 1920 and was playing almost to the end.

From these brief sketches will be seen the sort of people with whom, in his good judgment, Alexander surrounded himself, and the standard of acting he set at the St. James's from the start. In that same year, 1891, he added an additional one-act play called *Molière*, by Walter Frith, to *The Idler* bill. He himself played the great dramatist and with him were Herbert Waring, Alfred Holles, Ben Webster, and Marion Terry. Only a fragment, it portrayed the death of Molière. The critic Cecil Howard said:

> "Though the subject is impressive, only Mr. Alexander's fine acting saved the piece from being wearisome. Miss Marion Terry has really nothing to do but to look bewitching and almost scornful. Mr. Ben Webster sketched the character of the dissipated Marquis skilfully and Mr. Waring gave the idea of an attached friend as Dr. Dacquin. The author was called on the fall of the curtain. The piece was very handsomely mounted, the scene beautifully painted by H. B. Hall, the artist attached to the theatre, and the dresses by L. and H. Nathan were rich and thoroughly appropriate."

Although *The Idler* had had a considerable run, it went over as freshly as ever on the last night, which was also the last of the season. Alexander, in a few parting words of thanks for the patronage afforded him through his first season, announced that he would reopen at the end of September, again with *The Idler* and *Molière*. He had come to the end of his first season and was flushed with pride and pleasure at the support he had won. He had done more. He had brought the St. James's out of the shadows into the sun, and it remained there as long as he lived.

CHAPTER 12

Enter Oscar Wilde

ALEXANDER reopened as announced, with *The Idler* and *Molière*, following them on 17th November, 1891, with *Lord Anerley*, by Mark Quinton and Henry Hamilton, who so often collaborated with Cecil Raleigh in the great Drury Lane dramas. Here again was melodrama, but its scenes varied from a corral in the Wild West to a stately home in England. It was a most involved and wildly improbable tale, in which Alexander again played a man of dual nature. Once more the play was elaborately mounted and dressed, especially the Wild West scene, and again there was high praise for all and everything concerned. One critic remarked: "Mr. Alexander has of late achieved success by portraying characters in which good and evil are constantly warring, and it was this quality which probably caused him to accept the play under notice."

The cast included, besides Alexander, Nutcombe Gould, Arthur Bourchier, Ben Webster, Herbert Waring, Gertrude Kingston and Marion Terry—the semi-stock company again. On the first night the play was well received and it looked as if it would win. But the public did not respond. Was the hoodoo of the St. James's going to return? Alexander did not think so. Everyone could make a mistake and he had made one now. He swiftly replaced *Lord Anerley* with *Forgiveness*, by J. Comyns Carr, which went into the bill on 30th December, 1891. Alexander knew when to take off a play, which is as important to success as knowing when to put one on. *Forgiveness* did not last long, despite moderately good notices:

> "For general elegance and refinement of language," said a typical notice, "constantly brightened by clever repartee, epigram and wit, it would be difficult to find a superior play to Mr. Comyns Carr's *Forgiveness*. Its faults consist in the light comedy element, the silly

loves of Tommy Muir and Lucy Badger, the weakness of the character of Mrs. Badger, and the introduction of the Rev. Maitland Muir, a bore, having no proper connection with the play."

Another weakness was the extreme complexity of the plot. The critics were not unkind, but the public wouldn't have it.

Disappointed but not defeated, Alexander now tried a shot of a very different calibre. This was *Lady Windermere's Fan*, by Oscar Wilde, who took his place in the St. James's tapestry on 20th February, 1892. The production was the first of the great landmarks which Alexander was to set up at the St. James's. It is a matter of considerable importance, not only to that theatre but to the history of our stage in general, because it was Wilde's first play.

Wilde was already famous as the man who had set a new fashion in literature. He was an accepted wit and his epigrams were quoted everywhere. As a best-seller, he had become accustomed to having his own way and loved to demolish opponents with a witty, biting phrase. When he turned to writing plays he was, like all novelists, inclined to let his ideas and language dominate the characters and give the speeches priority over the action.

It would seem that Alexander, who had just suffered a couple of failures, wanted to attempt something new in methods of construction. Rehearsals began and almost at once the brilliant dilettante and the equally brilliant practical man were at loggerheads. While Alexander knew exactly what he wanted *qua* play, Wilde knew exactly what he wanted *qua* dialogue. Alexander was firmly set on two things: he was going to have a comedy twist at the end of the second act instead of the traditional emotional outburst. He was equally insistent that Wilde's desire to keep the relationship between Mrs. Erlynne and Lady Windermere a secret and suddenly spring it on the audience would ruin the play. He knew audience mentality and was not going to offend it. Wilde pleaded that nothing like the character of Mrs. Erlynne had been seen on the stage before. That, however, was not Alexander's point. He was concerned about the proper construction to achieve success. Wilde would argue and storm and then rush away and take to his bed. He would write long and rather pompous letters to Alexander, claiming he had been insulted, and in return receive short, pithy answers from the cool concise Scot, who refused to be side-tracked and grimly stuck to his guns. Finally, Wilde surrendered and attended the last rehearsals. Maybe he realised he was learning a new craft at the hands of a master.

The announcement of the play evoked much excitement. Oscar Wilde bestrode the world of fashion and his name was a magnet among the élite. Everyone who was anyone, and a great number who were not, simply had to see his play. It was produced on a Saturday, which was a fashionable night in the time before week-ends were invented. It must have been an anxious time for Wilde, on trial in a new line, and for Alexander, who was risking a new play by a man new to the theatre and whose very brilliance in other fields might make the critics hypercritical. He was, moreover, experimenting with a new kind of treatment and a new kind of play. He was, courageously, taking a triple, even a quadruple risk. Naturally, he gave it every possible chance. The cast was:

Lord Windermere .... Mr. George Alexander.
Lord Darlington .... Mr. Nutcombe Gould.
Lord Augustus Lorton .... Mr. H. H. Vincent.
Mr. Charles Dumby .... Mr. A. Vane-Tempest.
Mr. Cecil Graham .... Mr. Ben Webster.
Lady Windermere .... Miss Lily Hanbury.
The Duchess of Berwick .... Miss Fanny Coleman.
Lady Agatha Carlisle .... Miss Laura Graves.
Mrs. Erlynne .... Miss Marion Terry.

It will be seen that he relied largely on a well-tried team, only Vane-Tempest and Lily Hanbury being new to the St. James's. Alexander knew how much familiar faces in accustomed surroundings helped actors to a good performance. The "stock" members we have already met. A word now about the newcomers.

Francis Adolphus Vane-Tempest was an elegant young man of titled parentage, educated at Harrow and Oxford, who became an actor after twice failing for Parliament. His rejection is not surprising, as he looked the typical brainless aristocrat. Brains he had, however, and with them an appearance ideal for Society roles. After some preliminary experience under Charles Wyndham at the Criterion in 1891, he went to the St. James's to play Mr. Charles Dumby—a part which fitted him like a glove. Many will remember this clever actor, who was never better than as the Envoy from Dublin Castle in *General John Regan*. In this episode of Irish rebellion he was morally coerced into removing his hat when the band played "The Wearing of the Green", thinking it was the National Anthem! His look of shocked surprise, his bewildered air, his removal of his hat (because everyone else had done so it must be the thing!) and his mumbled complaint that somehow the tune seemed a little different—linger affectionately in the memory.

Lily Hanbury, at this time very young, was already showing signs of what she was to become in her tragically short career. Her beauty was astounding and, although it was suggested hypercritically that the part was rather beyond her experience, the average playgoer did not think so. Born in London in 1874, sister of Hilda Hanbury (another beauty) and cousin of Julia Neilson, after touring the provinces she played at the Vaudeville with Tom Thorne, then joined Wilson Barrett in town and on tour. She also toured for Tree in *The Dancing Girl*, playing the part created at the Haymarket by her cousin Julia, and immediately afterwards made a great hit at the Court Theatre with Ellaline Terriss and Pattie Browne in Pinero's *The Amazons*. Indeed, those three ladies startled the town in this piece by appearing in male attire. But this was after her appearnace in *Lady Windermere's Fan*, by which time Clement Scott had picked her out and commented not only on her beauty and talent, but on her devotion to her work.

Lady Windermere's Fan is too well-known to need description here. Its reception healed any breach that might have remained between author and actor-manager. One of the most elegant audiences that ever gathered at a West End première received it with enthusiasm. It was something new, they said. Here was that clever Mr. Wilde being more brilliant than ever. Here, too, was dear George Alexander giving of his very best. This was evidently the stuff to bring the people in: something fresh and intriguing, something to discuss at dinner-parties and over the teacups at the At Homes. A new play was always an event; but a new play by Oscar Wilde in which George Alexander appeared was an Occasion. Soon, the first-night flutter filled the town, extended to its suburbs and far beyond. It must have been on this night of wild excitement that Alexander stepped up to his throne as the idol of the ladies and the envy of the men.

The critics were divided. Some were shocked by its suave iconoclasm, other rejoiced at its courage. It evoked once more the recurrent conflict between the advanced thinkers and the boys of the old brigade. William Archer asked: "How comes it that, for the past twelve years or so, we have been entertaining a dramatist unawares, when he ought, on the contrary, to have been entertaining us?" Walkley almost threw critical caution to the winds. "For two pins," he wrote, "I would say *Lady Windermere's Fan* is an admirable play." Both gave it unmitigated praise. But Joseph Knight and the older thunderers pulled it to pieces. Bernard Capes, an eminent critic, picked some holes. Others found minor faults, as critics often do when not sure of their ground. One doubted if the average playgoer was educated up to the level of this new constructional technique. He need not have worried. The play was the most discussed thing in town and the people flocked to see it. They feasted their eyes on the lovely settings, chuckled and roared at Wilde's trenchant wit, surrendered themselves to the magnificent acting, and felt no need of further education. *Lady Windermere's Fan*, blazing as it did a new trail in the theatre, was itself an education. Mr. Capes thought the part of Lord Windermere rather beneath Alexander but was enthusiastic about the setting, saying:

> "The scenic accessories are worthy even of Mr. Alexander, who has been remarkable ever since he took to management for the lavish care he has bestowed on his *mise-en-scène*. Not often has any set been seen on the stage more complete or in better taste than the Morning Room at Lord Windermere's, in which the play begins and also ends. The other two scenes are also extremely good. *Lady Windermere's Fan* deserves to have a long run."

It ran, in fact, for 156 performances, went for a short tour and returned to town until replaced by *Liberty Hall* on 3rd December, 1892.

Liberty Hall, by R. C. Carton, was as unlike *Lady Windermere's Fan* as chalk from cheese. It marked a return to sentimental comedy with human feelings in place of epigrams and sentiment instead of cynicism. It was essentially a woman's play, specially designed to delight the ladies of the 'nineties, compounded to evoke happy laughter and a few tears. It made no demands upon intelligence but told a simple story of the sort fashionable at the time. Of its kind, *Liberty Hall* is a splendid play, although moderns would not find it to their liking. The story concerns two delicately nurtured sisters, one much younger than the other, who decide to leave their ancestral home rather than be obliged to the new heir whom they regard as an upstart. They take refuge with an old shopkeeper—a real Dickensian character—and the younger nearly falls for the wiles of a wicked young sprig of the aristocracy. She is saved from "a fate worse than death" by the presumed upstart, who has fallen in love with her sister. She, however, rebuffs him in true Victorian style and casts to the ground the roses he has given her. He stands regarding her, tells her of his hopes and says, as the act-drop falls: "Like my flowers, they are fading at your feet!" A real sob-packing curtain line. In the end—the heir being really a gentleman—everything comes right. A smashing success, the play scored 183 performances in town and made a pile of money on tour. Amateurs afterwards played it for years.

Staged and cast in the manner which had now become the hallmark of the St. James's, it won universal approval. One notice said: "Mr. Alexander sees, as none but Mr. Irving does, that justice is done to every play he handles, and *Liberty Hall* is made the utmost of. As a producer of modern plays, indeed, Mr. Alexander stands head and shoulders above any of his rivals." The critic was undoubtedly right, for it was largely by the beauty of his staging that Alexander banished the St. James's hoodoo.

Once again the cast was drawn almost entirely from the masterly St. James's team. The outstanding successes were Edward Righton, a fine actor, as Todman, and Fanny Coleman, as the maid-of-all-work who terrified and dominated the family. Alexander as Mr. Owen was, of course, Prince Charming and won all female hearts. Many ladies will remember his efforts to make ham sandwiches in the supper-party scene, and how, while sympathising with his helpful intentions, they could not but laugh at his obvious clumsiness.

Liberty Hall was an unquestionable money-spinner, pulling in much more than did *Lady Windermere's Fan*, and receiving eventually the supreme honour of a Royal Command Performance at Balmoral.

For the sake of the record it should be added that during the run of *Lady Windermere's Fan* there were two curtain-raisers, *Midsummer Day*, by Walter Frith, staged on 30th March, 1892, and *Kit Marlowe*, by W. L. Courtney, on 31st October, 1892.

George Alexander now stood in his rightful place, high among the leaders of his profession, rivalling Irving, Tree, Wyndham and the rest. He had raised the St. James's from comparative obscurity to as fashionable a theatre as could be found anywhere.

CHAPTER 13

Re-enter Pinero

WHILE the prettiness of *Liberty Hall* held the crowd enchanted, much was happening behind the scenes. Alexander was not the man to rest content on a current success nor was he blind to the need for progress. Like a good cricket captain, he knew the advantage of changing his bowling. He had been getting together with Pinero, who had made his name at the St. James's and who now had a play which he considered dynamite. It had been in the market before Alexander produced *Liberty Hall*, having been rejected by John Hare at the Garrick: an astute man, he feared it might offend his public, but Hare had by now become somewhat set in his ways and was as much a representative of the old school as Alexander was of the new. Perhaps Alexander was a little scared, too, but if he had lacked courage and resolution he would never have ventured at the St. James's at all.

Having set a new standard in the mounting and dressing of his shows, he was now acutely conscious of the ideas emanating from the new school of drama, which argued among other things the need to break through the old convention and replace the inevitable happy ending with something more approximate to real life. He had made a tentative move in this direction himself with the chancy *Sunlight and Shadow*, and had been encouraged by the way it turned out. He probably considered the time now propitious to attempt another advance.

Many will recall possibly, how in the early 'nineties the theatre world seethed with controversy, most of it pivoted on the works of Henrik Ibsen and Bernard Shaw. Shaw's early provocative piece, *Mrs. Warren's Profession*, like Ibsen's *Ghosts* was regarded by the conventional majority as positively unclean if not downright disgusting. Such subjects as these plays paraded were simply not discussed. If in practical life such odious things existed the best people simply declined to notice them. They were hidden away under the social carpet, swept discreetly out of sight (but they afforded grand opportunities for gossip, for all that!).

While the contestants debated *pro* and *con*, Alexander read Pinero's play and found it both disturbing and absorbing. He admired its craftsmanship and was not himself repelled by the theme. But he must have found it difficult to repress his Scottish caution when he turned his mind to his affluent clientèle, drawn as it was from the West End with a large leavening of ladies from the wealthy suburbs. Here was a play which boldly uncovered some of Society's most cherished conceits and which might well outrage many feelings. Its leading character was a lady of more than doubtful morals, a "woman with a past". Such ladies of the sort as had previously appeared on the stage had always redeemed their wantonness in hearts of gold and finally expiated their lapses in a death scene of impeccable respectability. There was not much of that in *The Second Mrs. Tanqueray*!

Well might John Hare have shied away, and well might Alexander ponder. Like all impresarios, he was dependent upon the box-office, all the more so since his own money was at stake, for he had no syndicate of backers. But he was no mere commercial manager, he was a professional manager, a connotation in which—for him at least—achievement shared equally in the reckoning with financial success. If he was ever a cautious man he was also an artist and, as generally conceded today, a great one. All the actor in him responded to the play. All the theatre in him impelled him to put it on.

His first idea was to test public reaction with a series of matinees. But Pinero did not want that, he, very naturally, wanted his play given a proper place in the evening bill, with a full cast and the whole weight of Alexander and the St. James's behind it. Somewhat to Pinero's surprise Alexander came round to his idea with no trouble at all.

The play was accepted and the contract signed. There remained the casting. None of the parts was easy, and it was imperative that the piece be given a perfect cast. Picking the female lead was no small problem, since it called for an actress capable of playing a new kind of character. Pinero proposed Olga Nethersole as Paula Tanqueray. She was still in her prime as the best emotional actress of the day. But she was under contract to John Hare and therefore not available. So Pinero thought again and suggested Janet Achurch, whom he had admired in an Ibsen matinee; but after seeing her again he thought she had developed mannerisms, and became less sure. Alexander's suggestion was Winifred Emery, but the author showed no enthusiasm. He said she might be otherwise engaged or might be ill. He envisaged all sorts of potential disasters, but Alexander was not put off.

What is important in these negotiations is the amicable way in which these two, author and actor-manager, worked together on the preparations for this and many subsequent plays. The prevalent idea today is that actor-managers were conceited, limelight-grabbing fellows who subordinated everything to their own glory. Nothing could be further from the truth. They worked in close collaboration with all concerned. Alexander and Pinero were closer perhaps than most, because each was aware how well the other knew his job.

Pinero could be a tyrant at rehearsals, but he knew better than to bludgeon Alexander. He never offered violent rebuff to his suggestions —he simply manœuvred them out of the way! Alexander had an idea that Mrs. Beerbohm Tree could play Paula. Pinero did not think so, and so he skilfully winkled her out of the manager's mind. Alexander, clinging unconsciously to old traditions, thought the play would be better for a spot of incidental music. Pinero tactfully disposed of that, too.

By March, 1893, it was settled that *The Second Mrs. Tanqueray* should be a full evening show, but Alexander had, meanwhile, gone off at a tangent. He thought he would like to try his hand at a version of *Rip Van Winkle*, and suggested Pinero might adapt it for him. But the dramatist quietly sidestepped that distracting notion. He was set on promoting his own play, and patiently persuaded his manager to travel his way. The matter of the leading lady was still not settled and both were aware that, important as the other parts might be, the play would stand or fall by her. Many ladies were discussed, among them Lily Hanbury and Julia Neilson.

Then Pinero decided they would have to take a chance. He was not so much concerned with a big name and popularity as with getting the right woman for the part. Very wisely, he considered that the part would make her, if she were right to play it. He told Alexander he would go out and look for a likely girl, and would begin his search at the Adelphi. Now, the wily Pinero knew something when he set out on this quest. And what he knew was that the Adelphi might hold the key to their problem. Herman Vezin, a magnificent actor, had recently invited managers to one of his touring dates near London, saying he had a "discovery". It may surprise the present generation that the managers went to see this girl, but none engaged her. Instead, they all took a fancy to another actress, who was playing a comedy role. It was not a scintillating role either, because the comedy in the old drama was usually weak. Nevertheless, this woman "had something"—beauty of form, face and voice, and also that indefinable quality, a compulsive vibrancy of personality which refused to be confined by the old-fashioned shackles which hemmed her round. As a result of the managerial visit she was soon at the Adelphi where, in *The Black Domino*, by George R. Sims and Robert Buchanan, she coruscated like a jewel. Her name was Mrs. Patrick Campbell.

This was just a routine melodrama, but a discerning critic said:

> "Mrs. Campbell's sensitive talent was employed upon Clarice. Upon her the interest centred, though the character was vaguely drawn. The method of the actress compelled attention, extorted admiration and set one marvelling why the clever authors deliberately withheld from such an artist a study worthy of her quite exceptional powers."

A previous notice, following *The Lights of Home*, by the same authors at the same theatre, had said:

> "Mrs. Patrick Campbell's nervous frame vibrates with emotion. Her artistic instinct serves her truly. In her picture of Tress she is never at fault. Of singular pathos, of unutterable mournfulness, exquisite in womanly feeling in her playing of the great scene."

No wonder Pinero began his search at the Adelphi Theatre! Yet, though not unresponsive to that charming lady's talent, he could not at once make up his mind. He was, however, sufficiently impressed to advise Alexander to see her. Now, just at this time Mrs. Pat was decidedly under a cloud. She has herself reported that her luck was dead out. She had almost died of typhoid fever, had in fact been given up for lost. But she recovered and, as it was necessary to work, went into *The Black Domino* at £8 a week. When the play got a bad Press the management blamed her, saying that her voice was weak, her gestures ineffective, and that nothing she said or did ever got over the footlights. Perhaps they were right. In any case, they gave her a fortnight's notice, and life looked black indeed.

And then, one evening, into a box came Mrs. George Alexander. She had come on behalf of her husband, to see what this girl was like. It would seem that Mrs. Pat got over the footlights all right that night because the next thing she knew was a letter from Alexander asking her to call and see him and Pinero at the St. James's Theatre. Hardly able to credit it, she went along. Her autobiography tells how she dressed herself for this ordeal, this tremendous chance. She wore a chic yellow straw bonnet trimmed with cherries, took its black velvet ribbon under her chin and tied it beneath her left ear, leaving the long narrow ends dangling down to accentuate the length of her neck. Contrary to the fashion of the day, her throat and neck were bare, not muffled up in lace.

Alexander looked at her, asked a few questions; then Pinero read her the play, beginning at her own entrance. She reports how she listened, enthralled. This was a real play—nothing like the fustian to which she was condemned at the Adelphi. Here was a living part—and one that she could play. Alexander told her it was hers. Back she went in triumph to the Adelphi. But her jubilation was short-lived, for when the management learned the reason for it they withdrew her notice. In despair she appealed to Alexander, but nothing could be done. So *The Black Domino* dragged along and then, when it was due to end, they told her she could go to Alexander. She got in touch at once, but it was too late: the part had been given to Elizabeth Robins. It was a distressing blow. But Pinero, impressed at the interview, and Alexander, impressed also by what he had seen and by his wife's report, got busy. They wanted this woman for Paula Tanqueray. They told Miss Robins the position. She was a great lady of the theatre as well as a great actress. She withdrew and wrote Mrs. Pat a most charming letter. So the part of Paula Tanqueray was cast at last.

The other roles were chosen with almost equal care. Amy Roselle was cast for Mrs. Cortelyon; Maude Millett, a St. James's "regular" had the important part of Ellean. Both men wanted Cyril Maude for

Cayley Drummle, the one spot of brightness in the play, but it was doubtful whether he would be available. Seymour Hicks was the next suggestion—a very young man then, and looking younger still. Pinero, who liked his acting, feared he would "look too much like a young man with a wig on". At that point Cyril Maude became available for that coveted but very difficult part. Ben Webster, another regular, had the important and almost equally difficult role of Captain Ardale. When the arguments were over, author and actor-manager found themselves armed with an ideal cast which redounded to the credit of both.

The thought arises that the notice which Mrs. Pat received from the Adelphi management—the Gattis, men of irreproachable integrity—might not have been so much on account of her alleged inability to project herself over the footlights as to the fact that she was a terrible "headache" when in the theatre. Nobody knew what she would do or say next. Stories of her vagaries are legion and she is herself legendary. It may well be she had upset them so badly that they gave her notice, but withdrew it when she had another offer. The Gattis were always kind, fair and generous folk. But Mrs. Pat was a law unto herself—always. Not even the dignity and decorum of the St. James's rehearsals could curb her spirit completely. She herself has told how strange and out of place she felt in that most West End theatre, and from time to time she kicked over the traces. Yet she got on well with the company, and in her book she remembers particularly the kindness of Pinero, who gave her Brand's essence when she appeared exhausted. What impressed her still more was that he even brought the teaspoon to enable her to take it!

After two dress rehearsals the big night of Alexander's new Pinero production arrived, with high tension for all concerned. There was as much in front of the curtain as there was backstage. This was an occasion such as had seldom been known in any theatre, and the first really big event at the St. James's, greater even than the launching of *Lady Windermere's Fan*. Word had gone round that Alexander harboured a bombshell and everyone wondered whether it would splutter or really explode. The house filled with eager, expectant people, while behind the curtain the company battled with their nerves. In front the patrons consulted their programmes—free as usual—and this is what they read:

THE SECOND MRS. TANQUERAY
An Original Play in Four Acts
by Arthur W. Pinero.

Aubrey Tanqueray .... Mr. George Alexander.
Sir George Orreyed, Bart. .... Mr. A. Vane-Tempest.
Captain Hugh Ardale .... Mr. Ben Webster.
Cayley Drummle .... Mr. Cyril Maude.
Frank Misquith, Q.C., M.P. .... Mr. Nutcombe Gould.
Gordon Jayne, M.D. .... Mr. M. Hathorn.
Morse .... Mr. Alfred Holles.
Lady Orreyed .... Miss Edith Chester.
Mrs. Cortelyon .... Miss Amy Roselle.
Paula .... Mrs. Patrick Campbell.
Ellean .... Miss Maude Millett.

Success was never for a moment in doubt. At the end of the second act came a tremendous ovation—a most unusual thing. *The Globe*, an important London paper, said on the Monday evening:

"A new custom seems to have sprung up among first-nighters. At the fall of the curtain on the second act there was a tremendous outburst of applause. The curtain was raised again and again. Mrs. Campbell had taken the house by storm. Then there were loud calls for 'Author!' Mr. Pinero's appearance, however, was not made until the final fall of the curtain."

Did any other play ever receive a call for the author when it was only halfway through? It was not that first-nighters had adopted a new fashion, but that they had been carried away by a great play magnificently produced and superbly acted—especially by a little-known actress who played Paula and whose name was Mrs. Patrick Campbell. It was, perhaps, the greatest of all the great nights at the St. James's. That night was Saturday, 27th May, 1893.

CHAPTER 14

Days of Glory

"WITH his new play, Mr. Pinero has at one blow accomplished a revolution." Thus in one bold confident phrase a typical report summarised the general response. Enthusing at great length the critic seized on the substance of the piece and continued descriptively:

> "He beckons us on from smooth ways to rough, from pleasant levels of cheeriness and ease, down declivities of sadness, till we stand in the valley of the shadow of death, and then he uncovers the face of his lantern and throws its light upon a woman's form. There is nothing theatrical about the exhibition. She smells neither of patchouli nor midnight oil. There she is, just as God (and devilish man) made her—the good and evil in her inextricably blent—a woman who has passed through heaven knows what defiling orgies and who yet preserves something of the heart of a child. The type is not a new one. Since the Magdalene crouched at her Saviour's feet and bathed them with her tears, two thousand years ago, Paulas innumerable have stumbled pathetically through the world, but the transfiguring light of genius has not been shed upon a single one of the tearful band till now . . . Before the naked reality of the figures in this enthralling tragedy, this haunting picture of a soul upon the rack of this rough world, the critic is almost dumb."

That, however, did not prevent him carrying his applause over a number of columns, in the course of which he handed out elaborate bouquets to all the leading players. Of Mrs. Campbell he said: "It is the most unforgettable piece of acting seen for years and it stamps her at once as a genius." To Alexander, he offered praise as warm and emphatic, an approval he also extended to Cyril Maude. "And the rest," he concluded, "sustained the reputation of the St. James's for unassailable ensemble. The play produced a profound impression. It is a great play, the greatest of modern times."

Students of the theatre will not need to be told how rarely a critic rises to such unmitigated enthusiasm. But all the bouquets were well deserved. Even William Archer, the archpriest of criticism, had no fault to find. He, too, handed out the bouquets and then addressed himself to the leaders:

> "Well now, Mr. Pinero and Mr. Alexander," he asked oratorically, "whatever your box-office returns may say, don't you feel you have done a fine thing, a thing that enhances your self-respect and makes you realise that a man's a man for a' that and not the slave of a booking-sheet?"

And he went on to assure them that they were not going to suffer for it even in pocket:

> "To dare greatly is to succeed; it is the man who dares feebly that pays for his feebleness. I think it very probable that *The Second Mrs. Tanqueray* will not run as long as *Charley's Aunt* and will not show, on the whole, as heavy a balance of profit as *Liberty Hall*. Perhaps it will not pay you more than a fair day's wage for a fair day's work, and I know that is not considered enough by the punters round the theatrical roulette table. But you are no common gamblers; you could not have done this at all if you had not done it for the pleasure of the thing—that is to say, in the only true artistic spirit . . . It is possible that *The Second Mrs. Tanqueray* may bring in only, say, five per cent on the time and money invested, whereas a piece of screaming buffoonery or trivial sentimentality might have brought in fifteen. But, frankly, isn't the pure joy of effort and triumph cheap at the money? Now that the thing is done—and not in a tentative, apologetic, afternoon fashion but with straightforward courage and confidence—don't you feel that if art is not virile it is childish, and that virile art alone is really worth living for?"

Mr. Archer's estimate of the play's monetary value was an underestimate. Naturally, it had not the run of *Charley's Aunt*. Its first London season hit up 227 performances and took £36,668 13*s*. In

July Alexander broke the run and went on tour, as was his custom. He believed in keeping in touch with provincial audiences—and how wise he was! He played out of town for ten weeks, his only suburban date being the Grand, Islington. His repertory was four plays: *The Second Mrs. Tanqueray*, *Liberty Hall*, *Lady Windermere's Fan* and *The Idler*, of which the first was the biggest draw. It swept provincial no less than London audiences off their feet. Then he brought it back to town, where it ran until the following 21st April, 1894. His courage had justified itself. It did more; it put the seal of supremacy upon him and his theatre.

Forgotten altogether were the bad old days. The St. James's was now the most brilliant playhouse in London, where the most exciting plays, the finest acting and the best *mise-en-scène* could be found. The theatre which stood the farthest west had indeed become the most "West End". Alexander's progress had been steady and on the whole continuous. After barely four years at the St. James's, and now only thirty-five years old, he stood the equal of anybody on the English stage, save perhaps his great master, Irving. That was certainly an achievement. It is true that Tree also had ventured into management at an early age, but he had taken over a big theatre, The Haymarket, already established, famous, and situated in a main street. Alexander had taken a house that was almost a synonym for poverty and had placed it in the very front rank.

All that is worth remembering today when theatres vanish and actors are forgotten.

As has already been remarked, one found at the St. James's an atmosphere of quiet splendour and unobtrusive dignity. Alexander bestowed this, his hall-mark, on everything he touched. He brought it into his business relations and into his theatre. Nothing was done in an off-hand manner. And his staff behaved as he did. Any other behaviour would have been severely castigated. But his dignity was shaken when, on about the fourth night of the Tanqueray run, it seemed to him that his leading lady was not comporting herself on stage with the decorum that the St. James's demanded. Not that she was giving a bad performance—far from it—but he detected (or thought he did) a hint of levity, which seemed to him the more deplorable because directed apparently against himself.

He did not remonstrate verbally: that was not in accordance with

Alexandrine or St. Jamesian dignity. He delivered his admonition in writing. His note said: "Mr. George Alexander presents his compliments to Mrs. Patrick Campbell and begs that she will not laugh at him on the stage." That will be that, he thought. The note was delivered by hand. In due course his leading lady wrote back: "Mrs. Patrick Campbell presents her compliments to Mr. George Alexander and begs to inform him that she does *not* laugh at him on the stage . . . she waits until she gets home." What could you do with such a woman? Alexander did not pursue the matter. He knew when to give up.

Much space has been devoted to *The Second Mrs. Tanqueray* because it is a landmark not only in the history of the St. James's but in that of the English theatre. Imparting an unaccustomed freedom of thought, it signalised a turning-point in the development of the stage. To modern eyes the play may seem old fashioned, but that does not detract from its merits as a piece of dramatic writing. The world has altered much since Othello slew Desdemona, Macbeth murdered sleep, and even since Sheridan wrote *The School for Scandal*, but that does not diminish the quality of these pieces. Pinero is difficult to revive nowadays because the style of acting has greatly changed. Though actors sometimes think the dialogue stilted and artificial, that was the way decently educated English people used to express themselves. They are English plays, appropriate to the time when most people spoke very good English. Slang expressions and mispronunciations from overseas had not crept in. If occasionally there was slang—well, it was British slang and none the worse for that.

Paula Tanqueray's impact on Victorian society may readily be imagined. She and the play, not to mention Alexander, became the universal topics. Dinner-tables found the subject inexhaustible, drawing-rooms and boudoirs echoed to the personalities and the theme—and suddenly George Alexander's portrait began to appear in every home where playgoing was popular. As formerly with *Lady Audley's Secret*, not to have seen *Tanqueray* was to be right out of the swim, an omission that had to be repaired at all costs. Thus conversational recommendation brought in the patrons. The pit and the gallery added their boost in their own impressive way. All of which spelled Success, with the largest possible S, to Alexander, Pinero, Mrs. Pat and all concerned.

Alexander followed up the immense excitement with a piece by Henry Arthur Jones, who could turn out light comedies, social satires, and gripping melodramas like *The Silver King*, with equal facility. Essentially a man of the theatre, he could pack a story with tension and hold it without deviation to its conclusion. He pronounced and practised his excellent axiom that a good play should, like Euclid's straight line, move directly from point to point. His characters were never allowed to stand in the way of the action, nor a secondary plot to detract from the central interest. Like Pinero, he had his own ideas on staging, and often held up rehearsals while he fought for his own way. But at last *The Masqueraders* was ready for the curtain, and on Saturday, 28th April, 1894, Alexander put it on.

Alexander led, and with him were Herbert Waring, H. V. Esmond, Mrs. Patrick Campbell, and—a name to top the bill later—Irene Vanbrugh. *The Masqueraders* was quite unlike *Mrs. Tanqueray*, in accordance with Alexander's policy of variety. Had he tried to follow Pinero's epoch-making play with another bombshell, it might have turned out a squib. So, in *The Masqueraders*, he presented a straightforward, romantic story, written in a style that was definitely "theatre".

The high spot of the play was a gripping gambling scene at Nice, where the hero and the villain cut the cards for a fortune on one side and a wife and child on the other. That scene, as played by Alexander and Herbert Waring, became the talk of the town. Archer said:

> "The gaming scene . . . is one of the most telling pieces of romance I ever saw on the stage and is admirably acted by Mr. Alexander and Mr. Waring. It quite justly determined the success of the play. Mrs. Pat, whose part was radically different from that of Paula, played it with quiet reserve but great artistry and won praise all round."

Said another critic:

> "Best among the minor characters were the heartless young cynics of Mr. Elliot and Mr. Vane-Tempest, the unscrupulous 'wife of the world' of Miss Irene Vanbrugh, and the dreamy mystical boy of Mr. H. V. Esmond. There is not, however, one part which is not well played, and several of Mr. Alexander's scenes are most elaborate

and beautiful. To all intents the first-night enthusiasm was universal and beyond doubt Mr. Jones has provided the theatrical sensation of the season."

The Masqueraders ran right up until August—139 performances—when Alexander took it on tour with *The Second Mrs. Tanqueray*, then brought it back to the St. James's to play out the season.

It may surprise playgoers who remember Irene Vanbrugh—Dame Irene, so quietly dignified, yet so alive—to learn that her first part at the St. James's was in "character". Lady Charley Wishanger was the "new woman" of the period and Miss Vanbrugh played her in red wig and monocle. Touring with Alexander the same year, he offered her the part of Lady Orreyed in *Tanqueray* as well. But Miss Irene was horrified, for she had taken a particular aversion to that character when she saw the play. So Alexander, who was always considerate of promising young players, asked her what part she thought she could play, and on her choosing Ellean he rehearsed her in that on approval—and approved. That was Alexander's way. Not all modern producers are so patient, or so wise.

Glancing back over the short road which had brought him to his present eminence, Alexander was aware that his two major lifts had been heavily sprung with novelty. In *Lady Windermere* and *Mrs. Tanqueray* he had brought to the theatre ideas and attitudes on which the arbiters of quality had preferred to stay mute. They constituted, therefore, not only a break with a long stage tradition but also a challenge to the prim insincerities of the established social code. Having thus violated the furrow of Victorian complacency—so much to his own satisfaction and profit—it behoved him now to whip up the horses and keep on ploughing.

To this end he cast around in search of ideas not hitherto, or not usually, brought to the boards. He was not seeking sensation but rather plays which, while exhaling the spice of novelty, would appeal by their own dramatic content. His choice fell on Henry James, who was living at Rye in Sussex. Born in New York in 1843, James was a man of cosmopolitan education. Intended for the Bar, his sympathies lay in literature, and after a brief journalistic career in America he published his first novel at thirty-two, following it with a number of others. Migrating to Britain, whose intellectual climate he preferred, he earned renown for the subtlety and poignancy of his stories, which, though not wildly popular, were almost sacred to the discriminating few. One of his novels, *The American*, he had already dramatised, and it had been presented by Edward Compton at the Opéra Comique off the Strand where, though highly praised, it had aroused little public interest.

Alexander asked James to provide a play—something of taste and power, appropriate to the St. James's. Henry James agreed, but warned Alexander it would not have the conventional happy ending, which did not at all trouble the actor-manager. Neither he nor the author then foresaw exactly what this was to mean. The title was *Guy Domville*. Alexander mustered a fine cast, including himself, Mr. Elliot, Herbert Waring, H. V. Esmond, Frank (Franklin) Dyall, Marion Terry (back in her old home), Mrs. Edward Saker, Evelyn Millard and Irene Vanbrugh. It was produced on 5th January, 1895.

They opened before an elegant and encouraging audience, many of whom, devoted admirers of the author, had come to acclaim him in his new field. The majority, of course, had in their minds the stark strength of *Mrs. Tanqueray* and the tense drama of the gambling scene in *The Masqueraders*. Henry James gave them subtle half-tones and static action. Clement Scott wrote:

> "The first act of *Guy Domville* is one of the most beautiful human documents that has been committed to the stage for some time. The man who can write that first act will, one day, write a play that will live. It is not only that Mr. Henry James took us at once to an old-world garden at the end of the last century, not only that we breathed the charm, the sweetness, the calm of repose in Old England in the Georgian era. He showed us not only the persons of two men and one woman; he showed us their hearts."

Unfortunately, the rest of the play did not live up to the promise of its opening: the whole thing lacked cohesion. The second act did not fit the first, and the third did not fit the second. Probably Alexander was aware of these weaknesses but could do nothing about them. Even the unhappy ending was a needless irritant.

Guy Domville was a dismal failure. But nobody was prepared for the pandemonium that broke loose at curtain-fall. This was probably due (as such things often are) to the quite unmerited enthusiasm of the author's friends, whose applause was entirely out of proportion and goaded the rest of the house into a counter-demonstration. That, in turn, provoked the faithful to further display, and brought the opposition screaming to their feet against the attempt to override them. Then some misunderstanding backstage added to the fury. Hearing calls for "Author!" and thinking the clamour enthusiasm, Alexander led on Henry James! That did it: the house fairly trembled with yell and counter-yell. It overwhelmed James, and he never wrote for the stage again.

Alexander now had to find something new, and quickly. With no fresh play in hand, he had nothing to revive either, for he had not been established long enough. But having recently turned down a play by Oscar Wilde, in the belief that it was too light for the St. James's, he quickly contacted the author. Wilde, badly in need of cash, had written the play in a month, and Alexander, who had relieved his need, had some kind of moral option on it. After some vicissitudes which are not of importance here, he put it into rehearsal. Its title was *The Importance of Being Earnest.*

Alexander took his choice of the two leading male roles and for the other engaged Allan Aynesworth, an actor of all the graces. He chose Rose Leclercq for the important part of Lady Bracknell, Evelyn Millard and Irene Vanbrugh for the two girls, and H. H. Vincent and Mrs. George Cannings for Canon Chasuble and Miss Prism respectively. The menservants were Franklin Dyall and Kinsey Peile. It was just the right mixture of talent. For a number of days Wilde turned up at rehearsals and made himself obnoxious, hindering everything and upsetting everybody. Alexander took him on one side and told him firmly to keep away, and that the company would do their best to please him.

Wilde kept away, and the rehearsals went on. On the eve of the production, a reporter asked him if he thought the play would be a success. Wilde was more than equal to him. "My dear fellow, you have got it all wrong," he said. "The play *is* a success. The only question is whether the first-night's audience will be one."

Well, that first night is history now. Alexander had never been better, nor had Aynesworth. They played together with the slickness and understanding of a music-hall double act, and there is no higher praise than that. Everyone was as near perfection as human frailty and stage limitations would allow. The audience was just as big a success as the play. And the play—so frequently revived—is now a classic. The night was 14th February, 1895 (which shows the short run of *Guy Domville*).

Some of the critics did find it too light and airy, but who cared about that? It had filled the theatre with wave upon wave of delighted laughter. The only disappointment of the evening was that Oscar Wilde did not make a speech. He lit a cigarette in the wings—against the Lord Chamberlain's orders, but what cared he for such things?—and went on to face an ovation. He stood there quietly smoking and bowed to the applause, but he said not a word. Wilde was a master of timing. He had a speech all right but he kept it for the proper time and place. He went round to see Alexander, who was dancing with delight. "Well, wasn't I right?" he asked. "What do you think about it?" Wilde gazed at him benignly and then, nodding his head, delivered his speech: "My dear Alex, it was charming, quite charming. And, do you know, from time to time I was reminded of a play I once wrote myself called *The Importance of Being Earnest*." No curtain speech could have bettered that!

Rose Leclercq, the Lady Bracknell, may not be so well remembered as the rest of that cast. But Dame Irene Vanbrugh, speaking of that play in her delightful book *To Tell My Story*, leaves a charming description of her:

> "A great personal success was made by that famous old actress Rose Leclercq, the natural *grande dame* of the stage with all the true polish and innate dignity of the unmistakeable 'lady'. Her walk, her voice, her carriage, her every detail was marvellous. The handkerchief she used, the long bottle of eau-de-Cologne, the way she sat—such details marked her as the blue-blooded lady she portrayed; and she was never stagey or exaggerated. She held a position which has never been filled, to my mind, by any other actress."

The Importance of Being Earnest, triumph though it was, did not at first play to capacity. It simply grew and grew—which is often the best way—and Alexander felt sure he had something which would recoup him for the loss and disappointment of *Guy Domville*. (He had also spent a good deal on the Wilde comedy, but with business steadily increasing, was not worrying about that.) And then—disaster fell. The first shock came when Wilde lost a libel action against Lord Queensbery, though it was compensated to some extent by the publicity. But right on its heels came Wilde's arrest and trial. Business fell off badly. Bookings were cancelled, many irate customers throwing their tickets at Arnold, the trusty box-office manager. Alexander deleted Wilde's name from the bill, hoping to save the day. On this score his memory has often been attacked, but he probably acted as he thought best for all concerned. Inevitably, Wilde's conviction meant the end of the play. It was withdrawn after a bare three months, leaving Alexander much "in the red".

With two disasters within five months he may well have been ready to write 1895 down as a bad year. He may even have feared the old hoodoo was about to return. Wilde's scintillating comedy only came into its own on its second revival, in 1909.

Alexander fell back on a play by Henry Arthur Jones, who had given him *The Masqueraders*. Called *The Triumphs of the Philistines*, it was produced on 11th May, 1895, the night after the withdrawal of *The Importance*. It was no triumph for anybody, not even the Philistines: it was Jones in his heaviest satirical mood and he was doomed from the start. It achieved only forty performances, but as it had not cost much to produce it made little difference to the funds. Up went a revival of *Tanqueray*, but it was too soon to draw them in, so Alexander resorted to *The Idler*. It was indeed a pretty bad year. His tour recouped some of the losses, but even there the profits were not up to previous standards for he had nothing new to offer. The only consolation was a Command Performance at Balmoral. This signal honour was not without effect on the public, very sensitive then to Court favour. Despite bad luck in a dismal year, Alexander was building up a steady following at the St. James's and his reputation was undiminished. His good looks, his impeccable manners and unfailing courtesy charmed all comers—especially the ladies—even in a day when courtesy and good manners were the general rule.

His autumn season opened with another revival—*Liberty Hall*—with Royal approval stamped on it. After a fortnight this was replaced with a new play, one by an actor-dramatist who, as an actor, was no stranger to the St. James's. He was H. V. Esmond, a charming man and practised playwright, and as good an actor as ever walked the English stage. But his experience was limited at that time. The play, titled *The Divided Way*, was produced on 23rd November, 1895, and ran for twenty performances. Doubled with it in the bill was *The Misogynist*, by G. W. Godfrey. The cast of *The Divided Way* included George Alexander, Allan Aynesworth, Herbert Waring and Evelyn Millard. It could not have been bettered. The fact that Alexander played a woman-hating septuagenarian in the curtain-raiser did not help, despite the art of Allan Aynesworth and H. H. Vincent and a young actress destined for fame whose name was Ellis Jeffreys.

The St. James's had lost money steadily all through the year, but Alexander was not in financial difficulties. He did not stint money but he never wasted it; and he never kept a play on when he knew it should come off—and that is the great secret of solvency in the theatre. His losses in that black year of 1895 totalled £3,341, from which must be deducted the £80 weekly that he had drawn in salary, leaving an actual loss of just over £1,908. In the midst of his frustration he must have felt grateful for the companionship of his ever-helpful wife, who, whenever he tended to get introspective, would boost his morale by reminding him of the magnitude of his progress and the comparative modesty of his reverses. It always did the trick.

It was at this critical juncture that Alexander got hold of a play which soon altered the shape of his accounts. It was based on a novel by Anthony Hope (whose real name was Anthony Hope Hawkins). After a brilliant career at Oxford, Hope had been called to the Bar. He had also worked for Henry Herbert Asquith—one day to be Prime Minister—and contested seats in the Liberal interest. Then he turned to writing novels which earned him quite creditable sales. He hit the best-seller bracket with a dashing, swashbuckling romance entitled *The Prisoner of Zenda*, which swept across the country like an epidemic. It was the book of the year, indeed of many years. Edward Rose, himself an actor with other dramatisations to his credit, prepared it for the stage.

But managers fought shy of stage versions of popular novels. Forbes Robertson, one of our greatest actors, gave it serious consideration, but perhaps it is as well for him and for the play that he did not do it. At length it had an American production, by Edward Sothern, Alexander's counterpart across the Atlantic. It swept America like a tornado. Alexander sent a representative over to see it and, on his favourable report, at once secured it for London.

The romantic character Rudolph Rassendyll—a double role of Englishman and Ruritanian king—was right up Alexander's street. It might, indeed, have been written for him. For Princess Flavia he selected Evelyn Millard, who had played in his company before. She had beauty, a quiet dignity and inherent charm and could also rise to emotional heights. *The Prisoner of Zenda* needs no description here, for the book—progenitor of many similar novels and plays—is still read. Hope set the action in "Ruritania", thereby adding a word to our language.

The play, produced on 7th January, 1896, formed yet another landmark in the St. James's saga, as well as in theatre history. Here is the original cast:

THE PRISONER OF ZENDA

Adapted from Anthony Hope's Story by Edward Rose.

Characters in the Prologue

Prince Rudolph .... Mr. George Alexander.
Duke Wolfgang .... Mr. Herbert Waring.
Gilbert, Earl of Rassendyll .... Mr. Charles Glenny.
Horace Glyn .... Mr. Vincent Sternroyd.
Jeffreys .... Mr. Henry Boyce.
Giffen .... Mr. F. Featherstone.
Amelia, Countess of Rassendyll .... Miss Mabel Hackney.

Characters in the Play

Rudolph the Fifth / *Rudolph Rassendyll* .... Mr. George Alexander.
Michael, Duke of Strelsau .... Mr. Herbert Waring.
Colonel Sapt .... Mr. W. H. Vernon.
Fritz von Tarlenheim .... Mr. Arthur Royston.
Captain Hentzau .... Mr. Laurence Cautley.
Detchard .... Mr. William H. Day.
Bertram Bertrand .... Mr. Allan Aynesworth.
Marshal Strakencz .... Mr. Henry Loraine.

Lorenz Teppich	Mr. F. Lomnitz.
Frank Teppich	Mr. George P. Hawtrey.
Lord Topham	Mr. George Bancroft.
Ludwig	Mr. I. Dawson.
Toni	Mr. Robert Loraine.
Josef	Mr. Frank Dyall.
Princess Flavia	Miss Evelyn Millard.
Antoinette de Mauban	Miss Lily Hanbury.
Frau Teppich	Miss Olga Brandon.

It was a galaxy of talent. There were St. James's stalwarts like Herbert Waring—a magnificent "Black Michael"—and W. H. Vernon whose Sapt might have stepped out of the pages of the novel. There was Allan Aynesworth, now a St. James's regular, whose gracious ease and polished style were so right for the role and theatre; and there, in a small part, was young Robert Loraine, who was to make such a name for himself later. Alexander's genius as a caster of feminine roles was particularly marked in this play. He contrasted Evelyn Millard's demure loveliness with the statuesque beauty of Lily Hanbury—both of them ideals of exactly what the author must have had in mind. And, for himself, Alexander had an easy ride. Here was Romance—and he was a great romantic. He had his portrait painted in the role of Prince Rudolph—and there in profile, in his satin knee-breeches, white shirt and ruffles, his powdered wig and buckled shoes, rapier under his arm, stands the *preux chevalier* of them all—George Alexander in his prime and his glory.

ALLAN AYNESWORTH

MATHESON LANG

SIR JOHNSTONE FORBES-ROBERTSON

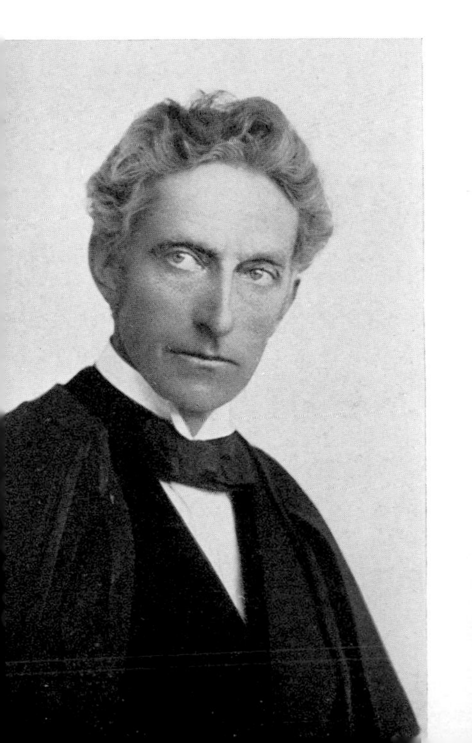

HENRY AINLEY

GLADYS COOPER

MIRIAM CLEMENTS

MRS. PATRICK CAMPBELL

PHYLLIS NEILSON-TERRY

CHAPTER 15

Romance—and Shakespeare

AS the curtain came down on *The Prisoner of Zenda* that first night there was no doubt about the popular verdict. The frenzied applause revealed beyond any dispute that, in current phrase, this was the stuff to give 'em. Next day the critics did a little sneering, but anyone who puts up romantic drama must expect the highbrows to scoff. Yet Ruritania is real stage country, as those who have since travelled the territory (Ivor Novello notable among them) have had good reason to tell. Giving Edward Rose full marks for the adaptation, the critic Archer, never easily pleased, said he had transferred the novel to the stage without losing anything of its spirit and had in the process clarified the action.

And Archer went on to give a slap on the back all round. Alexander, he said, played his three parts with ease, spirit, humour and feeling, while Miss Millard looked charming in her ruddy locks and played with all needful grace and sincerity. He thought Herbert Waring had too little to do as Black Michael, but conceded that he did it decidedly well. He also thought Miss Lily Hanbury good as Madame de Mauban, and that nothing could have been better than W. H. Vernon's Bismarckian embodiment of Colonel Sapt. Coming from Archer, that was approval indeed. It may well be that he wrote with his tongue in his cheek, for a few days earlier he had made a slashing attack on Wilson Barrett's *Sign of the Cross*, damning it as "Salvationist pantomime", and had in the meantime discovered his mistake.

Zenda quickly restored Alexander's finances and put the St. James's on top of the world. It contained no flashing epigrams or abstruse social discussions, but it sparkled with honest-to-goodness romantic drama. The cast played it for all they were worth, and for all it was worth, and both were worth a great deal. There was nothing "relaxed" about their performance. Each tackled his part with sincerity, so that the audience was not allowed to relax either. They brought their listeners right on to the edge of their seats—many, indeed, rose enraptured to their feet.

If one who witnessed that romantic wonder as a boy of nine may intrude his impressions, he would think it almost enough to say he has never forgotten it. Every word, every line, seems to linger in his mind, every movement, every spot of "business". He really lived that night in Ruritania. More than once he had to be held in his seat, and when he got home could not divest himself of that exquisite illusion. For weeks and weeks he reproduced it all alone amid a perfect armoury of pistols, swords and guns, playing every part in a version of his own. Years afterwards when the erstwhile boy went to its revival the magic remained. Yet film versions never touched the same degree of thrill. The truth is, Ruritania only comes to life in flesh and blood. In St. James's it got both.

Looking back on that wondrous night over the gap of sixty-two years, the difference in life seems incredible. In those far-gone days when *Zenda* represented something all but real—for there were many countries then near akin to it—humans were the masters and machinery hardly existed at all. When they travelled they mounted a horse, and for dramatic effect the flurry and thud of galloping hooves leaves the high-powered car and the growling aeroplane standing. Even the rattle and chatter of trains had nothing on the concentrated rhythm of cloppity-cloppity steeds. (Doesn't your heart jump as you hear the Derby thundering by on the radio?) The telephone was not, motors were not, nor machine-guns either. The handiest weapon was the sword, varied with the rapier and cavalry sabre, and the revolver sometimes backed them up. In Ruritania—as in many places else—uniforms glittered, spurs rang and top-boots glistened to a resolute stride. Steel clanged on steel and pistol shots rang out. There was no radio to spread the news, no television to make distant scenes part of the lounge, and no camera-men clamoured around King Rudolph to have today's picture in the next edition. Ruritania, and those Ruritanian times, were nearer the Wars of the Roses than the life of today. The internal combustion engine, science and two world wars have wrought enormous change. It seems a pity, for the Ruritanian way was much more picturesque, and so much more individual . . .

Zenda ran from 7th January to 18th July, 1896—254 performances; then, after the summer tour, resumed from 20th October until 28th

November. St. James's capacity in those days was £200. During the first run Alexander took in £40,000. He spent on the production more than £3,000—an almost unprecedented sum then. His net profit, including receipts from tours and sub-lets, exceeded £18,000, which was big finance for a theatre in the 'nineties.

Alexander followed Hope with Shakespeare, but instead of doing *Hamlet*, as he had long desired, he reached out to the other extreme and put on *As You Like It*. This ran from 2nd December, 1896, to 28th March, 1897, and averaged £200 a performance—just about capacity. Alexander was well satisfied. Naturally, he had given it a magnificent cast:

AS YOU LIKE IT

Duke	Mr. James Fernandez.
Frederick	Mr. C. Aubrey Smith.
Amiens	Mr. Bertram Wallis.
Jaques	Mr. W. H. Vernon.
First Lord	Mr. H. H. Vincent.
Second Lord	Mr. George Bancroft.
Le Beau	Mr. Vincent Sternroyd.
Charles	Mr. J. Wheeler.
Oliver	Mr. H. B. Irving.
Jaques de Bois	Mr. R. Loraine.
Orlando	Mr. George Alexander.
Adam	Mr. Henry Loraine.
Dennis	Mr. A. W. Munro.
Touchstone	Mr. H. V. Esmond.
Corin	Mr. W. H. Day.
Silvius	Mr. Arthur Royston.
William	Mr. George P. Hawtrey.
Hymen	Miss Julie Opp.
Rosalind	Miss Julia Neilson.
Celia	Miss Fay Davis.
Phoebe	Miss Dorothea Baird.
Audrey	Miss Kate Phillips.

As will be seen, it was a regular St. James's ensemble, reinforced by some outsiders. They were all—or were to become—grand players.

James Fernandez was an actor of great power; C. Aubrey Smith, who bowled for Sussex and England, became in his old age a Hollywood film star; H. B. Irving (Sir Henry's son) was making his St. James's début. He had already worked with John Hare and toured with Ben Greet, under whose guidance he had played Hamlet the previous year. Robert Loraine was there again, gathering experience for his brilliant after-career, especially as a magnificent portrayer of Shavian parts. Bertram Wallis was to become the most popular of all the musical comedy matinee idols. He was an upstanding, handsome fellow, a fine actor and singer, too. Julie Opp (Mrs. William Faversham), a noted American journalist, came to England and wanted to go on the stage. Alexander gave her this, her first chance, and she more than justified his confidence, although Archer complained that she "put rather too much dash and energy into her performance. A calmer dignity would have been more to the purpose." As a beginner, she was probably over-anxious; but she did much fine work later at the St. James's. Fay Davis, another American, came to England with a fine reputation and appeared at the Criterion. She had played in *The Prisoner of Zenda* when Lily Hanbury was away, and now she made a charming Celia. Archer again detected too much eagerness. She married Gerald Lawrence and remained at the St. James's to play many notable parts. Dorothea Baird was fresh from her triumph as Trilby. As Rosalind, Julia Neilson had every possible requisite for the part. Those who were present treasure the memory of the best Rosalind they ever saw. A critic described her in the part as "a being of infinite loveliness and womanly feeling . . . revealing in the swooning scene a measure of realistic expression calculated to surprise her warmest admirers."

In later years Julia often told her friends how she had enjoyed playing it. Abhorring a wig, she wore her own hair clubbed into a "bob". They gave her Arne's setting of "The Cuckoo Song" out of *Love's Labour's Lost* and she sang it delightfully. Once, when she spoke her lines in the Epilogue: "If I were a woman I would kiss as many of you as had beards that pleased me, complexions that liked me and breaths that I defied not," an eager voice came down from the gods: "Me first, please, Miss"!

Alexander received full marks all round for production and cast. His own Orlando brought this from William Archer: "Mr. George Alexander, one of the best speakers on the English stage, makes an excellent Orlando, playing with spirit and grace, humour and feeling." Another critic said: "Apart from an occasional tendency towards sedateness, Mr. Alexander's Orlando is the best the London stage has witnessed for many years. He speaks the lines with a fine regard for their rhythmical significance, and is at all times a gallant, manly and romantic figure." The reference to sedateness was doubtless justified.

As You Like It proved very much as they liked it. Pursuing his bent for variety, Alexander turned again to Pinero and staged *The Princess and the Butterfly*, subtitled *The Fantastics*. It opened on 29th March, 1897, again with a well-chosen cast and masterly production. In it, besides Alexander, were H. B. Irving, H. V. Esmond, C. Aubrey Smith, Julia Neilson, Julie Opp, Rose Leclercq, Mabel Hackney and Fay Davis, who scored a major victory.

Opinions were divided, Walkley, Archer and Addison Bright being for the play, the rest mostly against it. It lost heavily and was succeeded, on 25th October, 1897, by *The Tree of Knowledge*, by R. C. Carton, who did not, however, repeat the success of *Liberty Hall* or even *Sunlight and Shadow*. This far-fetched and shallow piece was a bit too unreal even for late Victorian tastes, despite its splendid cast and setting. In it were George Alexander, W. H. Vernon, Fred Terry, H. B. Irving, H. V. Esmond, George Shelton (later the beloved Smee of *Peter Pan*), Carlotta Addison, Fay Davis and Julia Neilson. The critics rather chewed it up, and one said of Alexander:

> "In the negative part of Nigil, Mr. George Alexander plays with his usual earnestness, but even he cannot convince us that Mr. Carton's hero is anything but a very foolish and invertebrate individual." He continued, however: "Miss Julia Neilson invests the character of the despicable Belle with the necessary coolness and contemptuousness. An exceedingly clever sketch of the cynical Roupell is given by Mr. H. B. Irving and Miss Fay Davis is altogether delightful as Monica. The remaining characters are all admirably played."

Then the St. James's returned to Shakespeare, with *Much Ado About Nothing*. Meanwhile, the failure of *The Princess and the Butterfly* had occasioned a breach between author and actor. Alexander knew the play fell far below Pinero's usual standard, and during rehearsal had tried to have its weaknesses remedied. He advised, suggested and protested, but all in vain. Ill-constructed in five acts, the play failed to run even the 100 nights usually necessary to recoup the initial outlay. After the inquest Pinero swore he would never write for the St. James's again. Alexander, who had lost £2,000, expressed his deep regrets but kept his own counsel. Pinero later relented, and did in fact write for him again. As though to add to Alexander's annoyance, during the dispute *The Tree of Knowledge* lost money, too, though not so heavily as Pinero's play.

As regards *Much Ado*, William Archer said: "It has never been so richly caparisoned nor (in our time) acted with more gaiety and gusto. Mr. Alexander's Benedick is one of the best things he has ever done—gay, gallant, humorous, incisive, amusing from first to last." And Benedick had Julia Neilson as his Beatrice. She was as good a Beatrice as she had been a Rosalind. Her beauty, her command, her grace and gaiety were something to behold. She had less malice than most Beatrices and more womanly wiles. She was as lovely as she looked. Fay Davis was applauded as Hero, and Robert Loraine jumped right into the front rank as Claudio. Fred Terry was a magnificent Don Pedro, and H. B. Irving was a convincingly sinister Don John. But *Much Ado*, with only fifty-three performances, was only half the success of *As You Like It*, which had registered 114.

This Shakespearean season put the crowning-touch on Alexander's reputation. He was now firmly entrenched in his theatre, and in high standing socially as well. Though he had hosts of friends and admirers his success never turned his head. He would entertain or go to dinner-parties when engagements permitted but he was never seen about casually. He was completely absorbed in fostering the fortunes of the St. James's Theatre.

But financially he again came a cropper with the next play—*The Conquerors*, by Paul M. Potter. Based on the Franco-Prussian War, it was a poor piece of work in every respect. It did not help that Alexander played a Sub-Lieutenant of Uhlans. He had with him J. D. Beveridge, H. V. Esmond, Robert Loraine, Bertram Wallis, Fred Terry, H. B. Irving, Julia Neilson, Fay Davis, Constance Collier and Ida Molesworth. That was an all-star cast, and the cost of a like combination today would be fabulous. But it ran no time at all.

Produced on 14th April, 1898, it was off by 2nd June, and Alexander hastily put *The Ambassador* into the bill.

In passing, a glimpse at the theatre's staff may be of interest. Robert W. Shone was the business manager, R. Legge the secretary, H. H. Vincent the stage manager, William Robins the musical director, and E. Arnold was in the box-office. Mr. Robins had an excellent small orchestra, and the music he provided for *The Conquerors* illustrates how the orchestra was integral with the play in those days. His selections reflected the spirit of the story: Ouverture, *Festival*, by Leutner; Pot-Pourri, *Deutsche Studentenlieder*; Valse, *The Conquerors*, by Mr. Robins himself; selection from *Tannhäuser*, by Wagner; March, *The Uhlans' Call*, by Eilenberg, and *Husarenritt*, by Spindler, and March; *Standard Bearer*, by Fahrbach. All of which helped to create the appropriate atmosphere.

The Ambassador, a comedy in four acts by John Oliver Hobbes, went into the bill on 2nd June, 1898, and immediately caught on. The cast included, besides the actor-manager, who played the British Ambassador at Rome, H. B. Irving, H. V. Esmond, C. Aubrey Smith, Violet Vanbrugh, Fay Davis and a very young lady named Mary Jerrold, whom modern theatregoers will remember as one of the best of our older actresses. There was no prospect of a long run, as Alexander, booked to tour himself, had let the theatre to the Kendals for the autumn; yet he gave it the best production possible. The scenes were laid in Lady Beauvedere's residence in the Champs Elysées; at Major Lascelles's place in a fashionable part of Paris; and in the garden at Lady Beauvedere's—settings replete with every element of taste and splendour. Added to this was Alexander striding the stage in all his magnificent finery as the Ambassador—just what his admirers liked to see!

A good story, beautifully dialogued and brilliantly dressed, *The Ambassador* was a perfect St. James's play. It ran for 169 performances and also did excellently on tour. The name of the author, John Oliver Hobbes, widely famed as a novelist, did much for the play's popularity. Hobbes was a pseudonym for Mrs. Pearl Craigie, but not everybody knew that. On the first night there were loud calls for "Author!", interspersed with cries of "Well done, John!", and when Alexander appeared, leading on Mrs. Craigie, the clamour momentarily subsided —then burst forth again with a vigour intensified by the surprise.

When the play was published, Mrs. Craigie said in a foreword:

"My permanent gratitude and friendship are due to Mr. George Alexander for the distinguished art he bestowed upon his rendering of the title role, for the support, interest and kindness he gave so generously from the first reading of the play, through the many anxieties of rehearsing, to the yet greater anxiety of its first production."

A charming tribute from a charming and gifted lady. And a just one, too.

Commenting on *The Ambassador*, Archer said of Mrs. Craigie:

"She has in an eminent degree the knack, the instinct of the scene. The knack of the stage, however, is not everything. There goes a great deal more than that to the making of a dramatist. Mrs. Craigie has one thing more—she has wit. She has another thing more —she has knowledge of society. Out of these ingredients an airy comedy like *The Ambassador* can readily be whipped up; and a delightful dish it is. What chiefly pleases one is the straightforward ease and simplicity of its technique and the delicate tact with which the tone of comedy is preserved throughout."

St. James's audience approved the delightful dish. It played out the season and was revived in the following February, preceded now by the same author's one-act drama *The Repentance*, a play about the Carlists in Spain.

In the interval before the revival run, the Kendals filled their autumn sub-lease with *The Elder Miss Blossom*. At its conclusion Kendal wrote to Alexander (who, it will be remembered, had played under the Kendal-Hare banner when a beginner), saying:

"My dear Alexander—I take the first opportunity—now you are back—of writing to thank you for having made us so comfortable during our too brief season at your theatre, and to say what a very pleasant time we had there—enhanced, not a little, by the uniform courtesy and attention of all the staff both before and behind the curtain—and I took on all your old hands. I never had occasion to utter a single word of complaint—on the contrary, only words of commendation. And it gives me great pleasure to record this fact. I am glad that everything was found satisfactory on our quitting the theatre and nothing to mar an altogether most gratifying little season, in more ways than one, and which has added another to the very pleasant memories we must always associate with the St. James's Theatre."

That letter from one famous actor-manager to another shows exactly the atmosphere that prevailed at the St. James's under Alexander.

Alexander's next venture was a mistake from the start and it is a wonder he let himself into it. He wanted to put on a play by that master romancer Stanley Weyman which had been adapted for the stage by Edward Rose, who had made the stage version of *The Prisoner of Zenda*. The title was *Under the Red Robe*. But Edward Rose had a play of his own called *In Days of Old* and Alexander, who usually had a mind of his own, allowed Rose to talk him into staging this instead of the other. It limped along for sixty performances and then had to come off. Meanwhile, Cyril Maude had accepted the other play and put it on at The Haymarket—where it pulled in full houses for over 250 performances! There is no record of what Alexander had to say about that.

This unfortunate production marked the end of his eighth year at the St. James's. But in that period his victories had far outweighed his defeats and he had no reason to be discouraged. He had achieved a high standard in acting, production and the quality of his plays and had graced his programmes with the names of dramatists established and new. He did not, of course, in this heyday of the actor-managers, stand alone in his achievement. His rivals, too, had much to their credit. Irving was still in harness, Tree also, and Cyril Maude, Charles Hawtrey, Charles Wyndham, John Hare, to mention only a few of his West End confrères whose combined endeavours made theirs the supreme era in the history of the British Theatre.

CHAPTER 16

The New St. James's

As soon as the run of *In Days of Old* ended, Alexander led his company off on tour and the builders and decorators descended on the St. James's. He had decided to modernise the place entirely, and it needed it. The work was entrusted to Blomfield Jackson, a leading light in the sphere of theatre construction. Blomfield's assistant on the architectural side was Emblin Walker, a genius in that line. Percy Macquoid designed the decoration scheme—a masterly job in the Louis XII and François Ier transitional style. The new act-drop, an exact reproduction of the "Pastoral Scenes" tapestry in the South Kensington Museum, was painted by D. T. White and H. Telbin; upholstery was in the hands of H. S. Lyon & Co. and Messrs. Rashleigh Phipps did the electrical work.

When the job was finished, patrons old and new were loud in their appreciation. They saw that the old theatre had not only been pleasurably modernised but considerably enlarged. Adjoining houses had been demolished and their area added to St. James's, the stage lowered and its depth increased, and the ceiling raised so as to acquire a perfect "rake". With the sinking of the orchestra pit below stage level, the musicians no longer obstructed the view from the stalls, which, along with the pit, dress and upper circles and gallery, had all been enlarged and their seating capacity increased. Two only of the boxes survived—the Royal box, with its own retiring room and separate entrance, and another facing it across the auditorium. The pillars, alas, remained, but they were looked upon as a structural necessity in all theatres.

When Alexander returned from tour and surveyed his sumptuous domain—which had cost him £7,057—he must have experienced a warm glow of pride at having been able, despite the setbacks, to convert Braham's Folly into this magnificent edifice. Nobody now thought the St. James's too far west, and he felt grateful to his patrons that henceforth his productions would be presented in a setting complimentary to them and creditable to himself. Now in the dawn of the new century he cast about for a play that should do justice to the reopening. He had hoped that Pinero would come up with something suitable to the occasion, but, like Achilles, he was still sulking in his tent. So Alexander put his faith in *Rupert of Hentzau*, an adaptation of Anthony Hope's sequel to his fabulous *Zenda*.

It went into the gay, rejuvenated playhouse on 1st February, 1900. The first night glittered with celebrities and brimmed with patrons from all walks of life. Pit and galleryites had waited for hours, queueing now under the more orderly arrangement which had banished the aforetime scramble at the doors. Those who could afford it could hire a boy from the District Messenger Company to relieve them of the tedious wait, and themselves arrive in comfort just before the portals opened. These perky lads of the D.M.C. in their blue uniforms with plated buttons and smart pill-box hats worn rakishly askew were then a feature of London life. Some of them rose to good positions—one, in fact, the cheery Bob Reynolds, eventually becoming general manager of the firm.

Once inside, the pittites discovered that their benches had been upholstered with carpet and provided with backs, but the galleryites still had to perch on the stone risers, though these had now acquired the doubtful comfort of a seating-board. Yet these first-night enthusiasts did not mind. What if another's toe did stick into one's back? It was all in the game, and anyway would become unfelt and forgotten once the show had begun.

That is not to suggest the galleryites were easily pleased. On the contrary, being free to carry their patronage where the goods seemed best, they had developed a sharp sense of value and if the fare offered failed to come up to standard had no hesitation in making their feelings felt. And managers everywhere were quick to respond. They never argued about it. If the patrons protested they took the play off and put on something else, even though in their hearts they sometimes rebelled at what they considered the uncultured verdict of ill-mannered louts. Not that the actor-managers ever despised any part of their audiences. There was, indeed, and especially at the St. James's, always a warm understanding between them. If Alexander rarely mixed with his clients he invariably considered them. His ready concern was recently recalled in a letter to the writer from Mr. F. W. Gladwell, himself a well-known theatre manager:

> "In my youth," says Gladwell, "I was one of a foursome, loyal fans of the late Sir George Alexander, and at the St. James's after dashing from work we would spend long periods on a dingy staircase, eating our sandwiches, trying to read in the gloom and playing cat's-cradle with a piece of string. Greatly daring, we wrote Sir George suggesting he should put a light in the gallery staircase for the great convenience of his modest patrons. We had a very polite reply from Sir George and the light was fixed within days. This would be round about the period of *Rupert of Hentzau* and *His House in Order*, which latter I saw at least a dozen times."

The only thing that worried those *fin de siècle* audiences—so long as the play was good—was that they sometimes had to miss the end of the show. The rich clientèle had their own equipages of various kinds, but the humbler folk had to make the best of public transport, such as it was. There were no tubes, so dwellers in the suburbs had to rush to Piccadilly and catch a horse-bus to the terminus for their train home. On the way they either re-read Alexander's monogrammed programme, or forgot the illusion of *Hentzau* in the Boer War casualty lists. This doleful tragedy had broken upon the world in the preceding October and now the euphemistic "reverses" were creeping into the Press.

The scarifying reports from Mafeking, Ladysmith and Kimberley made little difference to the routine of the theatres, and at the St. James's Alexander made no patriotic gesture in the way of the fare provided. *Rupert of Hentzau* decorated the boards on the re-opening night, with a cast and décor in full accord with the manager's usual perfection. It would be pleasant to record that this initial assault on the new century was a raging success, but *Rupert's* power had only the veriest semblance of *Zenda's* and it crashed at the end of eight weeks. Happily for Alexander, it broke even because of the *Zenda* matinees which accompanied its run. It proved once again the practical folly of attempting the same thing twice. Sequels seldom have the appeal of originals, and in the case of *Rupert* the novel fell as flat as the play. It was Ruritania with the same filibustering characters and similar incidents all over again. Inevitably the stale hash of *Rupert* suffered by comparison with the freshness of *Zenda.* Maybe, too, the painful reality of war had robbed the mimic Ruritanian battles of their splendour. Nor, under the circumstances, was the sad ending with Rudolph lying in state much to the patrons' taste . . . they were accustomed to seeing Alexander alive and cock-a-hoop at curtain-fall.

The programme during this run, though typical of the St. James's at this period, was in the nature of a souvenir—and free, as usual. Alexander had dropped his old trademark, the Yeoman of the Guard, in favour of his monogram and the masks of Comedy and Tragedy. Beautifully printed on parchment paper, the programme carried a number of advertisements, notable among them one for "Tatcho"—a hair-restorer—loudly recommended by the eminent and hirsute dramatist George R. Sims. Another, which called attention to the Best Riding School in London, might have served as a modern epistle to the horsey or as plug for a learn-to-drive school. In fact, it featured the bicycle—the first form of mechanical traction to occupy the roads—and offered a single lesson for 2/- and a full course for 10/6. If you bought your boneshaker at the school, the lessons were free, and you could buy at special cash discount or on the never-never at 10/- a month. A purveyor of mineral waters sought the custom of The Quality by announcing them: "As supplied to the House of Lords and to this theatre." The St. James's manager struck a note of his own in a panel which said: "Mr. George Alexander wishes to express the hope that the Ladies will avail themselves of the New Lounge above the Vestibule, where tea and coffee can be procured during the Entr'actes." As he ran his own refreshments the business instinct encased in that refined and elegant phrase could hardly have gone unnoticed. That, however, did not detract from the atmosphere of politeness which suffused the St. James's and its manager at all times.

The next venture was a play by Walter Frith, whose work had occupied the stage before, entitled *The Man of Forty*. Produced on 28th March, 1900, its cast included Alexander, H. B. Irving, C. Aubrey Smith, Dennis Eadie (later himself an actor-manager of note), Julie Opp, Carlotta Addison and Esmé Beringer. *The Man of Forty* ran until July, which was long enough to justify Alexander's going off for a holiday. When he returned in September he produced Sydney

Grundy's *A Debt of Honour*. This piece led to a bit of trouble, for Mrs. W. K. Clifford, an authoress of distinction, had written a play on very similar lines called *The Likeness of the Night*, which the Kendals had accepted as the buttress of their forthcoming tour. Mr. and Mrs. Kendal were present at the St. James's first night and were much struck by the resemblance. They did not, however, rush into accusations. They knew that dramatists sometimes thought alike, and they also knew Alexander and his author. Mrs. Clifford, too, though naturally upset, absolved Alexander from any possible blame. She was familiar with his methods, and had in fact negotiated with him over another of her plays. She knew there had been no wilful plagiarism. But the matter leaked out and Clement Scott stirred up a considerable disturbance about it. He recalled for public benefit that there had been similar disputes about *The Squire*, and a lesser one over *The Second Mrs. Tanqueray*, both at the St. James's. Mrs. Clifford's play had, in novel form, been serialised in a popular magazine and the Kendals had commissioned the play on the strength of it. Wisely, nobody went to law. Charges in such cases are very difficult to prove, and Grundy—a man of standing himself—was not likely to have wilfully stolen a plot. After all, how many plots are there? It is treatment that counts.

A Debt of Honour held the stage for eighty-three performances, which showed a profit to all concerned, and then made way for *The Wisdom of the Wise*, by John Oliver Hobbes (Mrs. Craigie), and *The Plot of His Story*, by Mrs. Oscar Beringer, *The Wisdom of the Wise* did not repeat the success of Mrs. Craigie's *Ambassador*: the story was thin and got nowhere. At curtain-fall the gallery manifested their dislike in a violent demonstration. Yet there was much good in that story, if also some rather obvious faults. Creaky and contrived, it ran for only fifty-four performances, coming off in December, 1900. The rumpus led to angry discussion and certain managers considered the possibility of closing the gallery on first nights and asking the critics to a dress-rehearsal. Happily, wiser counsels prevailed.

Thus, at the end of the first year in his new theatre, Alexander had added little to his fortune but a good deal to his reputation. Between February and November he had produced four plays and revived one for matinees—which would be a disastrous procedure today—and had lost £278. This, however, was but a nominal reckoning, for when his salary was taken into account he had actually made £1,030. He had even made a profit of £23 5*s* 8*d* on the seemingly hopeless *Rupert of Hentzau.* There was also a respectable balance from his provincial tour, during which, playing the smaller towns with *Rupert* and *Zenda*, he had netted a profit of nearly £500.

He opened his eleventh season in 1901 with *The Awakening*, a play in four acts by Haddon Chambers, which had in its cast, besides himself, A. E. Matthews, H. B. Irving, Gertrude Kingston and Fay Davis. But this again scored only sixty performances. He followed it with *The Wilderness*, by H. V. Esmond, the actor-playwright, whose plays, if not classics, were eminently such as the people liked and first-rate pieces of stagecraft. It was produced on 11th April, 1901, and ran for fourteen weeks to very good business, and did even better on tour. In it were Alexander, W. Graham Browne (that first-class actor who married Marie Tempest), Lennox Pawle, C. Aubrey Smith (who still remained business manager), Dora Barton, Eva Moore (Esmond's wife—as beautiful a woman as actress), and Miss Phyllis Dare (as a child). A one-acter, *Old Crimea*, by Cosmo Hamilton, was added to the bill on 11th July.

When *The Wilderness* closed Alexander went again on tour. Ever since he had been forced to withdraw *The Importance of Being Earnest* he had believed the time would come when this amusing play could be revived and really succeed. He wondered whether if by now the reason of its withdrawal had been forgotten and Wilde's disrepute softened in the public mind. At some risk, he played it on the tour in turn with *The Awakening* (a failure in town), *The Wilderness, Liberty Hall* and *The Idler*. It did better than *The Awakening*, but not so well as any of the others.

Whilst he was away the Kendals returned to the St. James's and on 28th October, 1901, presented the play which had figured in the recent controversy, Mrs. W. K. Clifford's *The Likeness of the Night.* Whatever there may have been in the charge of plagiarism, it went over well. It gave Mrs. Kendal a perfect part, of which she took full advantage. Its cast included Kendal, Mrs. Beerbohm Tree, Kate Bishop (an excellent actress and mother of Marie Löhr), Henrietta Watson, Grace Lane (who attained such eminence and died so recently) and Mrs. Kendal.

When Alexander returned to town he came to a decision on a problem that had long beset him. Some years earlier he had secured a poetic play, and though these were not in fashion he saw no reason why a thing of beauty should not succeed at the St. James's if properly handled. He had bought this play from Stephen Phillips, had indeed commissioned him to write it. But many things had stood in the way of its production, and meanwhile Phillips had enjoyed tremendous success with Tree's presentation of his *Herod* and also his *Ulysses* at His Majesty's.

Stephen Phillips was a strange character—a mixture of poetry and puckish impudence—a Bohemian unaffected by convention and whose life was at the end an even greater tragedy than anything he put into his verse. But as a poet-dramatist he was magnificent. Despite their disparate demeanours, he and Alexander got on very well together, for each appreciated the artiste in the other. The story was *Paolo and Francesca*, and Alexander was entranced by the majesty of its language and the music of its poetry.

He resolved to give it every chance. He knew he could ensure it an ideal stage production, but he wanted also a cast that would pull all London to see it. He himself would play Giovanni Malatesta. The ideal Francesca would have been Mrs. Patrick Campbell, but she could not accept. He wanted Mrs. Kendal for Lucrezia. She was strongly tempted, but her annual tour with her husband, now an institution, compelled her to decline. Finally, he engaged Evelyn Millard (who had already won many laurels at the St. James's) for Francesca, and it was a very wise choice. Margaret Halstan had the part of Tessa and played it beautifully. A superb actress, she still graces the stage today. As Mrs. Kendal could not play Lucrezia he made another apt choice in Elizabeth Robins. This savoured of poetic justice, for Miss Robins had, it will be remembered, surrendered Paula Tanqueray to Mrs. Patrick Campbell. A young man who was to go far, H. R. Hignett, had his first London engagement as Pulci, and Lilian Braithwaite, who was soon to rocket to fame, played Nita. Arthur Machen, actor as well as writer, played Carlo. Others in the cast were Lyall Swete, Herbert Dansey, R. E. Goddard, Lemprière Pringle, Beatrix de Burgh, Ada Ferrar and Italia Conti, later renowned for her stage training school.

There remained the choice for Paolo. Fate played a part, as it so often does in the theatre. A couple of years previously Alexander had been much struck by a young amateur who had "walked on" in the crowd during his visit to Leeds. (Amateurs were then afforded this

OWEN NARES

SIR GODFREY TEARLE

SIR GERALD DU MAURIER

CELIA JOHNSON with HUGH WILLIAM
in *Pride and Prejudice*

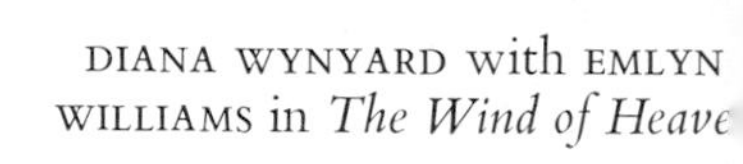

DIANA WYNYARD with EMLYN
WILLIAMS in *The Wind of Heave*

MICHAEL REDGRAVE and TOM
GILL with VALERIE TAYLOR in
A Month in the Country

privilege and made the most of it.) The youth—strikingly handsome and manly—was a bank clerk and did not like it. Humbly he asked Alexander's advice which, readily given, reinforced his urge to the stage, and after overcoming parental objection he joined the famous Benson company. Alexander had not forgotten this handsome young man from Leeds. His name was Henry Ainley. At this crucial moment Benson and his company were at Croydon, so Alexander went along to see for himself. He found Benson enthusiastic about Ainley but also pressing the claims of another young man in his company whom he thought would be still better for Paolo. This man's name was Matheson Lang. Alexander went to see them both. Of course, the great man's purpose in Croydon soon leaked out, and the two young rivals quickly learned what lay between them. Alexander chose Henry Ainley—and Matheson Lang, immeasurably the better actor of the two, never forgot it. This shadow lay between the two for the rest of their lives. Lang never mentioned it but Ainley, more ingenuous, never tried to conceal it. Lang had the better of it in the end. He became a great actor-manager and died a leading figure of our stage. Ainley's end was tragic, his life a list of lost opportunities and luckless mistakes. But he played Paolo and played it efficiently if not extremely well.

Paolo and Francesca was produced on 6th March, 1902. Nobody who was present will ever forget it. It was a night of exquisite thrill and excelling beauty. The settings in Rimini were supremely suited to the loveliness of the words. The voices, no less than the acting, sufficiently matched to the mood and movement of the author's verse. Evelyn Millard's dulcet grace held the audience entranced, and when young Ainley stepped on the stage an audible gasp betrayed his immediate impact on men and women alike. This man seemed hardly real. He hit them like a vision of splendour incarnate, the embodiment and sum of a dreamed Adonis. He and Evelyn Millard together composed a theme for a great artist's brush—the most perfect pair of lovers the stage had seen. But when it came to acting, Miss Millard was vastly superior to her Paolo. He had a glorious voice to match his appearance, but there was about him a restraint—due probably to lack of experience—a visible reluctance to let himself go. Still, nobody carped overmuch about that. The eye fed the mind and all critical faculties were submerged in the senses.

Alexander had stepped aside to give this young man a chance in a million, and had himself accepted a part which was at once "character" and unsympathetic. Nevertheless, his was the finest performance in that play and in its most difficult part. His role of an ageing, battle-scarred warrior, who saw his younger brother supplant him in the heart of the girl he loved, called for both subtlety and assertion. It got them, too. In many ways this was the outstanding performance of Alexander's whole career—he had to give it everything. Here his early training with Irving stood him in good stead. He assumed the grand manner, tempered assurance with quiet force. He thrilled, he quivered, he used his voice as well as he knew how—and he, who had played so many light comedy parts and evoked so much laughter, now held his audience spellbound with the stark tragedy of his murder of the two most dear to him—his brother and the girl on whom his hopes had been set. It was a genuine *tour-de-force*.

The next play was pure romance, costume romance, captioned *If I Were King*, by Justin Huntly McCarthy. Stage version of a successful novel, it was a massive success. Lavishly mounted and heavily cast, it told the story of François Villon, vagabond poet, who rose for one day to kingly power at the whim of Louis XI and used the occasion to smash the Burgundians, escaping the gallows because he had won the love of the high-born Lady Katherine de Vaucelles. It gave Alexander full scope for his versatile charm, and the St. James's a big and colourful production.

Produced on 30th August, 1902, it ran for 215 performances. Alexander played the poet and Charles Fulton made a remarkable Louis XI. Julie Opp first played Katherine but later gave way to Lilian Braithwaite, who after that performance never looked back. Suzanne Sheldon was outstanding as Huguette du Hamel, the light-o'-love who sacrifices her life for Villon. This stately actress married Henry Ainley, who also had a small but effective part in the production. Other names were E. Vivian Reynolds (who became stage manager), E. Lyall Swete (later to gain further triumphs there and elsewhere), and amongst the very minor parts Auriol Lee and Jean Mackinlay. This play, retitled *The Vagabond King*, eventually became an American musical hit.

Once more Alexander gave an impressive performance. From a dirty, unshaven, half-drunk and disreputable poet in the Fir Cone Tavern of the first act, he became the *preux chevalier* of the later scenes, displaying a quiet if slightly wondering nobility and adoring love. His entrance in full armour on a white horse after his defeat of the Burgundians was a memorable thrill—and down the years one hears his voice reciting:

"I wonder, in what isle of Bliss
Apollo's music strikes the air,
In what green valley Artemis
For young Endymion sets her snare,
Where Venus lingers—debonair?
The wind has blown them all away,
And Phyrne in her beauty bare?
Where are the gods of Yesterday?"

CHAPTER 17

The Age of Elegance

GEORGE ALEXANDER and his grand new theatre were now firmly established in the hearts of a large clientèle. Now in the middle of his career at the St. James's, he had every reason to congratulate himself on the eminence he had attained. A giant among the actor-managers, an idol to a multitude of theatre-goers and almost an icon in his own house, he was on an ascending spiral of triumph. If his fortune was not large, it was modestly sufficient, and his future looked as secure as any could be in the dicey game of illusion. He had had many a down among his far more numerous ups and, by no means giddy with his success, was not insensitive to the risk of having many more.

That he was becoming aware of his age—now over forty—was indicated by his wanting to play the aged tutor, Dr. Juttner, when, following the finale of *If I Were King*, he put on *Old Heidelberg*. This spectacular piece was adapted from the German of Wilhelm Meyer-Forster by Rudolf Bleichmann, and was the first play of foreign origin Alexander introduced to the St. James's. It contained two outstanding male roles—Karl Heinrich, princeling of an imaginary State, and his old tutor. He decided to play the latter—and immediately stirred up a revolt. His wife was horrified: it must not even be considered! When Alexander insisted, she enlisted the aid of the staff (among them Captain C. T. H. Helmsey—later general manager—who still kept his uniforms, helmets, swords and accoutrement in a glass case in his office), and all told the boss he simply *had* to play the Prince. Alexander put up a fight. How could he play a young man, almost a boy, at more than forty? His wife assured him he didn't look it, which was certainly true. So did the rest. Reluctantly, he surrendered. It was well that he did, for the part produced one of the best performances of his career.

It was no mean feat to project himself back over the years to the burgeoning torments of youth and portray the shyness and gaucherie of a lad held fast to the stifling tyranny of the Court, nor to reveal his emergence as a carefree student and his dawning love for the innkeeper's daughter and its sequel—the romance shattered by his accession to the throne; and, finally, his return to the scene long afterwards in a vain attempt to recapture his youth, only to discover that such things cannot be. It was a profound and touching character-study.

The aged tutor was played by J. D. Beveridge, an actor of genius who, however, never became a star. His performance also touched perfection. The leaders were admirably supported by Lyall Swete, Ernest Leicester, Henry Ainley, H. R. Hignett, Alfred Brydone, William Farren, Reginald Owen, E. Vivian Reynolds, Henrietta Leverett, Elinor Aickin, Claire Pauncefort and Eva Moore, who made a delightful Kathie, in which role she was later succeeded by Lilian Braithwaite. Among the students and other minor characters were some other significant names, such as Reginald Dane, Ernest Thesiger, T. Weguelin, Martin Lewis and Owen Nares. Undoubtedly, the St. James's was a training-ground for stars.

Old Heidelberg opened on the 19th March, 1903, and kept open for 189 performances. Years afterwards it again claimed public favour as a musical entitled *The Student Prince*. When it came off, Alexander went on tour and another notable actor-manager, E. S. Willard, took temporary possession and filled in his stay with *The Cardinal*, by Louis N. Parker, *Tom Pinch* (a version of *Martin Chuzzlewit*), by J. J. Dilley and Lewis Clifton, and a revival of *The Professor's Love Story*, by J. M. Barrie.

On his return Alexander put back *Old Heidelberg* for a while, and then a sketchy piece by Erich Hartleben and Rudolf Bleichmann called *Love's Carnival*, which soon made way for a light comedy by Frederick Fenn and Richard Pryce, in which Alexander played "Lord Culvert of Alcester, late Captain R.N." opposite Lilian Braithwaite. This piece was accompanied by a snappy one-acter by the same authors entitled *'Op o' My Thumb*, in which Hilda Trevelyan appeared. There followed *The Garden of Lies*, by Justus Miles Forman and Sydney Grundy, and a curtain raiser, *The Decree Nisi*. None of these made much history.

On 27th January, 1905, a dramatist new to the St. James's had his name on the bills with a one-act play entitled *A Maker of Men*. His name was Alfred Sutro, and he provided the next full play there, too, *Mollentrave on Women*, on 13th February. Bernard Shaw got a look in on 21st March with his one-act *How He Lied to Her Husband*, transferred from the Court Theatre.

On 1st May Alexander presented *John Chilcote, M.P.*, by E. Temple Thurston and Katherine Temple Thurston. This had a good deal of advance publicty and left a sartorial heritage. It required a "double" for Alexander. But could there be such a person? Could this model of form and courtesy, this man of grave demeanour and good looks, produce, even with plentiful make-up, another sufficiently like him to pass muster? It was most unlikely. Yet they did discover someone of vague resemblance. He was W. J. Thorold, the editor of a glossy and very popular magazine called *The Smart Set*. But nobody was deceived for a second. The play not unnaturally failed; but it was notable for one thing. In it Alexander wore a soft double-fold collar, a thing hitherto unknown. It immediately became the vogue. But as he wore it with country clothes everyone understood that neither he nor anyone else would tolerate such informal attire in town. The collar was fairly high and made of flannel, and the ends were kept together with a gold safety-pin. In no time at all every man with any pretence to smartness had acquired such a collar for country wear. And so it was that the soft collar, now universal, originated at the St. James's.

The Man of the Moment, by Henry Melvill, Alfred Capus and Emanuel Arene, filled out the season, and in the autumn Alexander went to the Theatre Royal, Drury Lane, to play in *The Prodigal Son* at a very large salary and with enormous success. During this time he took charge of the funeral of his great and beloved chief, Sir Henry Irving.

Whilst he pulled in the town at Drury Lane, the Kendals went back again to the St. James's and produced *Dick Hope*, by Ernest Hendrie, a well-known actor; and also a three-act farce, *The Housekeeper*, by Metcalfe Wood and Beatrice Heron-Maxwell.

The Kendals were followed by William Mollison, in partnership with Lilian Braithwaite, who presented on 23rd December, 1905, *Beside the Bonnie Briar Bush*, by Ian Maclaren, Augustus Thomas and James Macarthur, and later, Shakespeare's *As You Like It*.

In 1906 Alexander returned to his own theatre. He had now been fifteen years in management and stood in the very front rank of his profession. When Irving died his mantle as leader fell naturally on the shoulders of Sir Herbert Tree, his next in magnitude. But next to Tree stood Alexander. He had placed a risky theatre securely on the map and in the process had given young players large opportunities, and had done the same for British dramatists. Only *Old Heidelberg* and *Love's Carnival* had been of foreign origin—two out of the fifty plays he had presented up to this date. He himself had made a tremendous impact on the public and brought much credit to his profession. Far from diminishing, his powers seemed to expand with every performance. He grew more handsome as the years advanced. His grave and courteous manner, his slow, pleasant smile, his straight gaze and his complete integrity all contributed to the genuine regard in which he was held. The ladies adored him, and his photo in a silver frame (or as good a frame as they could afford) adorned the home of every female playgoer. With them, he could do no wrong. That is why even his failures were hardly ever heavy financial losses. He had a most faithful following. And his theatre exuded the same gracious dignity as himself. They felt it as soon as they entered. It made playgoing not only pleasant but important. His attitude towards his patrons was one of responsibility and respect. This concern for the comfort of his clients is well illustrated by a programme note issued at a time when enormous hats were fashionable. They spread in a vast radius around the head, piled high with ornamentation of birds, flowers or fruit. Those behind them had small chance of seeing anything of the stage. Some bold spirits would ask the lady kindly to remove her hat—usually getting only a haughty glance for their pains. It was not that the wearer did not wish to oblige, but she did not want the trouble of putting the hat on again—a precision job which demanded a mirror to obtain just the right angle, and was achieved by perilously long hatpins that could inflict a nasty wound if mishandled. So the removal of a hat, once properly fixed, was a major operation.

These feminine monstrosities led to trouble at many theatres and inevitably came in question at the St. James's, which had a large female clientèle. The trouble was brought to Alexander's notice and he dealt with it in the following terms: "Mr. George Alexander would respectfully request those ladies who frequent the St. James's Theatre intent on viewing the performance to recollect the similar purpose in those who sit behind them. If, therefore, every large hat were left in the Cloak Room (for which there is no charge), the lady so doing would confer a great benefit on her immediate neighbours." Only the most granitoid lady could resist an appeal like that; yet it has to be confessed that many did—less perhaps from hard-heartedness than owing to the unmanageable magnitude of their hats.

The dignity and decorum that pervaded the St. James's is again highlighted by a young couple's adventure in Bond Street. They had taken a snack in a tea-shop and were returning arm-in-arm along London's most fashionable street, laughing and talking. The young man wore a Norfolk jacket (what would now be called a sports coat), tweed trousers and brogue shoes. His arty tie was large and floppy and much the same applied to his hat. The girl wore a costume neat and becoming, but of tweed. As they approached a corner they suddenly became aware of The Chief standing there watching them. He was perfectly dressed. On his head was a shining topper, and his collar and shirt were spotlessly white. He had a quiet grey tie in which twinkled a small diamond pin. He wore a perfectly cut morning coat and vest and you could have cut your finger on the crease of his grey trousers. From the V of his black vest peeped just the right amount—one-eighth of an inch—of white piqué. His boots were patent leather, his hands covered in skin-fitting gloves, and he carried a gold-knobbed cane. The young couple stopped. Alexander raised his hat and bowed. "I am pleased," he said, "to see two of my young people out together enjoying each other's company. It is what I like, it is what I encourage. It makes for good feeling, for *esprit de corps*. But I would remind them that this is Bond Street and at the fashionable hour, and that they are members of the St. James's theatre company. Membership of that company entails certain sartorial obligations. I need say no more." He bowed again, with a quiet, grave smile and passed on. Neither of those young people ever forgot that adjuration to the dignity of their profession. They were Henry Ainley and Lilian Braithwaite.

All that may suggest to the modern something stiff and formal, precious even and pompous. But Alexander was no poseur: he was perfectly sincere in his attitude. Manners such as his were the social currency of the day.

At the St. James's the staff, no less than the principals, spared no pains to cater to the needs of its patrons. They knew the likes and dislikes of most of them. Arnold in the box-office was a mine of information. He always wore a tall hat on duty, and his genial smile rarely left his large, fresh-complexioned face. He always looked freshly bathed—and in a sense he was, for every morning before work he took a plunge in the local swimming-bath. In their knowledge of the clientèle the whole staff were most meticulous. When the present author took over the management for a while, during the reign of Sir Alfred Butt, one afternoon he was apprised at short notice that the Princess Royal (Duchess of Fife) was coming to the matinee. H.R.H. was a wonderful patron of the Theatre. He made all arrangements and sent for the housekeeper, a regal and forbidding lady who kept the place like a new pin and always wore black silk. "The Princess Royal is coming this afternoon," he said. "No need to tell you, I'm sure, to have a nice tea ready in the Royal Room." The housekeeper folded her arms and regarded him with a mixture of surprise and disdain. He felt something was wrong. "Rightly speaking, Sir," she said, "Her Royal Highness does not partake of tea." "Oh," said the manager. "Of what then does Her Royal Highness partake?" "Rightly speaking, Sir, Her Royal Highness partakes of coffee." And coffee it was. But although coffee was served in the special silver service, Her Royal Highness did not partake. She and the manager spent the intervals discussing rheumatism, from which they both suffered at the time. They were, in fact, quite old friends—one of the few things the St. James's did not know.

The staff seldom changed: they knew when they were well off. Here, in the royal purlieus as it were, and in the Theatre of Distinction, ordinary life seemed to pass them by. Happy in a little world of their own, they regarded their theatre as the only possible place to work in, for it had its own special tone. For many years even the tickets were different from those of other theatres; while these used books of paper tickets the St. James's clung to cards. Even the name of the assistant-manager of the box-office held a hint of distinction—De Courcey. And if they granted complimentary tickets these were never the usual ones overstamped. No, they were special cards which carried instructions that evening dress was imperative if the bearer wished to be admitted. And if the manager desired to refuse what was known as "the courtesy of the house", he told Arnold to send Box C—as there were only Boxes A and B!

This was for the St. James's the age of elegance. When a play went into rehearsal, the company gathered on the stage for the first call, which was always at 10.30 a.m. They sat on chairs in a semi-circle and waited, for they always got there some fifteen minutes ahead of time. It was a tradition. And then at 10.29¾ minutes precisely the stage-manager would walk on and announce "Ladies and Gentlemen, Mr. George Alexander." (The occasion was heightened after he became "Sir".) They would all rise, and the Master of the House of St. James's would enter on the very dot of time. Bowing, he would greet them with a welcoming smile. In his immaculate frock coat, one of the most elegant of all male garments, he always conveyed the impression that it had been invented especially for him. The company would bow back, and he would say: "Ladies and Gentlemen, pray be seated." And then the rehearsal began.

CHAPTER 18

The Zenith

IT will be remembered that there had been a rift between Alexander and A. W. Pinero, arising out of disagreements over *The Princess and the Butterfly*. The actor had always wanted to bridge the gulf, but the playwright had remained aloof. In 1904, however, Alexander had set about patching things up. He was resolved to lure Pinero back to the St. James's, to which, in his opinion, he so properly belonged. His chance came when a play of Pinero's, produced at Wyndhams, called *The Wife Without a Smile*, turned out badly and did Pinero's reputation a good deal of harm. In these circumstances Pinero saw the wisdom of renewing the old association and was soon at work on a play. Alexander promised him a free hand for he wanted a Pinero play badly.

The dramatist was less demanding than usual but insisted that a pivotal character, a boy aged about eight, would need to be properly played. He thought it would be impossible to get a boy, so suggested young Iris Hawkins. She, however, was found to be under contract to Arthur Bourchier at the Garrick. Pinero wrote on and delivered the first two acts, with which Alexander was delighted. The dramatist wanted a real Frenchwoman to play the boy's governess, and Alexander was fortunate in securing Mlle Marcelle Chevalier, just the right person for the part. Rehearsals began on the due date, for luckily Bourchier had released Iris Hawkins, and there was no argument about the rest of the cast. This play, which marked Pinero's return to the St. James's, was produced on 1st February, 1906, and was called *His House in Order*.

Although some may disagree, the popular verdict acclaims this as the best play Pinero ever wrote—*Tanqueray* notwithstanding—and it was the biggest success of Alexander's reign. It set everyone talking and drew all London, time and again.

It was an ideal comedy in the best sense of the word, with an arresting plot, marvellous characterisation, wit, satire, drama—everything necessary for a successful play. As an example of craftsmanship it is outstanding. Everything that happens, every word spoken pushes it relentlessly along to its climax. Pinero did not strive for a conventional happy ending. He brought about the logical one—such as could happen in real life—and left it there. Humanity being what it was, there was every likelihood of happiness arriving.

Alexander put into the production of this well-remembered masterpiece everything he knew. It provided the vehicle for what was probably the best acting our stage has ever seen. The polish and integrity were almost beyond praise. Those who had the good fortune to see it, found it seared into their memory. Its four acts were essential to the proper realisation of the structure Pinero had created, especially as regards the "curtains"—and these were not the least remarkable things in *His House in Order*. Pinero did not miss one detail. This story of the mental persecution of a second wife, despised by the family of her predecessor, who had been placed on a pedestal and worshipped by all who knew her, had inherent drama. For the goddess proved no paragon. The beloved son, Derek, whom she had left when killed in an accident was not the child of her doting, dry, conventional husband, but of her lover. The secret had been well kept. It might never have been discovered but for the persecution of the second wife. She had been the boy's governess, and the father, when bereft of his adored Annabel Mary, had married her more or less for convenience—to "keep his house in order". She failed at the job, largely because of the determined efforts of the first wife's family, the Ridgeleys, to bring disgrace and contumely upon her. They defeated her every effort to please. They even deprived her of the conduct of the house, and as a final degradation relieved her of her cherished room because they considered it the right room for the son. It was this culminating act that brought about her victory and the Ridgeleys' downfall. The boy, ferreting about in his new room, discovered an old handbag of his mother's, and in it some letters of deadly import. Unaware of their significance, he gave them to his stepmother and thus put the weapon of retribution in her hands. That perfectly logical sequence shows the care and skill with which Pinero constructed his plays. Nothing was left to chance, there was no question of coincidence. It all happened as it could—and has—happened in real life.

It seems impossible today to revive that play and catch the real savour, the true essence of its greatness. It was, of course, of its period. It demanded the type of acting of its period, too, and that it got in full measure. The Ridgeley family might, today, seem comic; but in 1906 they were very real. They were the still powerful rearguard of the narrowest Victorian outlook. Everybody knew them and had suffered from them. The pity of it was, they were excellent people in their own way—doing what they considered the right thing—and Pinero showed you that. In point of years 1906 is not far away, in point of social usage it is a different era. But on that night of 1st February, 1906, the perfect play appeared in its perfect setting: Alexander, Pinero, and the St. James's Theatre reached their zenith. The cast must of necessity be recorded.

His House in Order

Hilary Jesson (British Minister to the Republic of Santa Guarda)	Mr. George Alexander.
Filmer Jesson, M.P.	Mr. Herbert Waring.
Derek Jesson	Miss Iris Hawkins.
Sir Daniel Ridgeley	Mr. E. Lyall Swete.
Pryce Ridgeley	Mr. C. M. Lowne.
Major Maureward	Mr. Dawson Milward.
Dr. Dilnott	Mr. Nigel Playfair.
Harding	Mr. Robert Horton.
Forshaw (a Provincial Newspaper representative)	Mr. E. Vivian Reynolds.
Servants	Mr. Anthony Fawcitt and Mr. Gerald Jerome.
Nina	Miss Irene Vanbrugh.
Lady Ridgeley	Miss Bella Pateman.
Geraldine Ridgeley	Miss Beryl Faber.
Mlle Thomé	Mlle Marcelle Chevalier.

The cast was as perfect as the play. Such complete artistry is seldom if ever achieved today. This play and this acting absolutely enthralled. The patrons came again and again. There is already the word of Mr. Gladwell that he saw it a dozen times, and many made even more frequent visits. The writer saw it fourteen times and always found something fresh at which to wonder—and he is a professional. There was not a single flaw. Lyall Swete was exactly right as the rich and pompous old Victorian father, narrow in outlook yet upright and virtuous according to his own lights. His killjoy attitude, loyally seconded by his wife and family, was typical of the kind and not in the least strained; and his final acceptance of defeat had all the dignity of Shylock's exit from the Court scene. There was no emotion, save that which the actor subtly conveyed by his general expression. He just retired from the scene saying: "It's time I had my na—ah—my nap."

C. M. Lowne as Pryce Ridgeley, the caddish son (who nevertheless belonged to the best clubs) acted beautifully in the best manner. This Pryce was a real man, one knew him. And Lady Ridgeley, as portrayed by Bella Pateman, froze all around her with her tremendous virtue, her complete and uncompromising Englishness. She detested foreigners and disliked the idea of her supposed grandson having a French governess. When that charming lady was playing the piano after dinner, Lady Ridgeley disapproved of the music—at which the Gallic blood of Mlle Thomé rose to the defence: it was Chopin, and he was a genius! Lady Ridgeley was not moved: geniuses to her were as bad as foreigners, and when a genius was also a foreigner, the nadir was reached. "It's high time that boy was in bed," she remarked. "We shall have him becoming a genius next!" Yet she and her family immediately sided with the despised French lady when one of poor Nina's dogs—forbidden the house—damaged her skirt. Anyone was good enough an ally to bring degradation on Nina, the despised second wife.

Beryl Faber as the icy Geraldine, who had usurped Nina's position as mistress of the house, by every polite word and frigid show of courtesy made Nina's position more and more unendurable . . . again, perfect casting. And Dawson Milward could not have been bettered as Major Maureward. Here was the regular army officer: a gentleman, polished, assured, exactly the sort one met in the best clubs, at Ascot, in the Row. Yet he had seduced the worshipped Annabel Mary—who really disliked her dry-as-dust husband Filmer—and the result was Derek, the cherished son and grandson, the Jesson heir. Maureward knew full well what he had done, yet he still came to the house, because he had loved this woman and he loved his son, who showed remarkable affection for him. Everything that Dawson Milward did told subtly how he realised his position and yet could not tear himself away.

But the two towering performances in this masterly cast were those of George Alexander as Hilary, brother to the deceived Filmer, and Irene Vanbrugh as Nina, the despised and persecuted second wife. This was really superlative acting. To hear Hilary tell his parable of the two French chefs, the one who followed a genius and was therefore belittled (a parable aimed against the Ridgeleys and understood by them) was to hear a beautifully written speech spoken as it should be spoken. Everything he did was a joy, not the least his grasp of the vital scene in the play. Up till then he had been a gay, light-hearted fellow, young for his years and a complete contrast to his dull brother. Yet, when Nina showed him the incriminating letters, all his brightness faded and youth crumbled to middle age. And—subtlest touch of all—having grasped their fatal import, in order to read them carefully he produced a pair of spectacles and put them on.

This scene remains in the writer's memory as the finest high comedy acting he has ever beheld, in a long life of playgoing. He can still see Irene Vanbrugh as Nina, those wonderful dark eyes seeming to occupy almost all her taut, tense face—can see her watching Alexander as he reads, taking in every moment of his growing horror and amazement—can hear her voice exclaiming, after he has read the final letter: "She was—his woman!" He can see her standing tense as a steel spring straining to burst forth, waiting to proclaim her victory and to shatter and humble to the dust those Ridgeleys whom she hated and who so hated her. It was quite unforgettable.

His House in Order ran for fifty-seven weeks, 427 performances. It took £78,189 at the box-office and showed a net profit of £23,443 on the London run alone, a sum augmented by tours and the letting of various rights. It remains an abiding memory, and will remain so when all trace of the St. James's has gone, the zenith of Alexander's achievement and maybe of the whole Edwardian theatre.

The next play, *John Glayde's Honour*, by Alfred Sutro, produced on 8th March, 1907, scored 138 performances and showed a modest profit. In this, Matheson Lang at last achieved the St. James's and did himself much credit. Then, on 12th November, 1907, came *The Thief*, adapted by Cosmo Gordon-Lennox from the French of Henry Bernstein. This provided another fine duologue between Alexander and Irene Vanbrugh, who was the St. James's leading lady *par excellence*. It was magnificently played but had not quite the compelling intensity of the letter-reading in *His House in Order*. Bernstein, a great dramatist and a stalwart man, was famed as one of the last of the duellists. *The Thief* was drawing-room melodrama and good of its kind. It ran for 186 performances.

In this year, 1907, George Alexander appeared in a new role—a real one this time. He was elected a member of the London County Council for South St. Pancras, standing as a Moderate (Conservative today). The ward had two members, and Alexander and Frank Goldsmith defeated the Rev. Sylvester Horne, of Whitefield's Tabernacle, and his associate. The novelist A. E. W. Mason, in his *Life of George Alexander* (to which the writer is greatly indebted), says that when the result became known Bernard Shaw declared that Mr. Horne and his colleague had been "beaten by the Comedian and the Jew". Alexander also considered standing for Parliament, but deferred to better advice.

The following year saw Pinero again at the St. James's with *The Thunderbolt*. It had not much thunder, however, and was far from vintage Pinero. This sordid story about unpleasant people made a mere fifty-eight performances. The cast included George Alexander, Louis Calvert, Kate Bishop, Norman Forbes, Mabel Hackney and Reginald Owen. It will be noticed how some names recur again and again in the St. James's casts. Alexander believed in maintaining the basis of a stock company and always put his people under long contracts, thus being able to use them as occasion required. He ended the year with *The Builder of Bridges*, by Alfred Sutro, which registered only a very moderate success.

About this period a certain young boy could often be seen running around in the St. James's. Maybe it was the call of the blood, for he was the son of a very famous American actor named Henry Miller, and his own name was Gilbert. Henry Miller, London-born, had gone to Toronto, where he made his first stage appearance, and then to New York. There he won prestige and became one of America's most distinguished actor-managers. Eventually he built the Henry Miller Theatre and exercised great influence on the American stage. He came often to this country and was a great friend of Alexander. His son,

Gilbert Heron Miller, used to come with him and was given the freedom of the theatre, where he was a great favourite among the staff. He drank everything in and, as after-events were to prove, probably quite unconsciously took the St. James's as his standard. Anyway, to this day he remembers with joy those boyhood visits and holds in reverence the memory of Alexander, to whom he was devoted and who always treated the youngster as a great pal. Although neither of them could know it then, this friendly association was forging a future phase in the chronicle of the St. James's.

CHAPTER 19

More Great Days

DURING Alexander's absence on tour, after topping the St. Pancras poll in 1907, a most distinguished tenant had taken over the St. James's. He was Edward Compton, a fine actor who had rendered yeoman service by touring Old English comedy and other plays, and by training recruits in the best of all possible schools—on the stage itself. He and his wife, Virginia Bateman, were both pillars of the theatre, and their children have inherited the talent and carried on the tradition. They include Fay Compton, one of our loveliest actresses, in every sense, and Sir Compton Mackenzie.

On 29th July, 1907, Compton produced a play called *The Eighteenth Century*—probably his own work, as no author's name was announced. *The Daily News* said it ought to draw all London. The cast was certainly strong, including Compton himself, Grace Lane, Suzanne Sheldon, Eric Lewis, Henry Ainley, Charles Groves and E. M. Robson (a little man who was a giant of comedy and the best Fluellen that ever appeared in *Henry V*). On 14th September Mr. Compton also staged a brilliant revival of *The School for Scandal*, for which Lilian Braithwaite was added to the cast. Both productions went a long way towards confirming the *Daily News*' prediction. The whole tenancy was in the best St. James's tradition.

When Alexander went on tour in 1908, Johnstone Forbes-Robertson (not yet knighted) stepped into the breach with one of his own most successful vehicles. This play, now a classic, first came to life on 1st September, 1908: it was *The Passing of the Third Floor Back*, by Jerome K. Jerome. Every famous actor has a play with which he is inseparably associated. With Irving it was *The Bells*; with Tree, *Svengali*; with Alexander, *The Importance of Being Earnest*; with Charles Hawtrey, *The Message from Mars*; with Lewis Waller, *Monsieur Beaucaire*; with Wyndham, *David Garrick*; with Martin-Harvey, *The Only Way*—and with Forbes-Robertson, *The Passing of the Third Floor*

Back. This curious play, so different from the author's hilarious story, *Three Men in a Boat*, introduced the Christ Figure, and did so—at least as Forbes-Robertson played it—with overwhelming effect.

Into a third-class Bloomsbury boarding-house, sordid and dim, and filled with wretched people at war with themselves and the world, came a Stranger. In that boarding-house, a microcosm of mankind, dwelt a Cheat, a Slut, a Painted Lady, a Shrew, a Snob, a Bully, a Hussy, a Satyr, a Coward, a Rogue and a Cad. And to them came the Stranger, the Passer-By. He was curiously old-fashioned to look at, with his cape and his old-type frock coat, but about him was some strange commanding power which expressed itself through his gentleness. Every denizen of that house had a problem, and each lived trembling on the brink of some disaster. The worst traits had come to the top in every one of them, and, remorseful of it, their dominant mood was despair. One by one, two by two, the Stranger dealt with them. With the utmost gentleness and compassion but with terrific power, he worked upon them, revealed them to themselves, opened their eyes and showed them the Truth. And, one by one, two by two, they turned from their fretful path and found the Better Way. He had found discord and despair: he left happiness and hope. His work done, he stood in the hall, quite alone. He faced the front door, to pass on his way. And as he stood in that dingy place, through the fanlight a ray of sunshine came and bathed him in its radiance. The Passer-By opened wide his arms as if to greet it, and a smile like the sun shone on that wonderful face. While he stood with arms outstretched, the sign of the cross, formed by his shadow, spread across the floor . . . and the curtain fell.

Words are quite inadequate to describe the grip of the play; but to see Forbes-Robertson in it was the experience of a lifetime. Nothing like it had been done before—nor has it since. It was one of the most beautiful pieces of acting that ever illumined our stage: it was sheer, cumulative artistry and effulgence of genius. Nobody but Forbes-Robertson could really play that part. Others have tried, but were mere shadows beside him. His wonderful, ascetic face, so much of the spirit, so little of the flesh; his amazing eyes—he riveted attention to the stage—and his voice, that peal of silver bells, fugued at times with his organ note, struck the ear like some celestial choir, so steeped was it in his tenderness, yet so full of strength. This must have been something of what the crowds saw in Galilee. It left an ineffaceable memory. It sent one out of the theatre humbled and hushed, yet immensely happy. It did more good than a century of sermons.

When Alexander returned in 1909, Forbes-Robertson transferred this great play to the now vanished Terry's Theatre, in the Strand, and the St. James's opened with a comedy by A. E. W. Mason, entitled *Colonel Smith*, preceded by *The Nursery Governess*, by M. Provins and P. G. Duchesne. *Colonel Smith*, presented on 23rd April, soon folded and was replaced by another Pinero play, entitled *Mid-Channel*. Alexander did not appear in this production and something went seriously wrong with it. The play had strength and dramatic power, but nearly all the characters were unsympathetic. Worse, they were unpleasant. In it Pinero showed that odd streak which marred his later work. The cast was excellent, yet the play did not catch on. It dealt with that awkward period in matrimony when the first romance has worn away and the binding force of comradeship and affection has not yet had time to cement the match. One of the characters, admirably played by C. M. Lowne, spoke the explanation of the title. There was, it seemed, a shoal midway across the English Channel which made the passage stormy and difficult at all times. Safely across it, all was well, but that was where shipwreck could occur. Masters of cross-Channel steamers, when interviewed, said they knew nothing of such a shoal, but everyone understood what Pinero meant. Though the play did not succeed, it left a deep impression on those fortunate enough to see it.

The next venture was *Lorrimer Sabiston, Dramatist*—an unfortunate piece by R. C. Carton, which had to come off within three weeks. That made three failures in a row. Then Alexander revived *The Importance of Being Earnest*. He rightly judged that the time was ripe. It ran for 324 performances. He played his original part of John Worthing and was fortunate enough to get Allan Aynesworth back as Algernon Moncrieff. Stella Patrick Campbell (Mrs. Pat's daughter) played Gwendolen; Rosalie Toller, a fair, pretty girl and excellent actress, was Cicely. Others in the cast were E. Vivian Reynolds as Dr. Chasuble, Alice Beet as Miss Prism, and Helen Rous as Lady Bracknell. Erik Stirling and Thomas Weguelin played the two menservants. The comedy came over as brilliantly as it had done originally, and all was again well at the St. James's.

This revival coincided with Alexander's twentieth year in management, and to mark the occasion he gave every member of the audience a handsomely bound copy of the play as a souvenir.

All through these years that young American, Gilbert Miller, had been coming and going between London and New York, and always spending much time with the Alexanders. He was now an actor and Alexander promised him a part in a forthcoming play, *D'Arcy of the Guards*. But the production was so often delayed that when at last it went into rehearsal young Mr. Miller was playing in New York and could not come. It is as well he did not, for *D'Arcy of the Guards*, by Louis Evan Shipman, became the fourth in Alexander's series of flops. Luckily, *The Importance of Being Earnest* had paid for all. However, young Mr. Miller missed his chance of joining the St. James's company, and he probably little thought then that the day was to come when he himself would control that theatre. Maybe that is not quite true, for perhaps the ambition was always there.

The ill-fated *D'Arcy of the Guards* was followed by *The Eccentric Lord Comberdene*, by R. C. Carton, which ran from 12th November, 1910, up to mid-December, when it gave way to a series of Christmas matinees put on by F. R. Benson's company. Alexander resumed on 1st February, 1911, with another of A. E. W. Mason's plays, *The Witness for the Defence*, which filled the bill for 150 performances.

No event of great importance happened that year. It was the coronation of King George V—which brought to Alexander the accolade of knighthood. Richly, indeed, did he merit it. Few, if any, had better earned it, and it is well to remember that the St. James's Theatre, where he had gained his title, deserved some share of the honour.

His first new play on the pinnacle of knighthood was a light, almost farcical comedy called *The Ogre*, by Henry Arthur Jones. At this point in political time Alexander had to assert himself as master of his house and did it by nailing his breeches above the mantelpiece. It was the era of the Suffragettes militant, and when they dared to stage a demonstration in his very august theatre he promptly had them ejected. In the cast of *The Ogre* appeared a very beautiful girl from the Gaiety, who had played for a short time in the revival of *The Importance* as well, and whose name was Gladys Cooper. The world was to hear of that lovely lady again!

After a short revival of *Lady Windermere's Fan*, in which Marion Terry filled her original part and Mr. Cecil Graham was played by the young Owen Nares, came, in December, 1911, *Bella Donna*, an adaptation by J. B. Fagan of Robert Hichens's popular novel. This piece brought back Mrs. Patrick Campbell to play the title role. She came with some reluctance, for she did not like the part, but, within the limitations imposed by the character, was never better in her life. Alexander risked his admirers' anger by playing Dr. Mayer Isaacson in a black wig. Not a showy part, he took it in his stride, giving quiet point to the several tense scenes, against the beauty, glamour and fire of Mrs. Patrick Campbell. In one of these scenes, set near Luxor, clad in a close-fitting dress of gleaming sequins, she really looked the Serpent of Old Nile. *Bella Donna* was a handsome success, running for 258 performances and proving a gold-mine on tour.

The programmes of this period throw considerable light on contemporary conditions. The one used for *Bella Donna* reveals that you could have afternoon tea at Hatchett's in Piccadilly for 1/-, a matinee luncheon for 2/6, a theatre dinner for 3/6 and supper after the theatre for 2/6. Landaulettes and open cars could be hired for two hours in the morning for 10/6 and for 12/6 in the afternoon. The evening charge, comprising time for dinner, waiting during the performance, and drive home, up to fifteen miles, was 10/6.

The Turning Point, by Henry Kistemakers and Peter de la March, which was produced on 11th October, 1912, had as leading lady that charming actress Ethel Irving, who had already scored a great victory in *The Witness for the Defence*. Now, she and Alexander played man and wife. The husband, an Engineer officer, took to gambling, whilst his wife solaced herself with a lover. When a crime was committed and the Colonel needed an alibi, the one person who could supply it was his wife, from whom he was hopelessly estranged. In this act, Alexander and Ethel Irving were superb. She had no rival when it came to expressing high nervous tension. Some people said that Alexander's performance rivalled Irving at his best. Their acting, supported by a perfect company, carried *The Turning Point* to 111 performances.

The cast included Athol Stewart, Godfrey Tearle, Lettice Fairfax, Norma Whalley and Olga Nicholson. The name of Norma Whalley is important, for she was an actress of both beauty and quality, who had distinguished herself also in musical comedy. She married Sir Percival Clarke, and after his death Major Beauchamp Salter. Their old home still bears her name although she passed on not long ago.

Alexander now played a season at the Palace Theatre, Shaftesbury Avenue, in a special sketch. The Palace was then a theatre of varieties (not just a music hall), and paid him a very large fee. He needed it. Back at St. James's he staged a curious musical version of *Turandot*—not the opera, but the same story used by Karl Vollmoeller and Jethro Bithell. Alexander gave it a beautiful production, with a large cast headed by Evelyn d'Alroy and Godfrey Tearle, who made his entrance in a little Chinese cart pulled by a live pony. It pleased the eye but little else and lost well over £6,000 in its run of twenty-seven performances. In an effort to recoup his finances Alexander revived *Lady Windermere's Fan* again and then put on A. E. W. Mason's *Open Windows*, preceded by *Playgoers*, a little one-act gem by Pinero, which ran until 10th May (ninety performances).

In 1913 Lillah McCarthy and Granville Barker ran a season at the St. James's, from September to December, as distinguished as the theatre itself. The plays presented were: *The Harlequinade*, by Dion Clayton Calthrop and Granville Barker; *Androcles and the Lion*, by Bernard Shaw; *The Witch*, by H. Wiers-Jensen and John Masefield; *The Wild Duck*, by Ibsen; *Le Mariage Forcé*, by Molière; *The Doctor's Dilemma*, by Bernard Shaw; *The Death of Tintagiles*, adapted by Sutro from Maeterlinck; and *The Silver Box*, by John Galsworthy. Most of these were, of course, revivals, but they all contributed to a most memorable season.

CHAPTER 20

The Old Order Changeth

THREE quite unremarkable plays occupied Sir George and the St. James's for the major part of the fateful year 1914. Suitably enough, he opened on 1st January with *The Attack*, adapted from the French of Henry Bernstein by "George Egerton" (a lady, well-known in theatrical and literary circles). In the cast was E. Holman Clark, an actor unrivalled in his characterisation of suave, persuasive, middle-aged or elderly men. Alexander took the lead and with him were his faithful stage-manager E. Vivian Reynolds, Gladys Storey, and a prominent actress, Martha Redman.

This piece brought in reasonable houses until 28th February and was succeeded on 8th March by Sutro's *The Two Virtues*, with a cast including Alexander, Herbert Waring, George Bishop, Martha Redman, Henrietta Watson and Athene Seyler. This play carried on until on 9th May Alexander revived Oscar Wilde's *An Ideal Husband*, first produced at the Haymarket in 1906. In this revival the part of Lady Chiltern was played by Phyllis Neilson-Terry, whose mother Julia Neilson had set the pattern for it in the original production. Wilde held the stage for seventy-seven performances, ending on 24th July.

The world stood now on the brink of war and within a few days the Continent was in arms. Britain went to the aid of her allies on 4th August. Momentarily, the whole nation was shocked. War was something strange to a people who, though accustomed to battling in distant lands, had not been involved in a European conflict since the Napoleonic struggle a century before.

The first reactions of disbelief and alarm gave way to a firm and quiet confidence; and as, in Earl Grey's words "the lights went out over Europe", somebody revived the old slogan "Business as Usual", and the country settled down to "beat hell out of the Kaiser". Alexander responded to the demand to carry on as usual with the production, on 19th September, of a new play by Michael Orme entitled *Those Who Sit in Judgment*. It was a courageous attempt to maintain the semblance of normality in difficult times. for things were now grim at the front, and life, even in the select St. James's area, was greatly disturbed. Almost everyone had taken up war work and the young men were flocking to the colours. Nevertheless Alexander, as a contribution to stability, gave the play a fine mounting, backed up by his usual competent cast, in which were, besides himself, Nigel Playfair, Henrietta Watson, Reginald Owen, Frederick Volpe, Helen Ferrers, Nicholas Hannen and Norman MacOwan. Among the numerous small parts, too, there were names which have since become prominent. But such of the public as went to "sit in judgment" on this play decided against it, and it was withdrawn on 10th October after only twenty-one performances.

Alexander fell back upon a revival of *His House in Order* with almost the original cast, except that the French governess was now played by an Englishwoman, Barbara Hannay, and two or three of the supporting parts were also changed. And this vintage Pinero held the boards until 19th December—seventy-five performances.

His first production in 1915 was *Kings and Queens*, by Rudolf Besier, that outstanding dramatist who was later to write *The Barretts of Wimpole Street*. Not allowing war to reduce his standards, Alexander mounted it in the real St. James's style and gave it a glittering cast. With him were Arthur Wontner, a player of real quality, Marie Löhr, now one of our foremost actresses, Frances Ivor, Ben Webster and Hesketh Pearson (famous now as a biographer). They kept it going for eighty-one performances, up to 27th March.

One of London's big war-time successes was *Peg o' My Heart*, written by J. Hartley Manners as a vehicle for his wife, that charming American red-head, Laurette Taylor. This piece, first produced in October, 1914, at the Comedy Theatre and then transferred to the Globe, had an original run of 710 performances, boosted by revivals to a total of well over a thousand. On 14th April, 1915, Alexander put on another play by the same author, called *The Panorama of Youth*. But, alas, its first night was greeted with an air-raid warning and a threat of fog—not at all a good evening and, as it proved, inauspicious for *The Panorama of Youth*. Dying after only twenty-four performances, it never saw old age.

Following this, Alexander put on another sure loser. His usually impeccable judgment must have failed him on this occasion. Perhaps he overlooked the fact that in war time people yearn for peace. One or two light-hearted comedies might get by, but the public—especially in those days—turns to the theatre for amusement in an escapist mood. Maybe Alexander had in mind the thrills of *Zenda*, but he must have forgotten *The Conquerors* and *D'Arcy of the Guards*. The new piece, called *The Day before The Day*, dealt with the coming of the war, with much emphasis on that famous German toast: "Der Tag!" Alexander did not play in it himself; nor did anyone else for long. It was withdrawn on 5th June, after only nineteen performances.

During this second year of World War I, Matheson Lang went to the St. James's as actor-manager with his own production of *The Merchant of Venice*. Last of the actors with the "grand manner", he made a memorable Shylock.

Alexander was now fifty-six years old, and he was ill, already suffering from the malady which was shortly to carry him off. Harassed by all the worries of a theatre in war time, he struck reverse after reverse. But he did not spare himself: in addition to his managerial responsibilities he was busily occupied in war work. And he kept his theatre open when many would have let it to the theatrical speculators who were cashing-in on the craze for Revue.

A play by Pinero took the stage on 1st September, 1915. It was *The Big Drum*, and again had a vintage cast with the actor-manager in the lead. Supporting him were Allan Aynesworth, Nigel Playfair, Leonard Boyne, Norman Forbes and Irene Vanbrugh. This comedy, though by no means in Pinero's best style, stopped the flow of failures. It ran from 1st September until 4th December—104 performances—and must have put new heart in the weary and stricken Alexander. At this stage he gave no sign of his illness: he just appeared his usual courtly, grave and distinguished self. But that, at least on occasions, he thought of the future was shown by his telling Gilbert Miller, who was now producing plays in Britain, how happy he would be if, after his own time, the St. James's could pass to him.

In 1916 came the last play but three which the man who had made the St. James's was to tackle. It was a comedy by "Clifford Mills" (a woman writer) entitled *The Basker*. Alexander played the part of George de Lacorfe, supported by Geneviève Ward (our finest tragedienne since Mrs. Siddons), Ellen O'Malley, W. Bridges Adams,

Helen Ferrers, Norman Forbes, Hilda Moore and Léon Quartermaine. *The Basker* came off after 112 performances, showing an acceptable profit.

Then came *Pen*, adapted by Horace Annesley Vachell from Morley Roberts's novel, *Lady Penelope*. Alexander did not play in it but gave it a strong cast. Though it lacked nothing of the St. James's polish, the play scored only sixteen performances, from 3rd May to 13th. Alexander put on a short revival of *Bella Donna* with Hilda Moore as leading lady, after which Sir Alfred Butt took over for a short season and revived *Peg o' My Heart*. But business was bad. Few people were about at night, for there had been a series of air raids. The manager who looked after Sir Alfred's interests opined that the only thing that would help business down in King Street would be the falling of a bomb there. On the night of Whit Sunday, 1916, one did indeed fall. It hit what had been Williss's Rooms, just a few yards from the St. James's. (Horatio Bottomley, who lived in a flat next door, claimed that it had been aimed at him!) The theatre suffered no damage save a broken glass in the canopy. But on the Whit Monday King Street was packed with sightseers and there was a very brisk matinee and evening business. But the excitement passed, and so, after a very few weeks, did *Peg o' My Heart*.

The year 1916 also saw another manager in the St. James's. He was Edwin T. Heys, who staged a play called *Lucky Jim* and followed it, after sixty performances, with a revival of *Charley's Aunt*.

George Alexander appeared in his last role at his beloved theatre on 25th January, 1917. The play was *The Aristocrat*, by Louis N. Parker. Had they known it was his swan-song, no title and no role could have fitted him better; for he had made the St. James's an aristocrat among theatres and he was certainly an aristocrat among the actor-managers. It was a story of the French Revolution, of the Terror, a subject which nearly always succeeds on the stage. It is most gratifying to record that this, Sir George's last active production, was successful. It was indeed what he deserved—and he did it magnificently. On the cover of his programmes was the announcement:

Sole Lessee and Manager, Sir George Alexander, 1890-1917.

He had been there for twenty-seven years, a third of its lifetime all but a year, and almost the half of his own life.

As it is the last time the name of George Alexander appears in a programme, the cast surrounding his final role should be given in full:

THE ARISTOCRAT
by Louis N. Parker.

Louis of Olonzac, Duke of Chastelfranc ...... George Alexander.
Louise, his daughter .... Mary Glynne.
Dame Ursula of Beauchastel .... Helen Rous.
The Duchess of Anteveille .... Geneviève Ward.
Félicien Gibert, Bishop of Carcassone .... William Lugg.
Baudouin of Batioz, Marquis of Béassac ...... Lennox Pawle.
Josselin of Bonassac, Count of Avantignan .... Edward Combermere.
Jacqueline, his wife .... Joyce Carey.
Gautier Lalance .... Dennis Neilson-Terry.
Gaspard Chépy .... Charles Glenney.
Augustin Phillibert Duroz .... William Stack.
Jacques, a Soldier .... E. Rayson-Cousens.
Toinon Chépy .... Miriam Lewes.
Urbain .... E. Vivian Reynolds.
Renaud .... Henry Oscar.
Bonami, Foreman of the Jury .... W. R. Staveley.
Lebrun .... Hector Abbas.
Louis II .... Sunday Wilshin.
Jacqueline II .... Phyllis Neal.

Servants, Soldiers of the National Guard, Jury, Mob.

It will be observed how the second generation was now entering the St. James's. Here is Dennis Neilson-Terry, son of Julia Neilson and Fred Terry, both of whom had played there, and his sister Phyllis had already appeared there. Here, too, is Joyce Carey, daughter of Lilian Braithwaite. The young lovers in the play, Dennis Neilson-Terry and Mary Glynne, actually fell in love and in due course married.

In this play Geneviève Ward gave the audience a wonderful moment. While being led to the guillotine, her courage broke: she wilted and whimpered—an old woman faced with a horrible death. Then, at a roar from the mob, she recovered and went out to face them as if she were entering the presence of her King, upright, noble and assured. And Alexander gave one of his most memorable performances.

How handsome he looked in that glittering costume, with his powdered wig, his lace and his silks, and a gleaming star on his breast. Here, indeed, was the Aristocrat! And he and the play held the house for 150 performances.

Only one more piece was done at the St. James's under Alexander's management—a comedy by Githa Sowerby called *Sheila*. It was staged on 7th June. By the autumn his health was deteriorating rapidly. This handsome and seemingly healthy man was a victim of consumption—and it had been to fight this disease and to aid a hospital which battled against it that he had first appeared, as an amateur, at the St. James's Theatre. The end came quickly. He died at his home at Chorley Wood, where so many of his happiest leisure hours were spent with his beloved wife. He passed away peacefully just after midnight on 16th March, 1918, at the age—the far too early age—of fifty-nine. He left £90,672.

Sir George Alexander performed a great service not only to the St. James's Theatre but to the whole British stage. He was a living example of integrity, talent, and high endeavour. Though often disappointed, he was never defeated and never despaired. He set himself the highest possible standard and lived up to it. He was proud of his profession and his profession has every reason to be proud of him. The whole nation mourned his passing.

As an actor-manager, he lifted an unlucky theatre from derelict depths and placed it at the pinnacle of success and approval. As an actor he never received full recognition. He was a very fine actor indeed, almost qualifying for the adjective great. Great he was in his own line, without question. He had all the personal attributes and he had command of his art. He could be as effective in the vast spaces of the Lyceum or Drury Lane as in the more intimate surroundings of the St. James's. In his own theatre he gave many people opportunities by which they profited. He made the St. James's a home for British acting and playwrights, and by his own example set a hallmark of competence on those who played with him. In bidding him farewell let it be said he was a great man who created a great theatre.

CHAPTER 21

The New Era

IT was a strange world that emerged from that holocaust of 1914-18. Much that belonged to the previous era had been distorted or destroyed. It was a hurried and precarious world in which the habits of leisurely elegance no longer found scope or encouragement. For more than four years the young people had been servants of the war machine, regimented in a way their fathers had never known. Reacting from the hazardous squalor of battle, they had devoted their short and precious leaves to obtaining what pleasure they could. They wanted the bright lights, warmth, acceptable food, happiness, laughter and freedom. In the process the old traditions tottered and moral values often went by the board. It was no use the purists complaining, for life seen through the eyes of impending dissolution conjures up a transcending ethic of its own.

Once it was over, the millions of young people matured in the mad abnormality of war were flung into a world well-nigh bereft of basic standards. What made it worse was that, having been trained to automata, they now had to think and fend for themselves. Inevitably, the expectations of peace out-dreamed the reality and old and young found it difficult and often impossible to resume life on the old foundations. Four years of war had changed the psychological climate of the whole world—and in a smaller but, within its own ambit, a no less important way, the death of Sir George Alexander altered the atmosphere of the St. James's Theatre. What was to happen in this Brave New World? As in the history of nations, so in the world of the theatre, the hour brought forth the man.

In the case of St. James's, the man was Gilbert Miller. As we have seen, he was no stranger to Alexander's distinguished establishment and had doubtless imbibed some of its tradition. Educated in New York, Paris, Dresden and Bedford, Miller was now thirty years old, and already experienced as an actor, producer and manager. As long ago as 1906 he had appeared at the Waldorf (later the Strand) in a minor part in *Julie Bon-Bon*. Early in the war he had been in Britain, where he was associated with a number of impressive productions. In 1916 he staged *Daddy Long-Legs* at the Duke of York's, where it scored 514 performances, due largely to the sweet insouciance of Renée Kelly and the bland assurance of C. Aubrey Smith. In the following year he produced *The Willow Tree* at the Globe and, with Charles Hawtrey *The Saving Grace* at the Garrick, both successful. Then in 1918 he put on *Nothing But the Truth* at the Savoy (578 performances) and, showing his versatility, staged a splendid musical version of *Monsieur Beaucaire* at the Prince's in 1919 and turned a handsome profit in a 221 run.

When the United States joined the Allies, Miller served in the American Army and was on an important assignment in Paris when he heard of Alexander's death. His remembrance of Alexander's wish and his own inclination determined him to obtain the succession. He immediately put his lawyers to work and soon, to his unbounded delight, the place was his, although not with immediate possession. So for the few months of the suspended lease the St. James's housed some fleeting productions. Notable among these was the musical *Valentine*, the first of its kind to occupy this theatre for many years. (In Alexander's ill-fated *Turandot* the music had been merely incidental.) Apart from that, no musical piece had been heard there since the seductive Hortense Schneider had appeared in Offenbach operas. Napoleon Lambelet composed the music for *Valentine*—a charming piece, enhanced by the presence of pretty Marjorie Gordon—but it did not have the success it merited.

When Miller at last took over towards the end of the year, he found plenty of trouble ahead. In the aftermath of war money was tight, and he had not only to finance his theatre but to effect the repairs and alterations demanded by the London County Council. One of these requirements was the installation of a secondary lighting system. This had long been compulsory in London playhouses and he felt certain an old-established house like the St. James's had not run free of the regulations. After much search and inquiry he found that his surmise was correct—there was a secondary system, but it consisted solely of some ancient oil-lamps! There had been no demand for improvement in Alexander's day, but now the world had altered.

Miller had to find a more substantial sum than his funds allowed. He solved the problem by letting the theatre bars to Westby & Co. (later, Grantley & Co.), a firm of contractors headed by Sir George Dance, the well-known millionaire theatre magnate. Mr. Dance (not yet knighted) for some queer reason hated to be identified with that firm and if anyone mentioned the connection was quick to accuse his staff of "blabbing". It seems never to have occurred to him that since he signed all the cheques himself he was the chief if not the sole source of the leakage. But he paid a handsome figure in advance for the rights of bars, cloakrooms and programmes and it must be agreed that Westby & Co. did the job efficiently.

The financial hurdle safely negotiated, Miller now had some more impalpable problems. For nearly thirty years the St. James's Theatre Company and Sir George Alexander had been for all practical purposes identical. Now the activating spark had gone, and gone, too, were the habits and tastes on which that grand synonymity had been founded and reared. How could the old customs be preserved? Was it possible in this new world to maintain the tone and discipline set by his predecessor? In Alexander's time the place was distinctly a workshop and no visitors were allowed backstage. Social life was excluded and only the facts and formalities of production were countenanced inside the doors. Alexander's custom of entering rehearsals preceded by his stage-manager and with his assistant bringing up the rear was less an evidence of pomp than an aspect of the discipline which he considered essential to the purpose and prestige of his house. As in a ship, no passenger was allowed on the bridge and none must exchange pleasantries with the man at the wheel. All of which may have served well enough in the old world but was hardly the thing for the new.

Miller was not unduly worried about abandoning some of the elegant detail, but he knew it was imperative to retain the essential order and polish which had made the St. James's attractive in the past and which he hoped would again make it a magnet for the older folk and perhaps for the younger public, too. The place had made its appeal largely as an actor-manager's theatre, but Miller himself, though at various times both actor and manager, had no intention of combining both roles. He, therefore, decided to link himself with a popular actor and operate in double harness. He had to find a man with a personality and a reputation suitable to the occasion and who could

PAUL SCOFIELD (*above*) with JOY PARKER in *Adventure Story*
and (*below*) with MAI ZETTERLING in *The Seagull*

RUTH DRAPER

HELEN HAYE with MARY KERRIDGE IN *Anastasia*

fit into the atmosphere of the St. James's, bringing with him, too, if possible, an acceptable following.

The search was not difficult. Right within his reach was a man already in the front rank and familiar with the St. James's. He was Henry Ainley, whose fascinating looks, manner and voice had spelt enchantment when he appeared there in *Paolo and Francesca*, back in 1902. Meanwhile, Ainley had come a long way and without losing anything of his appeal. Besides later productions at the St. James's, he had done a season in America, playing opposite the redoubtable Maude Adams. Then back in London at the Duke of York's, His Majesty's, St. James's again (in *Beside the Bonnie Briar Bush*), the Court, under the Vedrenne and Barker management, with Lena Ashwell, and at Drury Lane, where he had followed Gerald du Maurier as Raffles. But his best work had been with Sir Herbert Tree at His Majesty's, though he had also scored outstanding successes at the Kingsway in *The Great Adventure*—maybe his finest piece of acting—and at the Haymarket in *Quinney's*.

Linked now with Miller as actor-manager in the home of his first London triumph, he found the place very much to his liking. The partnership showed every promise of success. Both were practical men of the theatre, and both were conversant with the tradition they set out to maintain. With Ainley's resourcefulness and Miller's immense energy, the combination was aptly aligned to the job. Miller had a smile that would have melted an iceberg—he retains it still—and Ainley a friendliness that embraced everything in its glow. Both were of kindly disposition and neither lacked anything in the charm and courtesy to which patrons of their theatre had been so long accustomed.

There was no difference of opinion as to what they hoped to achieve at the St. James's. They agreed to reopen with something that would convince their potential patrons that the best of the old traditions still held sway. Shakespeare's *Julius Caesar* was their first intention, but—various obstacles having got in the way—they staged meanwhile, on 26th September, 1919, an adaptation of Tolstoi's *Reparation*. Appropriately to the occasion, they gave it a fine cast, including names already famous and others which were to become so.

That first Miller-Ainley cast included, besides Ainley, Meggie Albanesi, Ion Swinley, Athene Seyler, Claude Rains, Dora Gregory, Otho Stuart, Marion Terry and Ernest Milton. Clearly, the new management was keeping up the tradition. Their endeavour was widely appreciated. *Reparation* held attention for 116 performances, being withdrawn on 3rd January, 1920. It was a most promising and encouraging start.

The post-Alexandrine period of the St. James's really sprang to life with the Miller-Ainley production of *Julius Caesar*. Their choice was apt, for this stupendous drama is, like *Henry V* and *Henry VIII*, a sure-fire attraction where Shakespeare's plays are concerned. It is close-knit, cogent and cohesive, with a tensely woven plot, and characterisation that is at once widely universal and earthily individual. As befitted the piece and the occasion, they gave it all they knew and it emerged as a production of such perfect form and beauty as to merit the term grandeur. Nothing quite like it had been seen for years and the critics spared no adjectives in conveying their approval.

The quality of the players was appropriate to the demands of the play: rarely had a better cast been assembled. To look back on that night or to peruse a treasured programme is to wonder at the wealth of ability then available to the London stage. The list gathered together for this memorable production, on 9th January, 1920, is worth recording. Here it is:

JULIUS CAESAR

By William Shakespeare.

Julius Caesar............................Clifton Boyne.
Octavius Caesar ....Henry C. Hewitt.
Marcus Antonius ....Henry Ainley.
Publius ....Leonard Sickert.
Popilius Lena ....Sydney Bland.
Marcus Brutus ....Basil Gill.
Cassius ....Milton Rosmer.
Casca...................................Claude Rains.
Trebonius ....Howard Rose.
Ligarius................................Henry Morrell.
Decius Brutus ....Ernest Milton.
Metellus Cimber ....Henry Oscar.
Cinna...................................Julian Courtville.
Artemidorus ....Ernest Digges.
Varro...................................Sydney Bland.

Claudius .... Julian Courtville.
Lucius .... George Hamilton.
Pindarus .... Henry Morrell.
Servant to Caesar .... Stanley Vine.
Servant to Octavius Caesar .... Arthur Keane.
A Citizen .... Henry Morrell.
Calpurnia .... Esmé Beringer.
Portia .... Lilian Braithwaite.

Much could be written about that cast. Mention must be made of Basil Gill, an ideal Shakespearean actor and (next to Lewis Waller) the best Brutus for many, many years. Basil Gill had long been with Sir Herbert Tree. An inordinately handsome man, with a classical profile and a wondrous voice, he possessed sincerity and repose—maybe a little too much repose, but then he could just stand on the stage and compel everyone to look at him. It was a pleasure to see and a joy to hear him. He was, moreover, a most charming man, one of complete integrity, devoid of professional jealousy, who did his job as he best knew how—and that was splendidly. Perfectly at home in costume, he wore it as though it were his everyday dress. His performance as Brutus at the St. James's lingers in the memory: he looked "the noblest Roman of them all", and that was the way he lived. He died recently, mourned by all who knew him. The Cassius of Milton Rosmer was also excellent, and these two provided an outstanding "quarrel scene". Henry Ainley made a fine Marc Antony, a part which gave him full scope. Not so subtle, perhaps, as Antony should be, but his assurance, voice and majesty were all that could be desired.

Staging, décor and acting were in the true St. James's tradition—and in that of His Majesty's as well. To the public it appeared that the great days of the St. James's would continue in the hands of this new combination. But Gilbert Miller was not free from worries. Already Ainley, the partner whom the public would see, was showing signs of the weakness which assailed him—that same weakness which had brought down Edmund Kean, George Frederick Cooke and so many more. As the stage euphemism goes, Henry Ainley was not too "reliable".

Julius Caesar ran for eighty-three performances and was withdrawn on 20th March, 1920. The next play was *Uncle Ned*, a comedy by

Douglas Murray, which made forty-nine performances, between 27th March and 8th May. A name to note in the cast is Edna Best, then in the first phase of her career. Edna had begun at the St. James's in *Charley's Aunt* in 1917; then she had played Blanny Wheeler in *Fair and Warmer* on tour and succeeded Fay Compton in the same play at the Prince of Wales's. In 1919 she had played in *Caesar's Wife* at the Royalty; she had been Nibs in *Peter Pan*, and at the Little Theatre had taken part in a play called *Mumsee*.

Between May and August, Miller ran *The Mystery of the Yellow Room*, with a cast including Sybil Thorndike, Lewis Casson and Franklin Dyall. Then came *His Lady Friends*, a comedy by Emile Nyitray and Frank Mandel, from the novel by May Edginton—chiefly notable as being the origin of the famous musical, *No, No, Nanette!* This ran for 135 performances, up to 11th December, 1920, and was produced by Charles Hawtrey, who also appeared in it; among the supporting cast were Athene Seyler, Patrick Ludlow and Mercia Swinburne.

The Christmas attraction was *Peter Pan*, with Ainley as Captain Hook (there have been better Hooks!); this time Edna Best played Peter. From this point the name of Henry Ainley disappears from the record. Gilbert Miller had found it impossible to continue the association on which he had banked so much, and continued to run the theatre alone, as manager.

On 15th January, 1921, came *Daniel*, adapted by Sybil Harris from the French of Louis Verneuil. Despite an excellent cast, including Lyn Harding, C. Aubrey Smith, Edith Evans and Henry Oscar, it ran only until 26th February (forty-five performances). The next play, *Polly With a Past*, by George Middleton and Guy Bolton, had gained great popularity in America. It ran at the St. James's from 2nd March to 4th June, making 110 performances. In the cast were players whose names before long would be world famous, foremost among them Edith Evans and Noël Coward. Both the play and the cast maintained the top St. James's tradition. A play called *Emma*, by Herbert Thomas, which had been running at matinees, went into the evening bill on 5th June for a week.

In August Miller felt the need of a holiday and Lyn Harding took over the theatre for a season and, in association with Denys Grayson, produced *Threads*, a comedy by Frank Stayton. Despite a good supporting cast, this made only twenty-eight performances. Comedy was not really the forte of Lyn Harding, a magnificent actor in strong parts. *The Night of the Party*, a famous old farce, kept the curtain up for fifty-two performances; then Harding revived one of his great successes, *The Speckled Band*—a thriller based on a Sherlock Holmes story. His performance of the crazed Dr. Grimesby Roylott will be remembered as one of the most gripping our stage has ever presented: it was in the same class as Irving in *The Bells*, terrifying in its intensity. When a poisonous snake began creeping down the bell-rope the tension was such that many of the audience shrieked. This revival ran for ninety-two performances, from 22nd September until 10th December, 1921.

At Christmas *Peter Pan* came back (the St. James's had become its home) and was led by Joan McLean and Ernest Thesiger. It ran, for matinees only, until 28th January, 1922, and the evening bill carried another thriller, *The Bat*. This play, by Mary Roberts Reinhart and Avery Hopwood, came from America. It lasted until 4th November, its fine score of 327 performances providing Gilbert Miller with a success he badly needed. The programme during this run contained an innovation—a little slip which asked on one side "Can You Keep a Secret?" and on the other said: "If you like *The Bat*, now playing at the St. James's Theatre, King Street, W.1, please DO NOT DIVULGE the solution to the mystery. The pleasure of future playgoers will be enhanced if they, like yourself, are kept in suspense until the final curtain." It would appear that patrons observed the request. The splendid cast included Drusilla Wills, Eva Moore, Claude Rains, George Relph, Nora Swinburne, A. Scott-Gatty, Arthur Wontner, C. Stafford Dickens, Herbert Bolingbroke, and Allan Jeayes.

Peter Pan came back again for Christmas, filling the matinee bill, while *The Happy Ending* formed the evening bill. Again, the cast scintillated with first-class players, among them Miles Malleson, Ethel Irving, Jean Cadell, Robert Loraine, and Adèle Dixon, playing her first important role.

The year 1923 was as inimical to the theatre as to all kinds of business. Britain was then in the first grip of the post-war slump. But the St. James's carried on, though Miller was now temporarily engaged in America. The first play of that year was *If Winter Comes*, an adaptation of A. S. M. Hutchinson's famous best-seller, by himself and

Basil Macdonald Hastings. Produced on 31st January, it ran, disappointingly, only until 17th March (fifty-three performances), despite another excellent cast which included Grace Lane, Frederick Volpe, Owen Nares and Helen Spencer. *The Inevitable*, which followed on 21st March, met an "inevitably" early end, scoring only four performances; then *Plus Fours*, transferred from the Haymarket, lasted until 26th May.

The first "century" of the year was made by *The Outsider*, between 30th May and 1st September. This play, by Dorothy Brandon, provided that splendid actor, Leslie Faber, with one of his best parts as Anton Ragatzy, the so-called quack healer.

In September, Miller returned and put on *The Green Goddess*, which became at once a vast success, running for exactly a year, from 6th September, 1923, to the following 6th September, with 417 performances. This exciting melodrama was by the eminent critic William Archer, who had in his time poked fun at many such plays, but now wrote an outstanding example himself. It brought to the St. James's George Arliss, famed on stage and screen alike, and he never gave a better performance than now, as The Rajah of Rukh, supported, as usual at the St. James's, by a fine cast. It was a tremendous and well-deserved success.

Miller then brought over an American play called *A Nervous Wreck*, by Owen Davis, which he presented in association with Lewis and Gordon. Performed by an American company, it ran for ninety-three performances, until 6th December. He followed this with *Grounds for Divorce*, with Madge Titheradge in the lead, which during the first four months of 1925 recorded a moderate run of 118 performances. After this, Miller registered two most welcome hits in succession. The first was *The Last of Mrs. Cheney*, in which he was joined by another actor-manager, Sir Gerald du Maurier. Gladys Cooper was associated with the management as well as being in the cast. Produced on 22nd September, 1925, this Frederick Lonsdale masterpiece ran until 18th December, 1926—514 performances. Besides Sir Gerald and Gladys Cooper, its vintage cast included Dawson Milward, Ronald Squire, Basil Loder, Guy Fletcher, Frank Lawton, E. H. Paterson, A. Harding Steerman, Ellis Jeffreys, May Whitty, Mabel Sealby, Gladys Gray and Violet Campbell.

Then came *Interference*, by Ronald Pertwee and Harold Dearden, which ran over a year, from 29th January, 1927, until 27th February, 1928—412 performances. Again, Sir Gerald du Maurier headed a fine cast.

The St. James's was once more on the crest of the wave. Came now a minor sensation, *S.O.S.*, presented jointly by Miller and du Maurier. This play by Walter Ellis ran from February till July, 1928 (188 performances), and its cast included no less a personality than the inimitable Gracie Fields! The appearance of this genius of the music halls on the legitimate stage—and amid the distinguished St. James's company at that—raised many eyebrows. But Gracie, like the great artiste she is, took it neatly in her stride. Next on the scene was Arnold Bennett, but his play *The Return Journey* did not journey very far, only from 1st September until 24th November.

Then Ferenc Molnar, the great Hungarian dramatist, contributed *The Play's the Thing*. It was adapted by P. G. Wodehouse, and Sir Gerald du Maurier appeared in it, but surprisingly it lasted only eleven days, from the 4th to the 15th December, 1928. It has always distressed Gilbert Miller that this country has not taken to Molnar, who is such a big draw in America. Miller's admiration for his work is such that he would have the original Hungarian translated into English, German and French (all of which he speaks fluently), and then compare the different versions and select what seemed the best from each. Whenever possible he would consult Molnar in person, discussing the production with him in German, their only mutual language. By this means he believes he has been able to capture—for the English stage at any rate—the somewhat elusive charm of Molnar's art.

There followed *No Other Tiger*, adapted by A. E. W. Mason from his own novel, from 26th December, 1928, until 9th February, 1929, after which came *Fame*, by Audrey and Waveney Carten, produced jointly by Gilbert Miller and Sir Gerald du Maurier. It ran from 20th February until 27th May, 1929, reaching 180 performances. The cast is interesting for the many names that have since become notable: A. Scott-Gatty, Myles Clifton, Frank J. Arlton, Denis Mantell, Naomi Jacob (distinguished novelist and excellent actress), Cathleen Nesbitt, Nigel Bruce, Nora Swinburne, Gerald du Maurier, J. Disney-Roebuck, Ernest Haines, Frank Vosper, Walter Fitzgerald, Una Venning, Dorothy Monkman and Mignon O'Doherty.

Two short runs followed. These were *Caprice*, by Sil Vara, adapted by Philip Moeller and presented in association with the Theatre Guild of New York (5th June to 27th July), and *Heatwave*, by Ronald Pertwee, presented in association with Reandco (15th October to 14th December, 1929). Then *Peter Pan* came home once more for Christmas and marked a notable Yuletide by including Sir Gerald du Maurier and Marie Löhr, with Jean Forbes-Robertson in the title-role.

On 1st February, 1930, came A. A. Milne's *Michael and Mary*, presented by Miller in association with Charles Hopkins, and starring Edna Best and Herbert Marshall, then at the height of their joint popularity. It ran until 2nd June, its 159 performances pulling in a satisfactory return. And now Gilbert Miller got a big and well-merited thrill. He put on *The Swan*, by Ferenc Molnar, again starring Edna Best and Herbert Marshall, and it made 140 performances, from 30th June to 1st November. He had put Molnar over in London at last! It was a success even more pleasing than profitable.

Emlyn Williams's eerie thriller, evoking the atmosphere of a haunted theatre, *A Murder Has Been Arranged* (presented in association with the Daniel Mayer Co.), played out the year, until 31st January, 1931, and closed the annual book with an appreciable balance.

CHAPTER 22

The Last Years

CONTRARY to what might appear from the recent financial balance, the St. James's, in common with other theatres, faced the new decade in conditions of extreme economic difficulty. Caught up in the world-wide depression, the country seethed with social unrest. Stock-markets had crumpled, governments tottered, and personal incomes had shrunk to the lowest level of the post-war years. It was, therefore, not surprising that 1931 registered nothing in the way of substantial runs. Gilbert Miller in conjunction with Reandco, presented *Etienne*, by Jacques Deval and Gilbert Wakefield, in which Emlyn Williams, not yet famous, made one of his earliest West End appearances. The play soon came off, as did *Payment Deferred*, by C. W. Forrester and Jeffrey Bell, despite the appeal of Charles Laughton in the lead.

The following year was hardly better, though Marie Tempest held the interest for a while in *The Vinegar Tree*, and John van Druten's *Behold We Live* knocked up a helpful 158 performances. But in 1933 fortune smiled again and *The Late Christopher Bean* pulled in good business for more than a year. Adapted by Emlyn Williams from the French of René Fauchois, this remarkable comedy was both presented and produced by Gilbert Miller. Its cast, right up to the established standard, included Sir Cedric Hardwicke, Lucille Lisle, Edith Evans, Louise Hampton, Nadine March, Barry K. Barnes, Robert Holmes, Gilbert Davis and Frederick Leister. Its 488 performances provided a much-needed tonic.

This profitable run ended in July, 1934, and in the September Gladys Cooper and Raymond Massey took over temporarily from Miller and put on *The Shining Hour*, by Rex Winter. Both partners appeared in it, supported by Adrianne Allen, Marjorie Fielding, Cyril Raymond and Derek Williams. After a happy run of 213 performances, the same management staged, in 1935, *Worse Things Happen at Sea*, by Keith Miller, but it did not last long. Later in the year, Sydney W. Carroll transferred *The Mask of Virtue* from the Ambassadors'. This was an adaptation by Ashley Dukes from the original of Carl Sternheim. Max Wray produced and had in the cast Jeanne de Casalis, Frank Cellier, Lady Tree, Douglas Matthews, Jenny Barclay, Anna Burden, Olive Hinton, Antonia Brough and a new young actress, Vivien Leigh, whose success was really outstanding.

Gilbert Miller's return was marked by a beautiful production of *Pride and Prejudice*, neatly adapted by Helen Jerome. This was another winner, its first run making 316 performances between February and November, 1936. It was revived a month later. A large and brilliant cast included such names as Dorothy Hyson, Celia Johnson, Joan Harben, Viola Lyel, and Hugh Williams.

In association with Alfred de Liagre, Jnr., Miller than presented *Yes, My Darling Daughter*, by Mark Read, in which were Jessica Tandy, Evelyn Roberts, Margaret Bannerman, Ena Moon, Sybil Thorndike, Léon Quartermaine and Alec Clunes. This was followed by Keith Winter's *Old Music* and *The Silent Knight*, adapted by Humbert Wolfe from the Hungarian of Eugen Heltai, with Diana Wynyard and Ralph Richardson in the lead.

The St. James's was now past the centenary of its foundation and the standards of its second half-century were being well maintained, when once again the world was threatened with war. Gilbert Miller no longer stood in the programme as sole lessee, but he still figured in a dominant role among the partners of S. J. & L. Ltd., the syndicate in control to the end and of which Thomas H. Bostock was the general manager.

A notable play in those last years of uneasy peace was *Black Limelight*, by Gordon Sherry, originally produced at the "Q" Theatre and in which that fine actress Margaret Rawlings made a big success. It went to the St. James's on 22nd April, 1937, and later transferred to the Duke of York's, its total run of 404 performances being shared between these theatres.

On 21st June, 1938, was produced a much-publicised play by Clifford Odets, entitled *The Golden Boy*. It was not a real success although it ran for 109 performances. Many people liked it but it seemed to lack popular appeal, possibly because it dealt with boxing.

Terence Rattigan, who wrote the last of the big St. James's

successes, had his early play *After the Dance* produced there in 1939. That year also saw the production of *Sixth Floor*, adapted from the original of Alfred Henri by Rodney Ackland; but in September the war clouds burst and by Government order all theatres closed down. The Second World War brought problems of a number and magnitude hitherto unprecedented. In the expectation of mass air raids, all places of entertainment were shut down and a strict blackout imposed. Theatre-going was at the outset quite out of the question; but when the threatened raids did not materialise, one by one the theatres re-opened and though nobody could make a profit they somehow kept going. An early production at the St. James's, just after the enforced closure had been rescinded, was a season of Anglo-Polish Ballet—a brave attempt to brighten London.

Its first wartime production of any importance was *Ladies in Retirement*, by that practised pair, Edward Percy and Reginald Denham (the latter also produced). This grim, compelling drama, in which the suspense mounted as the play progressed, opened on 12th December and ran for 174 performances, which was really remarkable considering the conditions outside. In the cast were Joan Kemp-Welch, Mary Merrall, Mary Clare, Richard Newton, Margaret Watson, Nellie Bowman, Phyllis Morris and Olga Slade.

In 1942, Patrick Hamilton's play *The Duke in Darkness* was at the St. James's. This strong drama, superbly played by Leslie Banks and Michael Redgrave, had only a short run although it deserved more. London in war time was not yet attuned to stage tragedies. But in January, 1943, Donald Wolfit presented a short season of Shakespeare there and playgoers flocked to see his *King Lear*—the outstanding performance of this role in our time—and also *David Garrick*.

There followed a delightful revival, by Sir Bronson Albery and Tennent Plays, Ltd. (in association with C.E.M.A.), of Turgenev's *A Month in the Country*, adapted and produced by Emlyn Williams. Opening on 11th February, 1943, it made 318 performances. Its vintage cast included Michael Redgrave, Valerie Taylor, Ronald Squire, Michael Shepley, and, in a small part, an interesting name—Annie Esmond, the elderly sister of H. V. Esmond, who has been so often mentioned in this book.

On 17th November, 1943, there was a good Agatha Christie thriller, entitled *Ten Little Nigger Boys*. It nearly came to an untimely end because the roof of the theatre suffered bomb damage, but was able to resume after a few days closing, and eventually achieved 260 performances.

One of the biggest flops the St. James's ever knew was *Felicity Jasmine*, a play from America, produced in the autumn of 1944 (I think)—it hardly lasted long enough to make an impact on the records, or the memory. But in 1945 Anna Neagle deserted films to appear at the St. James's in an adaptation of Jane Austen's *Emma*, in which she gave a charming performance.

The last war-time Christmas—although nobody knew it then—saw a delightful production of *The Glass Slipper*, the Cinderella story told in a graceful, straightforward way and shorn of pantomime trappings, and in the following April, as the war in Europe neared its end, Emlyn Williams appeared in his own *The Wind of Heaven*, which, appropriately enough, greeted the resumption of peace with a run of 268.

When the last shots had echoed away in Asia, on 3rd September, 1946, Gilbert Miller and Peter Daubeny presented *But For The Grace of God*, by Frederick Lonsdale (201 performances), among the first-rate cast being A. E. Matthews, Michael Gough, Hugh McDermott, and Mary Jerrold. In the same year, Miller also presented *Dear Ruth*, by Norman Krasna.

The theatre was now under the joint direction of Gilbert Miller and Prince Littler, and in the programme Miller paid a tribute to the help and comradeship Mr. Littler had given him in recent ventures. At the end of 1946 they sub-let for a season to John Clements, who, during a gallant and distinguished spell of actor-management, produced *The Kingmaker*, a play about the great Earl of Warwick, and also *Marriage à la Mode*. It is a pity Mr. Clements was unable to continue, for these were both in the real St. James's tradition.

After Clements's short season, in 1947, Gilbert Miller and Henry Sherek presented *Truant in Park Lane*, by James Parish, with Roland Young and Lilian Braithwaite in the lead; and in the same year Tennent Plays, Ltd., in association with the Arts Council of Great Britain (formerly C.E.M.A.) presented *The Play's the Thing*, by Ferenc Molnar, and Gilbert Miller had the pleasure of seeing this revival run for quite a while. This brought Clive Brook, eminent alike on stage and in films, to the St. James's, where, at the head of a fine cast, he did great credit to the Molnar story.

Another interesting venture of 1947 was when Basil Dean's Theatre Group presented *All This is Ended*. It was one of those plays which endeavour to portray what happens after death, showing a little group of soldiers suddenly realising that they have been killed. It was not a success but was notable for excellent performances by Geoffrey Gomer and Hector Ross—who in this made a very early London appearance.

In 1948 the British Repertory Theatre Festival was held at the St. James's, given by members of the famous repertory companies at Liverpool (who presented *The Cherry Orchard*), Sheffield (*The Brontës*), Birmingham (*The Rivals* in modern dress), and Bristol, who played *Hamlet*.

A good play beautifully acted saw the light at the St. James's on 2nd September, 1948, and ran for 219 performances. Presented by Alec Rea and E. P. Clift it was called *Don't Listen, Ladies*, adapted from the French of Sacha Guitry by Stephen Powys and Guy Bolton. It was high comedy in the true St. James's style, excellently performed by that most talented actress Constance Cummings and that fine actor Francis Lister. A big success was made by the veteran Ada Reeve, playing an old-time musical comedy star. Betty Marsden also made a hit, and when Francis Lister was ill and had to leave the cast his part was taken by Jack Buchanan, who had already played it in New York.

The next major production was in 1949, when *Adventure Story*, a play about Alexander the Great by Terence Rattigan, ran for 107 performances; following which Paul Scofield appeared in a revival of *The Seagull*, transferred from Hammersmith.

Although much of Europe and not a little of London remained a shambles as reminder of the recent war, the theatres were now already regaining their attraction. And in 1950 came an announcement which made the hearts of the enthusiasts beat high with hope, for it told that Sir Laurence Olivier had taken over the St. James's as actor-manager. This seemed just what it needed. Gilbert Miller had kept the standard high and unsullied despite unprecedented difficulties. He cared little for profit, but had demonstrated again and again his regard for achievement, and the lustre of the St. James's had remained untarnished during his lengthy tenancy. But what was really needed was actor-management: a man or a woman—or a man and a woman—who would blend in one single authority the responsibilities of management and the pulling-power of public appearances. It needed a magnet to bring in the patrons by permanent habit, as Hare and the Kendals and Alexander had done. And here seemed the very thing—Sir Laurence, still young, a star of stage and screen, a fine producer, a man of the theatre, married to the brilliant and beautiful Vivien Leigh—here was the desired combination. There was every hope of the great days returning again.

Sir Laurence started off with *Venus Observed*, a poem-drama of immense eloquence by Christopher Fry. It was the right idea in the right vein. Besides producing the play, Olivier himself appeared in it. Opening on 18th January, 1950, it ran for 229 performances, a most auspicious start. His next production was *Captain Carvallo*, by Dennis Cannan, which he directed, without appearing in it himself. Diana Wynyard played the lead. It opened on 9th August, 1950, and held the stage for 190 performances. He followed with *Top of the Ladder*, produced and written by Tyrone Guthrie, with John Mills in the lead, which ran from October to December, and *The Madwoman of Chaillot*, from February to April, 1951.

Then the Oliviers came back again in person and, to celebrate the Festival of Britain, staged an experiment unique in St. James's history. This was a most exciting affair, for *Caesar and Cleopatra*, by Bernard Shaw, and *Antony and Cleopatra*, by William Shakespeare, were presented on alternate nights, with Vivien Leigh as Cleopatra in both plays, and Sir Laurence as Caesar in the first and Antony in the second. The season started on 10th May, 1951, *Caesar and Cleopatra* being the opening play. Here were two dramas, separated by 300 years, based on an amazing woman and two equally outstanding men. You could see both and pronounce your preference, and learn a lot from each. This novel and exciting brace made marvellous theatre and was in the real St. James's tradition. The place was again in the news and a topic of lively discussion.

The magnificent dual production ran until September, 1951—over four months—and might have continued longer, had not previous arrangements been made for a visit of La Compagnie Madeleine Renaud et Jean-Louis Barrault, which occupied the theatre for three weeks from 25th September. Then came another event—the first appearance on the English stage of Orson Welles, the highly controversial American stage and screen actor, whom Olivier presented in *Othello* on 18th October, 1951. Mr. Welles aroused tremendous argument, but all acknowledged him a magnificent actor and voted his Othello a fine one. It ran until the December of 1951.

The Christmas production that year was a stage version of Walt Disney's *Snow White and the Seven Dwarfs*, produced by Dennis Arundell. There followed, on 30th January, 1952, *The Happy Time*—Samuel Taylor's adaptation of the novel by Robert Fontaine, presented jointly by Olivier and Gilbert Miller. It had a short run and was succeeded on 3rd April, 1952, by Clifford Odets' *Winter Journey*. This had Michael Redgrave, Sam Wanamaker and Googie Withers in the cast, and held the public for 243 performances. November brought *Dead Secret*, by Michael Clayton Hutton, with a cast of four—Joyce Heron, Sophie Stewart, Ian Hunter and Hugh Wakefield. After a very short run, it left the stage to *Sweet Peril*, by Mary Orr and Reginald Denham, which lasted only six weeks.

The year 1953 opened with a very good play indeed—*Escapade*, written by Roger Macdougall and presented on 20th January. Original, controversial and striking, it ran for 448 performances. Among the admirable cast was the screen star Phyllis Calvert. An Italian Session followed, in which London saw for the last time the aged Ruggero Ruggieri, shortly before his death; and then a season by the Comédie Française, which presented *Tartuffe*, *Brittanicus*, *Le Jeu de l'Amour et du Hasard*, and *On Ne Saurait Penser à Tout*. Next came *The Uninvited Guest*, by Mary Hayley Bell, which lived for only a fortnight and died on 12th June.

Having let the theatre during most of the preceding twelve months, Sir Laurence Olivier came back in the summer of 1953, and on 5th August presented *Anastasia*, adapted by Guy Bolton from a play by Marcelle Maurette. This drama, based on the possibility of one of the Tsar's family having escaped the Bolshevik massacre, was first seen on television and created a deep impression. Olivier gave it a good cast, including Laurence Payne, Peter Illing, Anthony Ireland, Mary Kerridge, Geoffrey Tyrrell, Susan Richards, Michael Godfrey, Helen Haye, Ruth Goddard, Ralph Michael, Verena Kimmins and Michael Malnick. Outstanding was the performance by the veteran Helen Haye as the Dowager Empress of Russia. This superb actress, who died recently in her eighties, provided a picture exemplary of everything acting should be. *Anastasia* ran for 117 performances, despite the fact that millions had seen it on their television screens.

It was now near the end of 1953 and only some half-dozen more productions were to bring the St. James's to the end of its life. The first of these was a revival of *Pygmalion*, on 19th November, with Kay Hammond as a very excellent Eliza Doolittle. It had a goodly run and then, on 21st April, 1954, Olivier presented *Waiting for Gillian*, a play by Ronald Millar from Nigel Balchin's novel *A Way Through the Wood*. With John McCallum, Googie Withers and Frank Lawton it reached 101 performances. This was followed by a revival of Pirandello's *Six Characters in Search of an Author*, which occupied the stage up to 14th September.

And now, on 24th September, 1954, came the last of the great St. James's successes. This was Terence Rattigan's *Separate Tables*. It was really two plays, or one divided into two, the first entitled *Table by the Window*, the other *Table Number Seven*. This profoundly human play, fraught with knowledge and insight, ranks as one of the best we have seen for many years; and it had, as it so well deserved, a long and successful run, filling the house from September, 1954, right up to the last day of June, 1956. Its cast was as distinguished as the author and is worthy of a place in this record.

TABLE BY THE WINDOW

Mabel ....Marion Fawcett.
Lady Matheson..........................Jane Eccles.
Mrs. Railton-Bell.........................Phyllis Neilson-Terry.
Miss Meacham..........................May Hallatt.
Doreen ....Priscilla Morgan.
Mr. Fowler ....Aubrey Mather.
Mrs. Shankland..........................Margaret Leighton.
Miss Cooper...........................Beryl Measor.
Mr. Martin ....Eric Portman.
Mr. Stratton...........................Basil Henson.
Miss Tanner...........................Patricia Raine.

TABLE NUMBER SEVEN

Mrs. Stratton...........................Patricia Raine.
Mr. Stratton...........................Basil Henson.
Major Pollock ....Eric Portman.
Mr. Fowler ....Aubrey Mather.

SIR LAURENCE OLIVIER
with VIVIEN LEIGH in
Antony and Cleopatra

ORSON WELLES with
GUDRUN URE in
Othello

A scene from *Caesar and Cleopatra*; with SIR LAURENCE OLIVIER, NIALL MACGINNIS, VIVIEN LEIGH and ROBERT HELPMANN

ST. JAMES'S THEATRE

Mrs. Railton-Bell ....Phyllis Neilson-Terry.
Miss Railton-Bell ....Margaret Leighton.
Lady Matheson ....Jane Eccles.
Miss Meacham ....May Hallatt.
Mabel ....Marion Fawcett.
Doreen ....Priscilla Morgan.

Acting, dress and décor were all in the true St. James's tradition. Eric Portman and Margaret Leighton, in widely divergent parts in the two halves, touched the very limits of perfection; so did Phyllis Neilson-Terry and Beryl Measor. But special mentions are really invidious here, for it was exquisitely played all round. The play was produced by Peter Glenville and remains a cherished memory.

About the middle of its run, the news broke that the St. James's was to be sold, and shops and offices erected on the site. At once a yell of protest rose and indignant letters flowed into the Press. In answer to the fury, Authority expressed its regrets and stated that the St. James's had not been scheduled for preservation as had so many other buildings: it had, as the official phrase put it, "slipped through the net". The facts and the pending position of the theatre were for a while somewhat obscure, but for the moment at least Prince Littler weathered the storm. Speculation diminished and the remonstrants calmed down. But the story of St. James's was rapidly drawing to its close.

CHAPTER 23

The Curtain Falls

THE St. James's Theatre, which had escaped damage in the First World War, was not so fortunate in the Second. It lost most of its roof and suffered much internal damage as well. In due course, however, it got itself patched up and reopened, though its new ceiling was not nearly as handsome as the one which Alexander had put there. Many of the other repairs were makeshift, too. Nevertheless, it was comfortable enough to seek a resumption of patronage and was soon in operation again.

After *Separate Tables* there was not much more to chronicle. A play by Agatha Christie, prophetically entitled *Towards Zero*, had a good run, and that eminent American artiste, Ruth Draper, made her last London appearance there. There was also *The Long Echo*, *Double Image* and *The Restless Heart*. The final play in the St. James's eventful history was *It's the Geography that Counts*, written by Raymond Bowers and well produced, with a cast including John Gregson, John Stratton, Michael Duffield, Liam Redmond, Jack Hedley and Jane Griffiths. It was not, perhaps, a very good play but it had not much of a chance. It died with the St. James's.

For suddenly the theatre became "news" again. There was a rumour—more than a rumour, although official statement was still lacking, that this time the place really had been sold and was to be pulled down. At the time of the first alarm, in January, 1955, there was a considerable outcry. Now there was more. Again, letters poured into the papers: *The Times* gave it a leading article, and the controversy raged. During the first crisis the present author, who has spent a lifetime serving the theatre, received a call from the British Broadcasting Corporation asking if he would tell the story of the St. James's on television. "How long do I get?" he asked. "Oh," came the complacent reply, "four and a half minutes." . . . The St. James's was first opened in 1835—it was now 1955! He did his best. He also told the story on "sound", where he got a bit more time.

Much odium having been thrown on the owners, who were accused of betraying their trust, he drew attention to the fact that the sale—if sale there was to be—was brought about because the theatre was not paying its way. If this happened, was it reasonable to expect men to continue to lose money to regale a public which did not respond? He declared that the most important thing about any theatre was the audience, and if that did not come in sufficient force, the theatre could not function. But he also emphasised that he himself would deeply regret the passing of such a fine and well-loved playhouse.

Next day he was rung up and taken to task by a very irate lady. She had, she said, expected him to champion the theatre, and if necessary to lead the forces arrayed against the dragon of commercialism which threatened it. She talked on and on, giving him little chance to say anything except to answer some rather impertinent questions. When at last she seemed a little exhausted, he said, "I suppose, madam, you regard yourself as a champion of the St. James's?" She replied that she most certainly did and would do her best to save it. "Well then," he said, "I've answered your questions, now just answer one of mine. How many times have you paid to go into the St. James's Theatre during the last three years?" It was the end—she admitted she had not been once.

The outcry soon had repercussions in official quarters. A deputation of influential people called on the London County Council. Questions were asked in Parliament, and on 22nd February, 1955, Mr. Sandys, Minister for Housing, in a written reply, said there "was no present intention of demolishing the theatre or selling the site". He admitted "the exceptional concern which this project had evoked", saying he had discussed the matter with the L.C.C. and that he sympathised with "the understandable fear that if, one by one, other West End theatres were similarly to disappear, London's renowned position in the world of drama would be endangered".

Sandys' statement allayed some fears, but by no means all. On 25th October, 1955, replying to another question, he said he "had modified the County of London plan to ensure that only in very special circumstances would planning permission be given for converting a theatre to office use or replacing it by an office building".

The folk more generally interested breathed a sigh of relief. But those closely attached to the theatre world felt no sense of security. And they were right—for not two years afterwards (one year and seven months, to be exact) rumours of the sale and demolition were rife again, despite a statement by an official of the L.C.C. in *The Times* of 27th October, 1955, that Mr. Sandys' statement had strengthened the Council's powers "to such an extent that they could refuse an application to develop the theatre site as offices, should one be made".

Yet here was the threat again, and this time more than a threat: it seemed a *fait accompli*. At this point Mr. V. C. Clinton-Baddeley, Chairman of the Society for Theatre Research, brought the whole matter into focus in a letter to *The Times*. The fat was now in the fire. For it became known that S. J. & L., Ltd., of which Prince Littler, Gilbert Miller, S. J. Passmore and T. F. Birch were the directors, had definitely sold the theatre to the Viarex Property Investment Co. Ltd. (*Viarex* being Latin for King Street), the active director of which was Mr. F. D. Fenston.

Now further letters poured in, not all of them in favour of saving the St. James's. The distinguished critic and dramatist St. John Ervine wrote, intimating that the St. James's was out of date and badly placed. He said it had again become isolated, since the residential population of the surrounding streets and squares had moved away, and conditions had changed since Alexander's time. Yet, after all, there had been no trouble in filling the St. James's with *Separate Tables* and other good plays, as Sir Laurence Olivier reminded him in a letter published 10th July, 1957, in which he also expressed the view that the L.C.C. had been wantonly neglectful and suggested that that body should buy the theatre and rent it to a responsible manager.

Lord Rosse, Chairman of the Georgian Group, wrote deploring the demolition and stressing the architectural qualities of the building. Felix Aylmer, distinguished actor and pillar of Actors' Equity, drew attention to the hardships which would fall upon those employed in the theatrical profession. Mr. James Wentworth Day, while not unduly worried by the fate of the St. James's, called for the protection of beautiful and historic places. So the battle raged.

At this critical stage Miss Vivien Leigh launched a campaign for salvation. She did not write to the papers, but took direct action. Maybe she remembered the means by which women had gained the

Vote. In any case, she made a highly sensational start. From the gallery of the House of Lords she interrupted their grave deliberations with an appeal to save the St. James's. Their Lordships were a little astounded but probably not displeased. But Parliamentary procedure had to be observed and Miss Leigh was very politely escorted from the Chamber by Black Rod (and, incidentally, later entertained to tea by some of the Members). In official parlance, she went quietly—her object achieved. Next day, the St. James's was headline news.

Miss Leigh did not let things rest there. With the eager support of Alan ("Jock") Dent, the erudite dramatic critic of *The News Chronicle*, she led a procession through the West End carrying sandwich boards demanding that the St. James's should be reprieved. More headlines—and again the crisis loomed large in the public mind. Then Miss Leigh organised a march of members of the theatrical profession, and also a mass meeting at which some fiery oratory prevailed. Miss Leigh gave it as her opinion that the theatre could yet be saved.

This remarkably well-organised agitation pushed the matter into Parliament, where it was discussed with some urgency. And urgent it was, for on the night of 20th July, 1957, the final curtain fell on the St. James's last play, *It's The Geography That Counts.* A full house, taut with excitement, watched that red and gold curtain descend, and applauded play and actors with genuine emotion. It fell to the leading man, John Gregson, to speak the final lines from the stage from which had spoken generations of famous players. He said: "In this historic, beautiful theatre, the scene of so many great successes, you share the awful distinction of being in at the death. The talk has now become a grim reality. It should never have been allowed to happen. I want you to make a resolution in your hearts that such a thing shall never happen again."

It was a sad and dispirited audience that dispersed that night. Many waited outside to see the celebrities arrive for a farewell party on the stage. Among them was Vivien Leigh, whom they loudly cheered. She deserved it. She had not yet lost heart. She said: "I still feel hopeful. Two American millionaires are interested, and so is a British body. Although the Americans do not wish to remain anonymous I am not telling who they are, just yet. You may know on Tuesday—perhaps in the House of Lords."

The stage party, attended by many of the staff who had worked in that theatre for years, was not a very gay affair. But Miss Leigh was still optimistic. Not so the management. "Most of the staff have been paid off," said the manager, "but some of us will remain behind, because you can't just close up a theatre at a day's notice." Already many fittings and fixtures had been removed.

In the meanwhile, the purchasers had announced that demolition would begin in August. The theatre was closed and the sands were running out. Some bowed to the inevitable but Miss Leigh and her supporters fought on. *The Times* had a leader headed "Farewell to a Friend", and on the Tuesday following the closure the subject was debated in the House of Lords—thus far had Miss Leigh's original interruption brought it.

Lord Silkin, opening the debate, said that two American millionaires, Mr. Huntingdon Hartford and a Mr. Cort, had promised sufficient money not only for compensation to the owners of the site but to put the theatre on an economically viable footing. He said also that the Piccadilly and St. James's Association was prepared to sponsor a fund to save the theatre, and asked the Government to delay the demolition until it was seen how successful these funds would be. He moved: "That, in the opinion of this House, no action should be taken to demolish or otherwise prejudice the continued use of St. James's Theatre as a theatre, pending a decision on the matter by both Houses of Parliament."

On the Government side, Lord Bancroft did not hold out much hope. Despite the fact that Mr. Henry Brooke, the Minister for Housing and Local Government, had said in the Commons that if sufficient money were raised by public subscription he would change his mind, his Lordship said that the Government would not intervene to prevent demolition. Yet Lord Silkin's motion was carried by twenty-two votes to eighteen, after a debate which had lasted to an unusually late hour.

After this Government inquest, however, it was found that the promised support was not quite what had been expected. The Mr. Cort who had been mentioned was not interested. There had been a misunderstanding: it was the St. James's Theatre, New York, that he had recently purchased. But the case of Mr. Huntingdon Hartford was different. A great theatre enthusiast and patron of the arts (he had built one American theatre), he was prepared to put up £35,000. Sir

Winston Churchill, the greatest living Englishman—that lover of battle and champion of seemingly lost causes—also rallied to the flag and offered £500. It was a most promising start.

Miss Leigh, still fighting, went to see Mr. Fenston, who then declared an armistice. He would hold his hand, would not start demolition right away, but would give the friends of St. James's time to see what they could do. If they could raise the necessary money to make it a business transaction, he and his firm would withdraw. Naturally, they would require compensation; the sum needed to repurchase the theatre and site being round about £350,000. He mentioned, also, that there should be an undertaking that the St. James's would be run as a theatre in perpetuity. Now, that was indeed asking something, and the hearts of those who, while they loved the theatre, were also people of some business acumen, sank considerably.

The question whether the building could be made to pay its way was foremost in the minds of all. Certain figures appeared in the Press but they were not always accurate. Then Mr. Prince Littler made a businesslike and straightforward statement in *The Manchester Guardian*, neatly summarising his case, and that of his associates, as vendors. He appended a statement from his auditors, Andrew W. Barr & Co., which read:

> "We hereby certify that for the twenty-five years that S. J. & L. Ltd. have operated it, there has been no profit made from the St. James's Theatre, no dividends have been paid on the share capital, no interest paid on loan capital, no remuneration paid either to Mr. Prince Littler or Mr. Gilbert Miller as joint managing directors, and no expenses of any kind have been charged by either of these gentlemen."

That was the St. James's death-warrant. A plain statement of fact, it swept aside the sentiment and the romance of old association and brought the economic realities into focus. It showed, too, the spirit in which Prince Littler and Gilbert Miller had worked. Mr. Miller's interest in the St. James's was about £125,000. He was the largest shareholder (although Mr. Littler had equal voting power) and he intimated that he would be prepared, if things could be properly arranged, "to leave his money in", meaning that he would allow it to remain as capital to help save the theatre. There was also a masterly statement on Theatre Finance in *The Times*, by Mr. F. C. Carter, General Manager of Associated Theatres. This period of reprieve was a time of anxiety for many people but it could not last for ever. Finally, as a result of negotiations between the solicitors for the purchasers and the Piccadilly and St. James's Association the fact emerged that the total capital necessary to save the building would be rather more than £500,000.

That was the end. The magnitude of that sum shattered all hopes. The long life of the St. James's Theatre was over. Unable to survive in modern conditions, it was doomed to vanish from the city which it had served so long. It held only 950 people and many seats were unsaleable because of obstructions to the view. That had not mattered much once, but it did matter now. It could not compete with the modern luxury of the Granadas and the Odeons. It was as out of date as the roads of today. Only, while people have to use the roads, they did not have to go to the St. James's. It was a part of yesterday and and held no place in the bustling new world today.

So the playhouse of Braham, of Charles Dickens, of Rachel, of Irving, of Toole, of so many of the great ones, the playhouse to which the Kendals and Hare had brought success and which Sir George Alexander had made so famous—which was indeed his own memorial—went into the shadows of the past. It was empty and it was dead—and there are few things so dead as a disused theatre. Demolition began in October, 1957.

Now only the memories remain. And one of the last of these—and which will be perpetuated into the new generation—is Miss Vivien Leigh's gallant battle to save something of value not alone for her own limited world of the theatre, but for the world at large. She failed, but failed gloriously, because the odds against her were too heavy. But we English always love a loser. And those of us who loved the St. James's will cherish the thought of Miss Leigh for her splendid fight to aid something in which she believed. It is a comforting thought that her place in history is now doubly assured, for in addition to her niche in the annals of theatre she stands famed in the chronicle of Parliament as well.

Largely due to Miss Leigh's intervention, the St. James's went down fighting. No other theatre ever attained the distinction of a debate in the House of Lords, and no other ever brought about a government defeat. If the theatre fell instead of the government, that too may be in accord with its aristocratic tradition. Having served under seven sovereigns—from William IV to Elizabeth II—it is meet that its obsequies should be sung in an atmosphere as august as that for which it had itself become renowned.

Its echoes will linger long after the memories have passed away.

CHAPTER 24

Other People's Memories

IN the midst of the controversy over the closing of the St. James's, it occurred to me that it might be helpful to my readers, present and future, if they could learn at first hand how this theatre had impressed others who knew it. So I wrote to the newspapers, asking playgoers to send me their recollections, and their letters flowed in by the dozen. It has been difficult to select from them, and I apologise to those who so kindly wrote but whose contributions, owing to lack of space, I have been unable to use. I would have liked to print them all—but that would have meant another book. Those which follow, I think, speak for themselves.

One of the most revealing came from Phyllis Barker, who was one of the loveliest of the Gaiety Girls at their most dazzling time, and still retains her beauty. She says:

> "It was always understood in the theatre that George Alexander did not want to recognise the minor members of his cast if he met them in the streets. I was told there was a notice to this effect on the notice board but I never saw it. One day I did meet him out somewhere and was so embarrassed that I turned away and pretended I had not seen him. That night when I was waiting in the wings he came up and said 'You never smiled at me this morning, although I tried to catch your eye.'" (So much for *that* story!) Miss Barker continues: "I had a charming dress to wear, very suited to my nineteen years, of spotted muslin on silk with a sash. At the dress parade Alexander admired it and said how attractive it looked; whereupon Mrs. Alexander said at once it was far too simple and had it sent to the wardrobe and covered with tinsel trimmings. Miriam Clements, who was always very sweet to me, was furious and said it was only done because 'George' had admired it, and that now it made me look like a Christmas tree.

"Of all the theatres I have played in I never knew any other as strict as they were at the St. James's. No visitors were allowed in the dressing-rooms, even for the leading players, and *no* man was ever allowed on the women's side . . . I loved the theatre and do hope it will be saved."

That provides a delightful glimpse of the St. James's and its methods.

Mr. W. H. Cairns strikes a note of comedy, showing how the irrepressible Cockney will break through even the greatest scene of dignity and decorum. He writes:

"St. James's Theatre—date I cannot remember—seated in front of stage Irene Vanbrugh and Herbert Waring. George Alexander opens french windows at back of stage. Voice from the gallery cries out 'Next station, Marble Arch!'"

One would have liked a glimpse of Sir George's face!

Keneth Kent, a splendid actor himself, writes:

"I played the lead there in *Lucky Jim*, *Charley's Aunt*, and *Treasure Island*. The latter is of no interest to anyone, but the following may be: in *Charley's Aunt* Leslie Howard understudied me as Babs, Edna Best made her first appearance on the stage as the Ingénue, and Barry O'Brien (the manager) played Charley."

This shows how the St. James's was a birthplace of stars, and one can only regret Keneth Kent's far too early retirement.

Mr. E. Dodd writes:

"Anyone who visited the theatre during Sir George Alexander's management could not fail to feel the atmosphere of dignity and quiet pleasure that always pervaded it. I consider that it was the best-dressed house in London. Not that it was overdressed at any time, but it seemed that good clothes, good manners, and good plays were all in keeping with the St. James's Theatre."

From Mrs. Carmen D. Oakshott who, as Carmen Woods, played at the St. James's, comes this:

"The atmosphere of perfection is one thing I could never forget. One staircase for the ladies and one for the gentlemen; Mrs. Evans, the housekeeper, who walked around with such a regal air and always dressed in stiff black satin; Irene Vanbrugh so often arriving with a string bag full of shopping—and always everyone in evening dress.

"I understudied the part of Derek and played it in the first tour of *His House in Order*, in 1906. Mr. Alexander came to nearly every rehearsal, always immaculately dressed. Never did I see him out of temper: he was one of the most perfect gentlemen one could meet. Mr. Arnold, the box-office manager for many years, had a most tragic death. He and his wife went to Clacton for a holiday and while walking along the front were run down and killed by a motor-bike. I worked at the St. James's again in *Peter Pan* in 1921, but somehow the theatre did not seem the same without Sir George and the gracious atmosphere that surrounded him."

Miss Judy Knight calls attention to a remarkable coincidence:

"In December, 1936, a play was produced at the St. James's called *O, Mistress Mine*, in which a character named Mrs. Billing was played by Helen Haye. She had to say 'Have you seen the papers? The King has abdicated.' Strangely enough, just at that time (11th December), King Edward VIII did actually announce his abdication."

Mr. J. Leonard Mallé sends his memory in the form of a story:

"Lennie was a very tiny boy who had not quite reached his seventh birthday in the year 1901. His widowed mother was left with a small confectionery shop at the junction of Rochester Row and Artillery Row. A neighbour, Mrs. Webb, was the wife of the limelight man at the Standard (now Victoria Palace), Pimlico, and—according to herself—an actress who had had a lot in common with the leading lights of Theatreland. She took a fancy to Lennie, who spent quite a lot of time playing with her canary. One day she gave Lennie's Mum two theatre tickets for a matinee at the St. James's. Poor Mum couldn't spare the time, so she asked Bill Fisher to take Lennie.

"Now, Bill lived opposite to Lennie in one of the tiny houses in Greycoat Street. He was a cheery, fat boy of fourteen summers, and although kind-hearted, polite and 'one of the best,' was hardly what one would call *presentable*. Picture a rather uncouth, large boy with untidy hair and clothing and wearing white boots, leading by the hand a small, pathetic-looking nipper, complete with stiff celluloid collar, through the carriages drawn up outside the St. James's and into the second row of the dress circle, where they were surrounded by a bevy of fashionably attired ladies. What amazes me to this day is why we were allowed to occupy those seats.

"The stage performance was above their heads. All Lennie remembers is that there were two plays. The first was called a comedy; then there was an interval, after which everybody on the stage acted very seriously. But that interval! Pretty ladies came round with cups of tea or coffee, dainty sandwiches and delicate cakes. Bill became the owner of a tray. He muttered 'How much?', went all red and dived his hand into his trousers pockets for some money which Lennie knew he hadn't got. The pretty lady said 'It's all right', and everybody smiled and looked so kindly. While Bill was fumbling about with the things on the tray, the lady sitting next to Lennie asked him all about himself. She patted his hand and was very nice. The next thing Lennie remembers is a coachman holding open a carriage door, and the luxury of the cushioned seats; then he was standing in the doorway of the little shop clutching a silver coin, and the lady was shaking hands with Mum. Oh, yes, one thing more: when he asked where Bill had gone, Mum said the lady had taken him to the Army and Navy Stores to buy something."

That true story of life in the "bad old days" at the St. James's is most illuminating.

Percy Merriman, a fine performer with a long record, whose concert party "The Roosters" did so much to amuse the soldiers in the First World War, was at the St. James's when young.

"You may be surprised to know," he writes, "that your little Percy was one of the pages who held up the coronation robes in *The Prisoner of Zenda*—George Alexander and the beauteous Evelyn Millard. Remember my hair being curled nightly in a little room off the prompt corner (would love to find it one day!), and I do particularly remember one charming fact—we two boys were allowed to use the green-room, often when only Sir George and the lovely Evelyn M. were there. No side! Got 10/- a week and 2/6 matinees, which helped the folks at home."

I am afraid my old friend will never see that little room off the prompt corner again.

Mrs. S. F. Bonasselle, whose stage name was Teresa Furtado Clarke, writes:

"I joined George Alexander's company in September, 1895. We were playing *The Importance of Being Earnest*, when there was the Oscar Wilde trouble. Poor Mr. Arnold in the box-office was quite shattered. People went and threw their tickets at him and, as you know, the play had to be taken off. How times have changed! Give me the old days every time. I did not then know what it was all about. We went on tour soon after, and to Balmoral with *Liberty Hall*. I still have that programme and the brooch Queen Victoria sent me."

Mrs. M. Jordan writes:

"I well remember Mr. and Mrs. Kendal in *The Elder Miss Blossom*. I was only fourteen years old, but the lovely acting and story remain a most pleasant memory. Later I saw them in *The Likeness of the Night*. I saw George Alexander and Henry Ainley, and quite recently took my daughter to see *Double Image*. As a playgoer, the theatre had many happy memories for me and I sincerely hope it will be allowed to remain."

Mr. Basil J. A. Alexander recalls another incident:

"As a boy, I still recollect sitting enthralled in the middle of the front row of the gallery, when a group of women suddenly ran round to the left side (facing the stage) and threw quantities of leaflets over the gallery rails, shouting 'Votes for Women!' The leaflets floated down into the stalls like a miniature snowstorm, and the demonstrators hurriedly withdrew. However, the play was not interrupted . . . I had a passion for my namesake and saw him whenever possible . . . At a sad farewell visit to the St. James's two or three weeks ago, I tested various end seats in the dress circle during an interval and was rather shocked at the poor view obtained of the stage."

A pleasant reminiscence comes from Miss Dorothy Badchase:

"Many years ago I used to go to the St. James's to see George Alexander. I remember well *Old Heidelberg*, and walking home with a friend silently—both feeling quite sad. I do not think many present-day actors could make such an impression on their audience. One very cold night Alexander sent out tea to the gallery people waiting for the doors to open . . . I may say that in those days all actors and actresses could be heard in the back row of the gallery, however big the theatre. It is not so today."

Mr. Ogilvie Mackay recalls an incident in the First World War and how the St. James's met it:

"On a clear evening in the autumn of 1915, during the early bombing (mostly by Zeppelins), I was in the gallery. The play, appropriately enough, was *The Big Drum*, by Sir Arthur Pinero, in which a leading part was played by Sir George Alexander. About 10 o'clock, at the beginning of the last act, there was a sudden outbreak of gunfire just above our heads. Then a bomb fell. It couldn't have been far away. The players paused, and a few members of the audience—a very few—began to leave. The silence on the stage was broken by Sir George Alexander, who stepped forward and said that if the audience were prepared to keep their seats the players were prepared to carry on. The play then proceeded to its end."

My friend Laurence Shelton, son of that splendid actor George Shelton, writes to remind me that it was at the St. James's that his father made his first appearance on the London stage in 1876, under the management of Mrs. John Wood in *The Sultan of Mocha*, and fifty-four years later, at the age of seventy-eight, he made his last stage appearance there, playing once again his immortal Smee in *Peter Pan*.

And Reginald Long recalls that, when all the London theatres were forced to close in the war emergency of 1939, it was the St. James's which first opened its stage door to allow a company to rehearse for a tour in the provinces . . . There was just the fireman there and they had only one lamp, but the courtesy of Mr. Tom Bostock, then the general manager, enabled the wheels of the drama again to be set in motion—on the stage of the St. James's.

An old colleague of mine in many theatres, Mr. R. Jordan, who is, I think, the doyen of them all, sends an amusing story:

> "An old tank or cistern was sent in for a thunder effect, and it was placed down under the stage. As time rolled on, it often became full of water. A huge kettle was placed beside it to bail out the water for cleaning purposes. This had a rope attached to the handle (for pulling up), and the 'gag' was for any new man to be sent down to see 'the water otter', much to the fun of the older staff when he came back and said he couldn't see it. But the 'otter' met its end one night when Sir George Alexander was on the stage, having tea in the play. He was remarking about the water in the jug being cold, and at once 'Props' sent a new hand to fetch some *very hot* water. He turned up with the kettle, complete with rope, and was only just prevented from going on to the stage with the 'water otter'!"

Grace Denbigh-Russell, an actress of charm and a stage-manager too, recalls a terrible night during the play O, *Mistress Mine*, when an actor "dried up" and just could not take a prompt. He was in such a panic that he left the stage and she had to ask Yvonne Printemps to go on at once. That lovely artiste's English being rudimentary, she had to rely on cues. The dried-up actor reappeared with his part in his hand and went on again, but although Miss Printemps never got a cue, she never missed a speech and carried the scene off with aplomb. That play, which only ran for nine nights, has already been mentioned as the one in which Helen Haye had to speak of the Abdication, and by some unlucky chance nearly every line seemed to have some bearing on the whole unfortunate occurrence. To crown it all, when the Abdication speech was made over the radio and the St. James's, like all other theatres, was prepared to relay it to the audience, the machine broke down and only gave out distorted noises. Evidently the St. James's did not approve of abdications!

A letter from that distinguished actress Viola Lyel is of the greatest interest, because it introduces a new character into the story of the St. James's:

> "When I was playing there in *Pride and Prejudice* (1936), the 'ghost' was quite in evidence. He haunted the top floor, and the old housekeeper was not in the least afraid of him. Quite often the door of her room would open or close by itself, or it would be very firmly pushed against on the other side when she tried to open or shut it, sometimes strongly enough to prevent her coming in or going out. Joan Harben, Lueen McGrath and I shared a room on the floor below, and several times there was a loud knocking on our door and definitely no one in the corridor outside—though in the end, of course, this became a joke: people used to knock to frighten us and then run away. Once I was helped on with my coat in the dressing-room when there was no one behind me, and that was terrifying."

I can reassure Miss Lyel I, too, know that ghost and while I was in charge of that theatre I encountered him twice, in the same way as Miss Lyel and probably in the same room. I had gone to see an artiste after the show and had my coat over my arm. On starting to put it on, I was helped very expertly by unseen hands. It happened again a few nights later, and this time the hands not only helped me on but flicked some dust off the shoulders! I make no apology or explanation: I just state a fact. I see ghosts if they are to be seen, but this one, like Buckstone's at the Haymarket, only manifests itself by actions. And here is Miss Lyel to bear me out! Some old dresser, maybe, who loved the St. James's so much that he cannot tear himself from it.

CHAPTER 25

Personal Farewell

WHEN I had finished this book I felt I must add a few personal words on the passing of my old and revered friend, the St. James's Theatre. For to me, a mad person who inhabits the mad world of the theatre, all playhouses are sentient things with personalities, qualities and failings of their own. If you belong to their way of life, you get to know them and they get to know you. They will talk to you and whisper their secrets. You can hear and understand if you are a subject of the land of illusion. For those places retain something of all the energy which has been generated in them—the emotions of players and audiences alike. It is never quite dissipated, it still fills the air. And if you happen to be a human receiving set, as most people of the greasepaint really are, you can pick up the messages they send you.

I have stood on a stage when the theatre has emptied after an enthusiastic first night and felt the fatigue which seems to fill both stage and auditorium. It is as if the strain on the nerves engendered by creation has eased and that the place is throwing itself back and relaxing, glad of the rest but conscious also of a glow of pride. I have sensed the frustration of a failure of which much has been expected but which has gone astray. You may say this is just innate personal feeling consequent upon association. I think it is not, for sometimes I have had no connection with the event at all, except as a spectator, but have got the message just the same.

No effort is entirely wasted. It is my belief that force—personal, mental force—does something to the ether. I do not know what the ether is, and I don't believe that scientists know either. But we all know it is there, and that it can work miracles. Thus there remains in theatres some vestige of all the force expended in them. That remnant becomes the ghosts of the old players who fought their battles there and still linger there in spirit. Sometimes they won their fight, sometimes they were defeated; but something of it remains and creates that curious thing called "atmosphere". Naturally, it is stronger in old theatres than in new ones. You can feel it intensely at Drury Lane and the Haymarket, and at Covent Garden. It is apparent at the Criterion, the Adelphi, and Her Majesty's; and one draws great whiffs of it at the Theatre Royal, Bristol, and to some extent, too, at the Old Vic. One always sensed it strongly at the St. James's, which was indeed old, as theatres go. But now all that stored-up force will be released by the housebreakers' picks and disintegrate in the wide open air.

I went along there on an afternoon just prior to its closing down—not the very last afternoon, but to the Wednesday matinee before its last Saturday. I did not want to see the last curtain fall. I don't like being "in at the death", as John Gregson so aptly put it. I like to say good-bye to my old friends in a quiet, personal manner, not amid a crowd. For the same reason I detest farewells on railway platforms, at airports or docksides.

There it stood, in King Street, once such a lordly thoroughfare, now swamped by commerce and trade. A quietly impressive edifice, not very large, not very imposing, not beautiful, but dignified and unchanged down the years, mellow with over a century and a quarter of service. Outside it had not altered. Its flagstaff stood above it but no flag flew. On its left, as you faced it, were quiet, serene Georgian houses, and on its right was Angel Court, that narrow, dark little passage which led to its workman's entrance, the stage door. How many distinguished feet had passed down that court and turned into that small, dingy and entirely unimpressive stage door.

Up four steps and into the vestibule, through the doors, and under the portico above which the name was emblazoned. That vestibule was not very large but had restful dignity. It still held Yesterday. On the left as one entered was the box-office and on the right, let into the wall, was a bronze tablet bearing a remarkably good profile of Sir George Alexander, recording his management from 1890 until 1918—a tribute from fellow-members of his profession. This was a place in which Show Business had no being. It was a workshop—or studio maybe—of the theatrical profession. There was no noise or hustle, the good carpets prevented sound. It was a symphony in quiet shades. Flowers abounded, and before one lay a few steps leading to the dress circle and the boxes. Of course the lighting was in fine cut-glass chandeliers. Women predominated among the staff, which still maintained the courtesy that had been the hall-mark of the St. James's.

My friend A. M. Wolstenholme, box-office manager and assistant house manager, asked me into the box-office, the holy of holies of a theatre. How well I knew that little place, which always seemed too small for the business transacted! I sat beside him and chatted when he was not occupied by people asking questions and getting the right answers. Most of the customers were middle-aged ladies. Almost everyone asked if the news was true—was the theatre really closing down? Mr. Wolstenholme had to confirm the dismal tidings. One and all expressed regret. Many of them grew quite reminiscent about their numerous visits and the plays they had seen. And they were all treated with real courtesy and respect.

The cashier at the gallery entrance came in to pick up her float and her "return" forms, and as we were talking an elderly lady came to the window. She wanted to transfer her seat, she said—was it possible? The manager assured her it was, and wanted the details. The lady had a reserved seat in the upper circle and wanted to transfer to the gallery! That really shook us! Even Mr. Wolstenholme was taken aback for the moment. The gallery cashier gasped: "Well," she said, "I've worked here twenty years and never heard the like." Nor had I—and I have worked in theatres for fifty-five years. With the utmost politeness, Mr. Wolstenholme assured the lady she would be much more comfortable in the upper circle and would have a better view. But she was adamant—she meant to transfer to the gallery. So in the true spirit of the St. James's—the out-moded idea that the customer is always right—her wishes were granted, although at financial sacrifice to the exchequer. The lady went off delighted!

But the next customer wanted four stalls, and that restored the balance. This elderly patron also lamented the end of the theatre and regretted she would not be able to come again. She was a lady of Yesterday, dressed quietly but in the best materials. The small amount of jewellery she wore was real. One almost believed she had stepped out of a brougham. She said she expected everyone felt sad—that Mr. Wolstenholme felt sad, and he assured her that was so. Picking up her change she thanked him, lingered a moment and glanced around. "So many years," she sighed, "and so many happy hours here!" And with a smile and a bow she passed on. One recalled the lady who had been so kind to little Lennie—this was the very same sort, the true St. James's patron—a vanishing and impoverished race nowadays.

In the vestibule I saw my old friend Laurence Atteridge, last manager of the St. James's—the last of a distinguished line of house managers, or business managers as we used to call them—and he had every qualification for the job: he "looks right" in the front of the house and he *is* right. He has the needful courtesy, tact and discrimination; integrity also and charm. He knows all about backstage too. The knowledge that he was the last of his line depressed him sorely, for he is very much a man of the theatre.

We went into the auditorium and I took my last look round. How well I knew that place, with its almost Georgian air, its dress circle which tapered to the sides, its two boxes, its real air of theatre. He drew attention to the ceiling—the one put up since the blitz—through which lights twinkled as though from stars in the sky. I did not like its colour scheme so much as the old one. But in the main it was the pristine St. James's, right up to and including the proscenium arch. And, although the curtain was not up, we spoke in whispers, feeling already in the presence of the dead.

I watched the curtain rise, and then I went away: I had seen it go up, I did not want to see it fall. I walked again up Angel Court and had a glimpse of old Donald McMinnies, the stage door keeper (or, to give him his correct title, hall keeper). He was busy, so I did not worry him. For twenty-eight years he had worked there, but even that was after I had been in charge. I had known a St. James's he knew not.

I walked back along King Street, across St. James's Square, up the Haymarket and across Piccadilly Circus, musing as I went. Things and people flocked into my mind. Far too many to register in this book, but one name must be enshrined—Gertrude Butler, for so long the secretary (and, indeed, chief of staff) to Gilbert Miller. She still graces the world but has retired to a well-earned leisure. How many years had I known her? Well, memory went back to the days when she was secretary to Frank Curzon at the Prince of Wales's. She, her colleague Jack Houston—a dear little bird-like fellow who was treasurer—my father-in-law (who was Loewe & Co. of the Haymarket, "the most famous pipes in the world") and myself used to lunch together daily at the Corner House in Coventry Street from 1911 onwards for many years. Gertrude Butler knew all about the theatre. She was energy personified and had sure judgment, tact, and above all, discretion. No official leakages occurred where Gertrude Butler was in charge. She was a pillar of strength at the Prince of Wales's, and then for years at the St. James's. When she retired her friends gave her a party in the saloon of that theatre, where a large gathering of important folk wished her luck, long life and happiness. That, one is glad to say, has come true.

Then there were Arnold and De Courcey, of the box-office. How well I remember them! And Whitaker, the treasurer, who when Alexander died left that peaceful backwater and found the world outside such a very different and difficult place. But, because he had the strength of the St. James's behind him, he succeeded.

There was Bratt (or was it Brett?), the landlord of the public house on the corner of Angel Court, who for some time ran the bars, and did the job in real West End style. I seem to recall that he was keen on horse racing, as befitted his surroundings, which then still retained something of the old Corinthian days.

There was also Helmsley, the manager, with his museum of uniforms and weapons, and who had at his home a flagstaff where every day the flag was hoisted with ceremony and struck at sundown. The housekeepers, too—Mrs. Evans and her successor Mrs. Quinn (who shared Miss Lyel's experiences with the ghost); and in the later period Miss Taylor, the bar manageress, who was of Westby's. The figure of Mrs. Murray crosses the mind, too, the travelling manageress for Westby's, who every night visited each theatre under contract to the firm. A real lady in breeding and education, she was tall, slim, perfectly poised, with clear-cut aristocratic features, and her manners were such as a duchess might have envied. She and I worked for Sir George Dance at the same time—fellow-sufferers who sustained each other. Yet Sir George had his good points and we became great friends towards his end.

I remember, too, a night outside the St. James's in 1897. It was Queen Victoria's Diamond Jubilee. In the morning I had seen the procession and the service in St. Paul's churchyard; and that night two aunts of mine, whom I bless because they always took me to see all that should be seen, escorted me, a boy of nine, to see the illuminations. About four million other people had the same idea. St. James's Street was one of the star spots, and I remember getting wedged into a crowd at the corner of King Street, just outside the St. James's, where two streams of people met. I remember being submerged, and my aunts screaming, and a man pulling me up and putting me on his shoulder. Eventually police forced their way through and got the crowd circulating again. I recall the gas lights outside the theatre, and a great illuminated crown shining overhead. The play was *The Princess and the Butterfly*, but the performances were suspended: Alexander and the other actor-managers had wisely closed down that week, knowing the streets would be choked and that there would be no getting to and from the theatres.

When I managed the St. James's and Sir George so kindly let me use his room and his dressing-room, it was my joy to sit in that office-cum-drawing-room, all very solidly Victorian, and muse upon what had happened in there—the interviews, the famous people, the plans, the discussions with dramatists: Pinero, Carton, Jones, Wilde, and the others—all had used that room. And I would change into evening dress—my livery—before the evening show and sit at Sir George's dressing-table and switch on the lights bordering the three-sided mirror. Often it seemed not my own features I saw, but the gravely handsome face of the actor-manager; and in my imagination I watched it take the likeness of Rudolf Rassendyll, Malatesta, François Villon, Prince Karl Heinrich, and the other characters which had grown with the application of greasepaint in front of that mirror.

I left the St. James's reluctantly that last afternoon. I had known and loved it so long. I had gone there as a boy, I had sat in the gallery, the pit, the upper circle, the dress circle and then the stalls. I had, perhaps without realising it, become one of those people at whom I had gazed with something akin to envy in my gallery and pit days. I had seen such lovely plays, such superb acting, such supreme quality. I hoped it had taught me something. I think it had.

And now all was to go. Even the memory would fade with the passing of time. The young people had not the affection for it that we older ones felt. For myself, the St. James's was not only the Theatre of Distinction but also a monument to Sir George Alexander—and now that monument was to fall. It will be gone before this book is published. My only hope was that in its demolition it might yet achieve a victory. It might halt the seemingly irresistible tide which is sweeping so many theatres to destruction. And perhaps it has achieved this. The public may think twice in future. If so, then it will indeed have achieved immortality.

As one says "good-bye", one cherishes the hope that the last fight of St. James's the Aristocrat may be the beginning of a new era in theatreland.

LONDON, 12th October, 1957

INDEX

Under the heading St. James's are given the salient points in the history of this theatre. Only the more important plays are listed; others will be found alphabetically in the list of Play and Song Titles.

Abbas, Hector, 188
A'Beckett, Arthur, 59
A'Beckett, Gilbert, 28, 29
A'Beckett, Mrs. G., 28
A'Beckett, William, 55
Abraham, Mr. (Abey Punch), 19
Abraham, Mrs., 19
Abraham, Master (*see* Braham)
Abram, Master (*see* Braham)
Achurch, Janet, 126
Ackland, Rodney, 203
Actor-Managers, 14–16, 87, 98, 127, 153, 155
Actors' Equity, 212
Adams, Maude, 193
Adams, W. Bridges, 186
Addison, Carlotta, 53, 149, 157
Addison, Fanny, 62
Aicken, Eleanor, 165
Aidé, Hamilton, 107
Ainley, Henry, 160–2, 165, 168, 178, 193–5, 196, 222
Albanesi, Meggie, 12, 193
Albert, Prince, 39, 73
Albery, Sir Bronson, 203
Aldridge, Ira Q., 70
Alexander II, Czar of Russia, 58–9
Alexander the Great, 205
Alexander, Basil J. A., 222–3
Alexander, Sir George (George Alexander Gibb Samson)
birth and parentage, 98; schooldays, 99; at work in the City, 99–100; as amateur actor, 100; as amateur at St. James's, 100; becomes a professional, 101; on tour, 101–2; first appearance in London, 102; with Irving at the Lyceum, 102–3; with the Kendals at St. James's, 86–7, 88, 103; marriage, 103; American tour with Irving, 103; further parts at Lyceum (Macduff, Faust), 105–6; in Adelphi melodrama, 106–7; takes Avenue Theatre, 107; signs lease of St. James's, 108; opening play, *Sunshine and Shadow*, 109–11 (for further productions, see under St. James's); at Drury Lane, 166; appointed to L.C.C., 176; knighthood, 181; illness, 186, 189; death, 189; theatre routine, 170; relations with public, actors and staff, 156, 167, 168, 218, 221–2, 223; dressing room, 231; passing references, 16, 36, 90, 97, 206, 216, 219, 220, 222, 224
Alexander, Mrs. George (Lady Alexander; née Florence Theleur), 103–4, 105, 107, 114, 129, 142, 164, 218, 227
Allen, Adrienne, 201
Allen, David, & Sons, 74
Allen, W. E., 74
Allison, Miss, 32
Almack's, 26

Anderson, Mary, 103
Anderson, Percy, 111
Animals, performing, 36, 37
Archer, William, 62, 77, 79, 111, 122, 133, 145, 148, 149, 150, 152, 198
Arene, Emanuel, 166
Arliss, George, 198
Arlton, Frank J., 199
Arne, Thomas A., 33, 148
Arnold, E., 141, 151, 169, 220, 222, 230
Arnold, Mrs. E., 220
Arts Council of Great Britain, 204
Arundel Club, 54
Arundel, Dennis, 207
Ashe, Mr., 20
Ashley, Henry J., 50
Ashwell, Lena, 193
Asquith, Lord H. H. 142
Aston & Mitchell, 40
Atteridge, Laurence, 229
Austen, Jane, 204
Avril, Suzanne, 54
Aylmer, Felix, 212
Aynesworth, Allan, 90, 94, 95, 139, 142, 143, 144, 180, 186

BADCHASE, Dorothy, 223
Baird, Dorothea, 147, 148
Balchin, Nigel, 208
Balfe, Michael, 39
Bancroft, George, 144, 147
Bancroft, Lord, 214
Bancroft, Mr. and Mrs., 15, 65–8, 69, 72, 80, 82
Bancroft, Sir Squire (Early stage name, Sydney), 66
Banks, Leslie, 203
Bannerman, Margaret, 202
Barclay, Jenny, 202
Barker, H. Granville, 183, 193
Barker, Phyllis, 218
Barnes, Barry K., 201
Barnes, John H., 79, 103
Barnett, John, 33
Barnett, Morris, 28, 29, 33, 40
Barnum, Phineas T., 42
Barr, Andrew W., & Co., 215
Barrault, Jean-Louis, 206
Barrett, Wilson, 121, 145
Barrie, J. M., 165
Barrington, Rutland, 15, 93–97
Barton, Dora, 159
Bateman, Colonel, 77, 80
Bateman, Ellen, 42
Bateman, Kate, 42
Bateman, Virginia, 178
Bavaria, King of (Ludwig II), 58
Beale, Willert, 77
Bean, A. W., 113
Beauchamp, John, 94
Beazley, Samuel, 25
Becker, Bernard H., 78
Beers, Mrs. Bernard, 64
Beet, Alice, 180
Bell, Jeffrey, 201
Bell, Mary Hayley, 207
Bennett, Arnold, 199
Benson, Sir Frank, 161, 181
Beringer, Esmé, 157, 195
Beringer, Mrs. Oscar, 158
Bernhardt, Sarah, 43
Bernstein, Henry, 175–6
Bésier, Rudolph, 185
Best, Edna, 196, 200, 219
Betterton, Thomas, 75
Beveridge, J. D., 150, 165
Billington, Mrs., 21
Birch, T. F., 212
Birmingham Repertory Company, 205
Bishop, George, 184
Bishop, Kate, 159, 176
Bismarck, Prince von, 58
Bithell, Jethro, 183
Bland, James, 35
Bland, Sydney, 194
Bleichmann, Rudolf, 164–5
Bolingbroke, Herbert, 197
Bolton, Guy, 196, 205, 207
Bolton, Miss (*see* Braham, Mrs. John)

Bonasselle, Mrs. (*see* Clark, Teresa F.)
Bostock, Thomas H., 202, 223
Bottomley, Horatio, 187
Boucicault, Dion, 49, 50, 52, 53, 54, 116
Bouffé, H. D. M., 41
Bourchier, Arthur, 14, 16, 97, 118, 171
Bowers, Raymond, 210
Bowman, Nellie, 203
Boyce, Henry, 143
Boyne, Clifton, 194
Boyne, Leonard, 186
Boz (*see* Dickens)
Braddon, Miss, 45, 46
Braham, Augustus, 34, 43
Braham, Charles, 34
Braham, Frances (Lady Waldegrave), 34
Braham, Hamilton, 34, 43
BRAHAM, John (Master Abraham, Master Abram),
birth and parentage, 19; early career, 20; at Drury Lane, 21; singing tours abroad, 21; at Covent Garden, 20, 22; marriage, 22; writes opera and songs, 22; as singer and actor, 23–4; residences, 24, 34; acquires site of St. James's, 25; opening of St. James's (1835), 28–9; in management (1835–8), 28–34; bankruptcy, 34; American tour, 34; concert at St. James's, 34–5, 53; death, 35; family, 34; passing references, 39, 43, 50, 67, 93, 216 (*see also* ST. JAMES'S)
Braham, Mrs. John (*née* Miss Bolton), 22, 34
Braham, Spencer, 34
Braithwaite, Lilian, 160, 162, 165, 166, 168, 178, 188, 195, 204
Brandon, Dorothy, 198
Brandon, Mr., 76
Brandon, Olga, 144
Bratt, Mr., 230
Brereton, Austen, 84
Bright, Addison, 149
Bristol Repertory Company, 205
British Broadcasting Corporation, 107, 210
British Repertory Theatre Festival, 205
Brook, Clive, 204
Brough, Antonia, 202
Brough, Fanny, 60, 61, 107
Brough, Lionel, 59, 60
Brough, William, 49
Browne, Pattie, 121
Browne, W. Graham, 159
Bruce, Edgar, 61
Bruce, Nigel, 199
Brydone, Alfred, 165
Buchanan, Jack, 205
Buchanan, Robert, 128
Buckstone, J. B., 41, 56, 225
Bunn, Alfred, 38–40, 42
Burden, Anna, 202
Burnand, F. C., 45, 50, 61
Burnett, Mrs. Hodgson, 86
Bush, Mr., 49
Butler, Gertrude, 229–30
Butt, Sir Alfred, 169, 187
Byron, H. J., 45, 115
Byron, Lord, 43

CADELL, Jean, 197
Cairns, W. H., 219
Calthrop, Dion Clayton, 183
Calvert, Louis, 176
Calvert, Phyllis, 207
Campbell, Miss, 86
Campbell, Mrs. Patrick, 128–33, 134–5, 136, 160, 182
Campbell, Stella Patrick, 180
Campbell, Violet, 198
Cannan, Dennis, 206
Cannings, Mrs. George, 139
Capes, Bernard, 122
Capus, Alfred, 166
Carey, Joyce, 188

Carr, J. Comyns, 85, 118
Carroll, Sydney W., 202
Carten, Audrey, 199
Carten, Waveney, 199
Carter, F. C., 216
Carton, R. C., 80, 108, 109, 112, 149, 180, 181, 231
Casalis, Jeanne de, 202
Casson, Sir Lewis, 196
Casson, Lady (*see* Thorndike, Sybil)
Cathcart, R., 76
Cautley, Laurence, 143
Cavendish, Ada, 64, 90
Cellier, Frank, 202
C.E.M.A., 203, 204
Chamberlain, Joseph, 92
Chambers, C. Haddon, 111–2, 159
Charles I, 25
Charles II, 25
Charles XV (of Sweden), 58
Chester, Edith, 131
Chevalier, Albert, 73, 74, 75, 107
Chevalier, Marcelle, 171, 173
Chippendale, Thomas, 15
Christie, Agatha, 203, 210
Churchill, Sir Winston, 215
Chute, James H., 70
Cimarosa, Domenico, 22
Clare, Mary, 203
Clarisse, M., 41
Clark, E. Holman, 184
Clarke, John, 66
Clarke, John S., 55–6, 66
Clarke, Sir Percival, 183
Clarke, Teresa Furtado (Mrs. Bonasselle), 222
Clay, Frederic, 85
Clayton, John, 59, 61, 62, 69, 84
Clements, John, 204
Clements, Miriam, 218
Cleveland, Duke of, 25
Clifford, Mrs. W. K., 158–9
Clift, E. P., 205
Clifton, Lewis, 165
Clifton, Myles, 199
Clinton-Baddeley, V. C., 212
Clunes, Alec, 202
Coffin, Hayden, 15
Coleman, Fanny, 120, 123
Collier, Constance, 150
Collins, Arthur, 15
Combermere, Edward, 188
Comédie Française (Company), 207
Compton, Edward, 138, 178
Compton, Fay, 178, 196
Conti, Italia, 160
Conway, H. B., 73, 105–6
Cook, Dutton, 85
Cooke, George Frederick, 195
Cooke, T. P., 78
Cooper, Gladys, 187, 198, 201
Coquelin, Benoît Constant, 54
Cort, Mr., 214
Cottrell, Adeline, 49
Couder, M., 58
Coughlan, Charles, 59
Courtney, W. L., 124
Courtville, Julian, 194, 195
Coward, Noël, 196
Crace, Mr., 25
Craig, Gordon, 104
Craigie, Mrs. Pearl (*see* Hobbes, John Oliver)
Critchett, Sir Anderson, 112
Critchett, Dr. D., 112
Cromwell, Oliver, 77
Crook, John, 108
Cross, Mrs. Catherine, 54
Cummings, Constance, 205
Curzon, Frank, 229
Czarina Maria (of Russia), 59

DAINES, Emily (*see* Pinero, Mrs. J. D.)
D'Alroy, Evelyn, 183
Dance, Charles, 44
Dance, Sir George, 192, 230
Dansey, Herbert, 160
Dare, Phyllis, 159
Daubeny, Peter, 204
Davide, Giovanni, 21

Davis, Fay, 147, 148, 149, 150, 151, 159
Davis, Gilbert, 201
Davis, Owen, 198
Dawson, I., 144
Day, James Wentworth, 212
Day, William H., 143, 147
De Burgh, Beatrix, 160
De Courcey, Mr., 169, 230
De la Ferté, Mlle., 59
De la March, Peter, 182
De Liagre, Alfred (Junr.), 202
De Verney, Mr., 84
Dean, Basil, 205
Dearden, Harold, 198
Déjazet, Pauline V., 41
Denbigh-Russell, Grace, 224
Denham, Reginald, 203, 207
Denny, Reginald, 165
Dent, Alan, 213
Deval, Jacques, 201
Dibdin, Charles, 23, 28
Dickens, Charles ("Boz"), 30, 31, 32, 53, 55, 62, 216
Dickens, C. Stafford, 197
Dietz, Linda, 85, 87, 88
Digges, Ernest, 194
Dilley, J. J., 165
Disney, Walt, 207
Disney-Roebuck, J., 199
District Messenger Co., 17, 155
Dixon, Adèle, 197
Dodd, E., 219
Dowton, William, 35
D'Oyly Carte, Rupert, 93, 95
Draper, Ruth, 210
Du Maurier, Sir Gerald, 12, 15, 198, 199, 200
Duchesne, P. G., 180
Duffield, Michael, 210
Dukes, Ashley, 202
Dyall, Franklin (Frank), 138, 139, 144, 196
Dyas, Ada, 49, 51, 54, 55

EADIE, Dennis, 157
Eccles, Jane, 208, 209
Edginton, May, 196
Ediss, Connie, 15
Edward VII (as Prince of Wales), 57–8, 59, 77
Edward VIII, 220, 224–5
Edwardes, George, 15, 66, 93, 94–5
Edwards, Sutherland, 60, 89
Egerton, George, 184
Eilenberg, R., 151
Eliot, George, 53–4
Elizabeth II, 217
Elliot, W. G., 136, 138
Ellis, Walter, 199
Elliston, R. W., 35
Emerson, Ralph Waldo, 111
Emery, Winifred, 103, 127
Ervine, St. John, 212
Esmond, Annie, 203
Esmond, H. V., 136, 138, 142, 147, 149, 150, 151, 159, 203
Evans, Dame Edith, 196, 201
Evans, Mrs. (Housekeeper), 169, 220, 230
Ewell, C., 103

FABER, Beryl, 173, 174
Faber, Leslie, 198
Fagan, J. B., 182
Fahrbach, Herr, 151
Fairfax, Lettice, 182
Fargueil, Anaïs, 62
Farren, Nellie, 70
Farren, William, 59, 60, 61, 67, 165
Fauchois, René, 201
Faversham, Mrs. William (*see* Opp, Julie)
Fawcett, Marion, 208, 209
Fawcitt, Anthony, 173
Fawsitt, Amy, 69
Featherstone, F., 143
Fenn, Frederick, 165
Fenston, F. D., 212, 215
Fernandez, James, 147, 148
Ferrar, Ada, 160

Ferrers, Helen, 185, 187
Fielding, Marjorie, 201
Fields, Gracie, 199
Fife, Duchess of (Princess Royal), 90, 169
Fife, Duke of, 89
Finck, Herman, 108
Fisher, Bill, 220–1
Fitzgerald, Percy, 106
Fitzgerald, Walter, 199
Fletcher, Guy, 198
Fontaine, Robert, 207
Foote, Lydia, 59, 62
Foote, Samuel, 12, 15
Forbes, Norman, 96, 176, 187
Forbes-Robertson, Jean, 200
Forbes-Robertson, Sir Johnstone, 178–80
Forman, Justus Miles, 165
Forrester, C. W., 64, 201
Foulis, William, 102
Fournier, M., 61
Frederick, Crown Prince (of Prussia), 58
Frith, Walter, 117, 124, 157
Fry, Christopher, 206
Fulton, Charles, 162

GAINSBOROUGH, Thomas, 15
Gallifret, Marquis and Marquise de, 58
Galsworthy, John, 183
Garrick, David, 12, 19, 37, 38, 102
Gattis, The, 107, 130
George V, 181
Gilbert, W. S., 11, 12, 15, 31, 53–4, 61, 62, 70, 92, 93, 95–7, 103, 115
Giles & Co., F., 114
Gill, Basil, 194–5
Gillette, William, 86
Gladwell, F. W., 156, 173
Glenney, Charles, 143, 188
Glossop, Miss, 29
Glover, Mrs., 35
Glynne, Mary, 188
Goddard, R. E., 160
Goddard, Ruth, 207
Godfrey, G. W., 74, 76
Godfrey, Michael, 207
Goethe, J. W. von, 42
Goldney, Philip, 73
Goldsmid, Mr., 20
Goldsmith, Frank, 176
Goldsmith, Oliver, 59
Gomer, Geoffrey, 205
Gordon, Marjorie, 191
Gordon, Max, 198
Gordon & Harford, Messrs., 76
Gordon-Lennox, Cosmo, 175
Gough, Michael, 204
Gould, Nutcombe, 96, 109, 110, 112, 118, 120, 131
Graham, Cissie, 73, 74
Grantley & Co., 192
Grattan, Henry, 107
Graves, Laura, 120
Gray, Gladys, 198
Grayson, Denys, 196
Greet, Ben, 148
Gregory, Dora, 193
Gregson, John, 210, 213, 227
Grey, Earl, 184
Griffiths, Jane, 210
Grimston, W. H. (*see* Kendal, W. H.)
Grossmith, George, 15
Grove, Sir George, 22
Groves, Charles, 178
Grundy, Sydney, 89, 93, 101, 158, 165
Guitry, Lucien, 54
Guitry, Sacha, 205
Guthrie, Tyrone, 206

HACKNEY, Mabel, 143, 149, 176
Haines, Ernest, 199
Handel, George Frederick, 23
Halévy, Ludovic, 58
Hall, H. B., 117
Hallatt, May, 208, 209
Halstan, Margaret, 160
Hamilton, Cosmo, 159
Hamilton, George, 194, 195

Hamilton, Henry, 118
Hamilton, Lady, 23
Hamilton, Patrick, 203
Hammond, Kay, 208
Hampton, Louise, 201
Hanbury, Hilda, 121
Hanbury, Lily, 120, 121, 127, 144, 145, 148
Hannay, Barbara, 185
Hannen, Nicholas, 185
Harben, Joan, 202, 225
Harding, Lyn, 196–7
Hardwicke, Sir Cedric, 201
Hardy, Thomas, 84–5
HARE, Sir John
early career, 65; with the Bancrofts (1865–74), 65–8; in *Caste*, 66; in *The School for Scandal*, 67–8; at Royal Court, 68–70; in partnership with the Kendals, 68–9, 92; takes over St. James's (1879), 71, 72; at St. James's (1879–88), 72–91; farewell speech, 91; at Garrick, 92; refuses *The Second Mrs. Tanqueray*, 125; passing references, 103, 126, 148, 152, 153, 206, 216
Harley, John P., 31, 32, 33, 41
Harris, Sir Augustus, 12, 15, 114
Harris, Sybil, 196
Hartleben, Erich, 165
Hastings, Basil Macdonald, 198
Hathorn, M., 131
Hawkins, Anthony H. (*see* Hope, Anthony)
Hawkins, Iris, 171, 173
Hawtrey, Charles, 15, 153, 178, 191, 196
Hawtrey, George P., 144, 147
Haye, Helen, 207, 220, 224
Hayes, Samuel, 64
Hedley, Jack, 210
Helmsley, Capt. C. T. H., 164, 230
Heltai, Eugen, 202
Hendrie, Ernest, 89, 166
Henri, Alfred, 203
Henson, Basil, 208
Herbert, Louisa, 44, 45, 47, 49, 50, 56
Heron, Joyce, 207
Heron-Maxwell, Beatrice, 166
Hewitt, Henry C., 194
Heys, Edwin, 187
Hichens, Robert, 182
Hicks, Sir Seymour, 15, 71, 130
Highett, H. H., 160, 165
Hill, Caroline, 94
Hill, William J., 61, 62
Hinton, Olive, 202
Hobbes, John Oliver (Mrs. Pearl Craigie), 151–2, 158
Hodson, Henrietta, 62
Holles, Alfred, 109, 110, 117, 131
Hollingshead, John, 32
Holmes, Robert, 201
Honey, George, 66
Honey, Mrs., 30, 33, 35
Hook, Theodore, 37–8
Hooper, Edward, 135
Hope, Anthony (real name, A. H. Hawkins), 142, 143, 147, 155
Hopkins, Charles, 200
Hopwood, Avery, 197
Horne, Rev. Sylvester, 176
Horton, Priscilla, 29
Horton, Robert, 173
Houston, Jack, 229
Howard, Cecil, 117
Howard, Leslie, 219
Howe, J. B., 103
Hullah, John, 30, 31
Hunter, Ian, 207
Huntingdon, Hartford, 214
Hutchinson, A. S. M., 197
Hutton, Michael Clayton, 201
Hyson, Dorothy, 202

IBSEN, Henrik, 125, 126, 183
Illing, Peter, 207
Ireland, Anthony, 207
Irving, Ethel, 182, 197

Irving, Sir Henry, 14, 16, 45, 51–3, 54, 55, 56, 63, 73, 74, 77, 80, 94, 99, 102–6, 108, 123, 124, 134, 148, 153, 166, 167, 178, 216
Irving, H. B., 106, 147, 148, 149, 150, 151, 157, 159
Irving, Laurence, 53, 54, 104
Isola, Signor, 22
Ivor, Frances, 185

JACKSON, Blomfield, 154
Jacob, Naomi, 199
James, David, 103
James, Henry, 137–9
Jay, Isabel, 15
Jeayes, Allan, 197
Jeffreys, Ellis, 142, 198
Jerome, Gerald, 173
Jerome, Helen, 202
Jerome, Jerome K., 178
Jerrold, Douglas, 77, 78, 79
Jerrold, Mary, 151, 204
Johnson, Celia, 202
Johnstone, Mr. (tenor, 18th cent.), 22
Jones, Henry Arthur, 136–7, 141, 181, 231
Jones, Sidney, 15
Jordan, Dorothy, 27
Jordan, Mrs. M., 222
Jordan, R., 224
Josephs, Fanny, 50
Josephs, Pattie, 45
Judith, Mlle., 41

KEAN, Charles, 41, 63
Kean, Edmund, 12, 38, 195
Keane, Arthur, 195
Kelly, Renée, 191
Kemble, Henry, 69, 81–2
Kemp-Welch, Joan, 203
KENDAL, Dame Madge (*née* Margaret Robertson) (*see also* KENDAL, Mr. and Mrs.; ST. JAMES'S)
her autobiography, 68–9; birthplace, 70; early career, 70; first London rôle (Ophelia), 70; as Desdemona (1865), 70; at Drury Lane (1867), 70; leading lady at Gaiety (1868), 70; at Haymarket, 70, 71; marriage (1869), 71; as actress-manageress, 71, 73; respectability, 71, 73; on social life of actors, 85–6; on George Alexander, 86; welcomes Mrs. Herman Vezin, 87–8; as Rosalind, 87–8; accident and recovery, 89–90; her husband's death (1917), 92; dies (1935), 92
KENDAL, Mr. and Mrs. (*see also* ST. JAMES'S)
discusses partnership with Hare, 68–9; at Royal Court Theatre, 68–70; with the Bancrofts, 72; take over St. James's (1879), 71; visit Tennyson, 76; in plays at St. James's, 72–91; farewell banquet, 92; American tour, 92; return seasons at St. James's, 151–2, 159, 166, 222; visit St. James's, 158; passing references, 65, 103, 110, 116, 160, 206, 216
KENDAL, W. H. (real name, Grimston) at Haymarket, 71; marriage, 71; farewell speech at St. James's, 91; letter to Alexander (re Staff), 152–3; death, 92
Kent, Duchess of, 41
Kent, Kenneth, 219
Kerridge, Mary, 207
Kimmins, Verena, 207
King, Thomas, 68
Kingston, Gertrude, 112, 116, 118, 159
Kistemakers, Henry, 182
Knight, Joseph, 122
Knight, Judy, 220
Krasna, Norman, 204

LACY, Walter, 35, 51, 53, 54
Lamb, Charles, 23, 24
Lambelet, Napoleon, 191
Lane, Grace, 159, 178, 198
Lang, Matheson, 161, 175, 186
Langtry, Lily, 97

Lankester, S. G. (real name Robert Reece), 102
Laughton, Charles, 201
Lavenu, Miss, 49
Lawrence, Gerald, 148
Lawton, Frank, 198, 208
Leaf, Son & Co., 99, 100
Leclercq, Carlotta, 107
Leclercq, Rose, 139, 140, 149
Lee, Auriol, 162
Lee, Leoni, 20
Legge, R., 151
Leicester, Ernest, 165
Leigh, Vivien, 202, 206, 212–13, 216
Leighton, Margaret, 208, 209
Leister, Frederick, 201
Lemaître, Frédérick, 41
Leoni (*see* Lee, Leoni)
Leroy, Louis, 41
Leutner, Herr, 151
Leverett, Henrietta, 165
Lewes, George Henry, 42, 53–4
Lewes, Miriam, 188
Lewis, Albert, 198
Lewis, Alwyn, 111
Lewis, Eric, 178
Lewis, Martin, 165
Lind, Letty, 15
Linden, Marie, 107
Lisle, Lucille, 201
Lister, Francis, 205
Litchfield, Frederick, 114
Littler, Prince, 204, 212
Litton, Marie, 61, 62
Liverpool Repertory Company, 205
Loder, Basil, 198
Loder, Edward, 43
Loewe & Co., 229
Löhr, Marie, 92, 159, 185, 200
Lomnitz, F., 144
London County Council, 176, 191, 211
Lonsdale, Frederick, 198, 204
Loraine, Henry, 143, 147
Loraine, Robert, 144, 147, 148, 150, 197
Lord Chamberlain, The, 59, 61, 140
Louis XI (of France), 162
Lowne, C. M., 173, 174, 180
Lucas, Hippolyte, 42
Ludlow, Patrick, 196
Ludwig II (of Bavaria), 58
Lugg, William, 188
Luis I (of Portugal), 58
Lyel, Viola, 202, 225
Lynn, Ralph, 15
Lyon, H. S., & Co., 154

MACARTHUR, James, 166
MacDougal, Duncan, 99, 100
Macdougall, Roger, 207
Macewan, Norman, 185
Machen, Arthur, 160
Mackay, Ogilvie, 223
Mackenzie, Sir Compton, 178
Mackinlay, Jean, 162
Mackintosh, William, 73, 76, 85, 89, 90
Maclaren, Ian, 166
Macquoid, Percy, 154
Macready, W. C., 38, 42
Maeterlinck, Maurice, 183
Malibran, Madame, 38, 39
Mallé, J. Leonard, 220–1
Malleson, Miles, 197
Malnik, Michael, 207
Manchester, Duke and Duchess of, 58
Mandel, Frank, 196
Manners, J. Hartley, 185
Mantell, Denis, 199
Marais, Léon H., 62
March, Nadine, 201
Marsden, Betty, 205
Marshall, Herbert, 200
Marston, Henry, 59
Martin-Harvey, (Sir) John, 103, 178
Masefield, Sir John, 183
Mason, A. E. W., 176, 180, 181, 183, 199
Mason, John, 113
Massey, Raymond, 201
Mather, Aubrey, 208
Mathews, Charles, 35, 41, 50
Mathews, Mrs. Charles, 50

Mathews, Helen, 103
Matthews, A. E., 159, 204
Matthews, Douglas, 202
Matthews, Frank, 35, 44, 45, 49, 50, 51, 53, 61
Matthews, Mrs. Frank, 35, 44, 45, 49, 50, 51, 53, 61
Maude, Cyril, 14, 60, 98, 129–30, 131, 132, 153
Maurette, Marcelle, 287
Mayer, Daniel (Co.), 200
Maynard, Walter, 76
McCallum, John, 208
McCarthy, Justin Huntley, 162
McCarthy, Lillah, 183
McDermott, Hugh, 204
McGrath, Lueen, 225
McLean, Joan, 197
McMinnies, Donald, 229
Measor, Beryl, 208, 209
Mellish, Fuller, 89
Melvill, Henry, 166
Mensiaux, Marie de, 104
Merivale, Herman, 62
Merrall, Mary, 203
Merriman, Percy, 221–2
Merritt, Anna Lee, 77
Meyer, Louis, 97
Meyer-Forster, Wilhelm, 164
Michael, Ralph, 207
Michaeleis, Mme., 40
Middleton, George, 196
Millar, Gertie, 15
Millar, Ronald, 208
Millard, Evelyn, 138, 139, 142, 143, 144, 145, 160, 161, 221–2
Miller, Gilbert Heron, 176–7, 181, 186, 190–200, 201, 202, 204, 205, 212, 215, 229
Miller, Henry, 176–7
Miller, Keith, 202
Millett, Colonel Ley, 116
Millett, Maude, 109, 110, 112, 116–7, 129, 131
Mills, Clifford, 186
Mills, John, 206
Milne, A. A., 200
Milton, Ernest, 193, 194
Milward, Dawson, 173, 174–5, 198
Mitchell, William, 40–42
Moeller, Philip, 200
Molesworth, Ida, 150
Molière, Jean-Baptiste, 183
Mollison, William, 166
Molnar, Ferenc, 199, 200, 204
Moltke, General von, 58
Monckton, Lady, 112
Monkman, Dorothy, 199
Montague, H. J., 50
Montgomery, Walter, 70
Moon, Ena, 202
Moore, Eva, 159, 165, 197
Moore, Hilda, 186, 187
Morgan, Priscilla, 208, 209
Morlay, Henry, 45, 49, 55
Morrell, Henry, 194, 195
Morris, Phyllis, 203
Munro, A. 147
Murray, Douglas, 196
Murray, Gaston, 49, 53, 59, 60
Murray, Mrs. Gaston, 73, 76, 84, 88, 89, 90, 96
Murray, Mrs. (Staff), 230

NAPOLEON I, 54
Napoleon III, 57
Nares, Owen, 165, 182, 198
Nathan, H. & L., 117
Neagle, Anna, 204
Neal, Phyllis, 188
Neilson, Ada, 109, 110
Neilson, Julia, 96, 121, 127, 147, 148, 149, 150, 184, 188
Neilson-Terry, Dennis, 188
Neilson-Terry, Phyllis, 184, 188, 208, 209
Nerot's Hostelry, 25
Nesbitt, Cathleen, 199
Nethersole, Olga, 94, 95, 126
Neville, Henry, 115
Newton, Richard, 203

Nicholson, Olga, 182
Norman, Mr., 49
Norreys, Rose, 96
North, Colonel, 94
Novello, Ivor, 145
Nyitray, Emile, 196

O'BRIEN, Harry, 219
O'Doherty, Mignon, 199
O'Malley, Ellen, 186
Oakshott, Mrs. Carmen D. (*see* Woods, Carmen)
Odets, Clifford, 202, 207
Offenbach, Jacques, 57
Olivier, Sir Laurence, 205–8
Olivier, Lady (*see* Leigh, Vivien)
Opp, Julie, 147, 149, 157, 162
Oppenheim, M., 54
Orme, Michael, 184
Orr, Mary, 207
Oscar, Henry, 188, 194, 196
"Ouida," 55
Owen, Reginald, 165, 185
Oxenford, John, 55

PARISH, James, 204
Parker, Louis N., 165, 187
Parry, John, 33
Passmore, S. J., 212
Pateman, Bella, 173, 174
Paterson, E. H., 198
Patti, Adelina, 23
Pauncefort, Claire, 103, 165
Pawle, Lennox, 159, 188
Payne, Edmund, 15
Payne, Laurence, 207
Pearson, Hesketh, 185
Peile, Kinsey, 139
Percy, Edward, 203
Perlet, M., 41
Pertwee, Ronald, 198, 200
Pettitt, Henry, 106
Phelps, Samuel, 63
Phillips, F. C., 93
Phillips, Kate, 73, 76, 84, 147
Phillips, Stephen, 160
Phillips, Watts, 59
Phipps, Rashleigh, 154
Piccadilly and St. James's Association, 216
Pinero, Arthur Wing, 79, 80–5, 88, 89, 90, 121, 125–33, 135, 136, 149–50, 155, 170–5, 176, 180, 183, 185, 186, 231
Pinero, Mrs. J. D. (*née* Emily Daines), 80
Pinero, John Daniel, 80
Pirandello, Luigi, 208
Planché, J. R., 44, 61
Playfair, Nigel, 173, 185, 186
Plessis, Mlle., 30, 41
Poeck, Herr, 40
Pope, Alexander, 52
Portman, Eric, 208, 209
Portugal, King of (Luis I), 58
Potter, Paul M., 150
Powys, Stephen, 205
Princess Royal (*see* Duchess of Fife)
Pringle, Lemprière, 160
Prinsep, Val, 75
Printemps, Yvonne, 224
Provins, M., 180
Prussia, Crown Prince Frederick of, 58
Prussia, King William of, 58
Pryce, Richard, 165
PUBLIC EVENTS
  Wars of the Roses, 146
  Napoleonic Wars, 23, 184
  Queen Victoria's Marriage, 39
  Queen Victoria's Jubilee, 230–1
  Boer War, 116, 156
  Coronation of George V, 181
  Suffragettes, 181, 222–3
  First World War, 184–7, 190, 223
  Abdication of Edward VIII, 220, 224–5
  Second World War, 203–4, 210, 224

QUARTERMAINE, Léon, 187, 202

Queensberry, Lord, 141
Quin, James, 15, 52
Quinn, Mrs. (Housekeeper), 225, 230
Quinton, Mark, 118

RACHEL, Mme., 21, 42, 43, 216
Raine, Patricia, 208
Rainforth, Miss, 33
Rains, Claude, 193, 194, 197
Raleigh, Cecil, 112, 118
Rattigan, Terence, 202, 205, 208
Rauzzini, Venenzio, 21
Rawlings, Margaret, 202
Raymond, Cyril, 201
Rayson-Cousens, E., 188
Rea, Alec, 205
Read, Mark, 202
Reade, Charles, 42
Reandco, 200, 201
Redgrave, Michael, 203, 207
Redman, Martha, 184
Redmond, Liam, 210
Reece, Robert (*see* S. G. Lankester)
Reeve, Ada, 205
Reinhart, Mary Roberts, 197
Réjane, Mme., 54
Relph, George, 197
Renaud, Madeleine, 206
Reynolds, E. Vivian, 162, 165, 173, 180, 184, 188
Reynolds, Sir Joshua, 15
Reynolds, Robert (Bob), 155
Richards, Susan, 207
Richardson, Ralph, 202
Righton, Edward, 123
Ristori, Mme., 43, 51
Roberts, Evelyn, 202
Roberts, George, 45, 55
Roberts, Morley, 187
Robertson, Thomas W., 55, 60, 65, 66, 69, 70, 72, 84
Robertson, Thomas (Junr.), 102, 116
Robins, Elizabeth, 107, 129, 160
Robins, J., 44
Robins, William, 151
Robson, E. M., 178
Romer, Frank, 40
Rose, Edward, 142, 143, 145, 153
Rose, Howard, 194
Roselle, Amy, 129, 131
Rosmer, Milton, 194, 195
Ross, Hector, 205
Rosse, Lord, 212
Rous, Helen, 180, 186
Rowley, Mr., 76
Royal Hospital for Consumption, 100
Royston, Arthur, 143, 147
Rubens, Paul, 15
Ruggieri, Ruggero, 207
Russia, Czar Alexander II of, 58
Russia, Czarina Maria of, 59
Russia, Tsarievitch Vladimir of, 58
Rutty, Herbert W. (*see* Waring, Herbert)

S. J. & L. Ltd., 202, 212, 215
ST. JAMES'S
General: Audiences, 16, 121–2, 155–6, 158, 168, 219, 221, 228–9; Building (description), 28, 227; Building (redecorations and enlargements), 30, 74, 111, 154, 191; Environs, 16, 19, 25, 50, 227; Ghost, 225; Organisation, 134, 170, 192, 219, 220; Programmes, 75, 157, 182, 187, 197; Staff, 111, 134, 151, 152–3, 168–9, 214, 220, 224, 228–30; Tickets and Prices, 17, 28, 43, 111, 169, 182
Foreign Plays: French, 1836, 30; 1839, 38; 1841–53, 41; 1868, 57–9; 1869, 59; 1951, 206; 1953, 207: German, 1840, 39–40; 1852, 42: Italian, 1858, 43; 1953, 207
History:
Braham (1835–38): site purchased, 25; building costs, 25; advertisement circular, 28–9; opening date, 28; first season, 29–30; second season, 30–2; third season, 32–3; Braham's bankruptcy, 34;

Braham's Concert appearance, 34–5; known as "Braham's Folly", 61, 91, 154
Interregnum (1839–79): Hooper (1839), 35; Bunn (1839), 38–40; called Prince's Theatre, 39, 40; Barnett (1840), 40; Mitchell (1841–52), 40–2; Barnum (1851) (sub-let), 42; Mrs. Seymour (1854), 42, 51; Ristori (1858), 43, 51; Chatterton (1858–60), 43; Wigan (1860), 44; Vining (1861), 44; Matthews (1862), 44–50, *Lady Audley's Secret*, 45–9; Webster (1864), 50; Miss Herbert (1866–69), 50–6; John S. Clarke (1867), (sub-let); 55–6 Schneider (1868), 57–9; Mlle. de la Ferté (1868–9), 59; Mrs. John Wood (1869–70), 59–61; Miss Litton (1875), 61; Wigan (1876), 62; Mrs. John Wood (1877), 62; Hayes (1878), 64
Hare and the Kendals (1879–88), 65, 72–92; Opening play, *The Queen's Shilling*, 73–6; First Pinero play, *The Money-Spinner* (1881), 81–4; *The Falcon* (Tennyson), 76–7; *William and Susan*, 76–9; *The Squire* (Pinero), 84–5; *Young Folks' Ways* (Alexander's first rôle at St. James's, 1883), 86–7; *As You Like It*, 87–8; Farewell performance (*The Squire*), (1888), 90
Interregnum (1888–9): Rutland Barrington, 93–7; Mrs. Langtry, 97; Arthur Bourchier, 97; Louis Meyer, 97
George Alexander (1890–1918), 109–189: First play, *Sunlight and Shadow* (1890), 109–11; *The Idler* (1891), 111–4; *Lady Windermere's Fan* (1892), 119–22; *Liberty Hall* (Dec. 1892), 122–3, Command Performance, 123, 141; *The Second Mrs. Tanqueray* (1893), 125–33; *Guy Domville* (1895), 137–9; *The Importance of Being Earnest* (1895), 139–41; *The Prisoner of Zenda* (1896), 142–7; *As You Like It* (Dec. 1896), 147–8; *Much Ado About Nothing* (1897), 149–50; *The Ambassador* (1898), 150–1; *Rupert of Hentzau* (1900), 155–7; *Paolo and Francesca* (1902), 160–1; *If I Were King* (1902), 162–3; *Old Heidelberg* (1903), 164–5; *His House in Order* (1906), 171–5; (Forbes-Robertson, sub-lease) *The Passing of the Third Floor Back* (1908), 178–80; *The Aristocrat* (1917), 187–9
Gilbert Miller (afterwards, S. J. & L.) with sub-leases as noted (1920–1957), 192–209; *Julius Caesar* (1920) (Miller and Ainley), 193–5; *The Rat* (1922), 197; *The Green Goddess* (1923), 198; *The Late Christopher Bean* (1933), 201; *The Shining Hour* (1934) (Gladys Cooper and Raymond Massey), 201; *Pride and Prejudice* (1936), 202; *Black Limelight* (1937), 202; *A Month in the Country* (Bronson Albery and Tennent Plays, Ltd.), 203; *The Wind of Heaven* (1945), 204; *Don't Listen, Ladies* (1948) (Clift and Rea), 205; *Venus Observed* (1950) (Laurence Olivier), 206; *Caesar and Cleopatra* and *Antony and Cleopatra* (1951) (Olivier), 206; *Escapade* (1953), 207; *Anastasia* (1953) (Olivier), 208; *Separate Tables* (1954), 208–9; Last play—*It's the Geography that Counts* (1957), 210
Demolition: war damage, 204, 210; rumour of closing, 209, 210; Press controversy, 210, 212; statement by Minister of Housing, 211; Vivien Leigh's campaign,

ST. JAMES'S: *Demolition*—cont.
212–213; questions asked in Parliament, 214; financial statement, 215; demolition began, 216
St. Paul's, Dean of, 106
Saker, Mrs. Edward, 138
Sala, George Augustus, 31
Sala, Mrs., 31
Salter, Major Beauchamp, 183
Salvini, Anton M., 54
Samson, George Alexander Gibb (*see* Alexander, Sir George)
Samson, Mr., 98
Samson, Mrs., 98
Sandys, Duncan (Minister for Housing), 211–2
Sardou, Victorien, 44, 60, 72, 88
Sass, Edward, 94
Schérer, M., 54
Schmerzer, Herr, 40
Schneider, Hortense, 57–59, 191
Schumann, Herr, 39, 40
Schwarzbock, Mme., 40
Scofield, Paul, 205
Scott, Clement, 84, 85, 87, 90, 94–5, 96, 103, 111, 115, 121, 138, 158
Scott, Sir Walter, 24
Scott-Gatty, A., 197, 199
Sealby, Mabel, 198
Selby, Mrs., 28
Seyler, Athene, 184, 193, 196
Seymour, Mrs., 42
Shakespeare, William, 42, 43, 47, 87, 147, 149–50, 166, 193, 194, 203, 206
Shaw, George Bernard, 125, 166, 176, 183, 206
Sheffield Repertory Company, 205
Sheldon, Suzanne, 162, 178
Shelton, George, 149, 223
Shelton, Laurence, 223
Shepley, Michael, 203
Sheraton, Thomas, 15
Sherek, Henry, 204
Sheridan, R. B., 32
Sherry, Gordon, 202
Shipman, Louis Evan, 181
Shone, Robert V., 111, 151
Sickert, Leonard, 194
Siddons, Sarah, 12, 186
Silkin, Lord, 214
Simpson, Mr., 49
Simpson, Palgrave, 44, 50, 62, 64
Sims, Albert, 89
Sims, George H., 106, 128, 157
Slade, Olga, 203
Slaughter, Walter, 111
Smith, C. Aubrey, 147, 148, 149, 151, 157, 191, 196
Society for Theatre Research, 212
Somerset, C. W., 89
Sothern, Edward, 142
South Kensington Museum, 154
Sowerby, Githa, 189
Spencer, Helen, 198
Spicer, Henry, 42
Spindler, Herr, 151
Squire, Ronald, 198, 203
Stack, William, 188
Staveley, W. R., 188
Stayton, Frank, 196
Steerman, A. Harding, 198
Stephens, Mrs., 61
Stephens, W. H., 44
Stephens, Yorke, 109, 110
Stephenson, B. C., 85
Sternheim, Carl, 202
Sternroyd, Vincent, 143, 147
Stewart, Athol, 182
Stewart, Sophie, 207
Stirling, Arthur, 45, 49
Stirling, Erik, 180
Stirling, Mrs., 33, 50
Storace, Anna (Nancy), 21, 22
Storace, Stephen, 21
Storey, Gladys, 184
Stratton, John, 210
Stuart, Otho, 193
Sullivan, Arthur, 11, 12, 15, 31, 62, 93, 95
Sullivan, Barry, 42
Sutro, Alfred, 166, 175, 176, 183, 184
Swanborough, Ada, 101

Sweden, King of (Charles XII), 58
Swete, E. Lyall, 160, 162, 165, 173, 174
Swinburne, Mercia, 196
Swinburne, Nora, 197, 199
Swinley, Tom, 193

TACCHNARDI, Niccolò, 21
Taglioni, Signora, 38
Tandy, Jessica, 202
Taylor, Laurette, 185
Taylor, Miss, 230
Taylor, Mr., 49
Taylor, Samuel, 207
Taylor, Tom, 42, 44
Taylor, Valerie, 203
Tearle, Godfrey, 182, 183
Telbin, H., 154
Tempest, Dame Marie, 15, 71, 159, 201
Tennent Plays, Ltd., 203, 204
Tennyson, Alfred (Lord), 76
Terriss, Ellaline, 15, 74, 121
Terriss, William, 12, 15, 73, 74, 75, 76, 103, 104, 107
Terry, Ellen, 44, 69, 92, 104, 115
Terry, Florence, 115
Terry, Fred, 107, 149, 150, 188
Terry, Kate, 44, 115
Terry, Marion, 109, 110, 112, 113, 114–5, 117, 118, 120, 138, 182, 193
Thackeray, W. M., 39
Theatre Guild of New York, 200
Theatre Tickets and Messengers, Ltd., 40
Theatres, "Atmosphere" of, 13, 15–16, 227
THEATRES (including Concert Rooms, Variety Theatres, etc.):
London: Adelphi, 11, 12, 15, 33, 43, 50, 74, 94, 106–7, 116, 127–8, 130, 227; Aldwych, 15, 16; Almack's, 26; Ambassadors, 202; Avenue, 107–8, 109; Belgravia (*see* Royal Court); Colosseum (Regent's Park), 25; Comedy, 15, 185; Court (*see* Royal Court); Covent Garden, 11, 12, 20, 22, 27, 29, 227; Criterion, 14, 120, 148, 227; Crystal Palace, 64; Daly's, 11, 15; Drury Lane, 11, 12, 15, 21, 27, 29, 35, 36, 41, 42, 43, 60, 70, 114, 118, 166, 189, 193, 227; Duke of York's, 191, 193, 202; Gaiety, 11, 14, 15, 70, 95; Garrick (Charing Cross Road), 14, 16, 92, 125, 171, 191; Garrick (Leman Street), 20; Globe, 80, 85, 185, 191; Goodman's Fields, 19; Grand (Islington), 194; Haymarket, 11, 12, 14, 16, 26, 42, 43, 50, 70, 80, 98, 112, 115, 116, 121, 134, 153, 184, 198, 225, 227; Haymarket (Little Theatre), 11, 15; Her (His) Majesty's), 11, 12, 14, 16, 41, 68, 98, 160, 193, 227; King's, 26, 27, 41; Kingsway, 193; Imperial, 116; Little, 116, 196; Lyceum, 12, 14, 16, 25, 80, 83, 98, 102, 103, 104, 108, 189; Marylebone, 70; Mirror (Holborn), 62; New, 12, 14, 16, 62; New Chelsea (*see* Royal Court); Novelty, 116; Old Vic, 227; Olympic, 44, 115; Opéra Comique, 138; Palace, 183; Park (Camden Town), 116; Playhouse, 107; Prince of Wales's, 15, 62–8, 196, 229, 250; Prince's, 191 (*see also* under ST. JAMES'S); Princess's, 44, 51, 59, 60, 63, 90; "Q", 202; Royal Court, 61, 68, 69–70, 73, 89, 94, 121, 166, 193; Royal Italian Opera House, 26; Royal Strand, 33, 51, 115; Royalty (Dean Street), 196; Royalty (Wellclose Square), 20; Sadlers Wells, 20, 63; Savoy, 11, 12, 15, 93, 191; St. James's (*see* detailed index); St. Martin's, 12; Standard, Shoreditch, 102; Standard, Pimlico, 220; Strand, 191; Surrey, 59; Terry's, 180; Vaudeville, 15, 103, 121; Victoria Palace, 220; Waldorf, 191; Wyndham's, 12, 15, 16, 171

THEATRES—cont.
Provinces: Bath, Theatre Royal, 20; Bristol, Prince's, 70, Theatre Royal, 227; Edinburgh, Theatre Royal, 80; Liverpool, Alexandra, 80; Manchester, Prince's, 82; Theatre Royal, 115; Margate, Theatre Royal, 116; Nottingham, Theatre Royal, 102
Abroad: Paris: Comédie Française (Company), 207; Théâtre Historique, 41; Théâtre des Variétés, 57: U.S.A.: Henry Miller Theatre, 177; St. James's, New York, 214
Theleur, Florence (*see* Alexander, Mrs. George)
Thesiger, Ernest, 165, 197
Thomas, Augustus, 166
Thomas, Brandon, 73, 74
Thomas, Herbert, 196
Thompson, Lydia, 42, 43, 44
Thorndike, Dame Sybil, 196, 202
Thorne, Sarah, 116
Thorne, Thomas, 103, 121
Thorold, W. J., 166
Thurston, E. Temple, 166
Thurston, K. Temple, 166
Titheradge, G. S., 64
Titheradge, Madge, 198
Toller, Rosalie, 180
Tolstoi, Leon, 193
Toole, J. L., 32, 42, 44, 216
Tree, Sir Herbert Beerbohm, 12, 14, 68, 92, 98, 104–5, 112, 116, 121, 124, 134, 153, 160, 167, 178, 195
Tree, Mrs. Beerbohm (Lady Tree), 89, 90, 127, 159, 202
Trevelyan, Hilda, 165
Turgeniev, Ivan S., 203
Turner, Godfrey, 106
Turpin, Miss, 35
Tyrrell, Geoffrey, 207

VACHELL, Horace Annesley, 185
Van Ambergh, Isaac, 36
Van Druten, John, 201
Vanbrugh, Dame Irene, 136, 137, 138, 139, 140, 173, 175, 176, 186, 219, 220
Vanbrugh, Violet, 151
Vanderhoff, George, 42
Vanderhoff, Miss, 42
Vane-Tempest, F. A., 120, 131, 136
Vara, Sil, 199
Vedrenne, J. E., 193
Venning, Una, 199
Verneuil, Louis, 196
Vernon, W. H., 101, 142, 143, 144, 145, 147, 149
Vertpré, Jenny, 30
Vestris, Eliza, 41
Vezin, Herman, 61, 62, 63, 68, 69, 87, 128
Vezin, Mrs. Herman, 59, 60, 63, 87
Viarex Property Investment Co., 212
Victoria, Queen, 36, 39, 41, 59, 73, 222
Victorians, The, 46, 178
Villon, François, 162–3
Vincent, H. H., 120, 139, 142, 147, 151
Vine, Stanley, 195
Vining, George, 44
Vining, Mrs. Henry, 59
Vladimir, Tsarievitch (of Russia), 58, 59
Vokes Family, 43
Vollmoeller, Karl, 183
Volpe, Frederick, 185, 198
Vosper, Frank, 199

WAGNER, Richard, 151
Wakefield, Gilbert, 201
Wakefield, Hugh, 207
Waldegrave, Lady (*see* Braham, Frances)
Walker, Emblin, 154
Walkley, A. B., 122, 149
Waller, Lewis, 15, 94, 95, 96, 178, 195
Wallis, Bertram, 147, 148 ,150
Walls, Tom, 15
Wanamaker, Sam, 207
Ward, Geneviève, 186, 188

Waring, Herbert (real name, H. W. Rutty), 85, 87, 88, 89, 90, 112–3, 115–6, 117, 118, 136, 138, 142, 143, 144, 145, 173, 184, 219
Warner, Charles, 62–3
Watson, Henrietta, 159, 184, 185
Watson, Margaret, 203
Webb, Mrs., 220
Weber, Carl Maria, 23
Webster, Benjamin (Senr.), 41, 50, 87
Webster, Benjamin (Junr.), 107, 109, 110, 117, 118, 120, 130, 131, 185
Webster, J., 32
Webster, Miss, 87
Weguelin, Thomas, 165, 180
Welles, Orson, 206
Wellington, Duke of, 26, 84
Wenman, T. N., 76
Westby & Co., 192, 230
Westminster, Dean of, 106
Weyman, Stanley, 153
Whalley, Norma, 182
Wheeler, J., 147
Whitaker, Mr., 230
White, D. T., 154
Whitty, Dame May, 110, 198
Wiers, Jensen H., 183
Wigan, Alfred, 32, 35, 44, 50, 51, 62, 67, 70
Wigan, Horace, 44
Wilde, Oscar, 119–22, 139–41, 184, 222, 231
Willard, E. S., 165
William IV, 27, 41, 217
William (of Prussia), 58
Williams, Arthur, 59
Williams, Derek, 201
Williams, Emlyn, 200, 201, 203, 204
Williams, Hugh, 202
Wills, Drusilla, 197
Wills, W. G., 63, 77–9
Wilshin, Sunday, 188
Wilson, Mr., 49
Winter, Keith, 202
Winter, Rex, 201
Withers, Googie, 207, 208
Wodehouse, P. G., 199
Woffington, Peg, 12
Wolff, Albert, 58
Wolff, Humbert, 202
Wolfit, Donald, 203
Wolseley, Sir Garnet (Lord), 78
Wolstenholme, A. M., 228–9
Wontner, Arthur, 185, 197
Wood, Mrs. John, 59–61, 62, 64, 94, 223
Wood, Metcalfe, 166
Woods, Carmen (Mrs. Oakshott), 219–20
Wray, Max, 202
Wrench, Benjamin, 35
Wright, Edward, 32, 33
Wright, Huntley, 15
Wyndham, Sir Charles, 12, 14, 55, 56, 61, 62, 120, 124, 153, 178
Wynyard, Diana, 202, 206

YOUNG, Mrs. Charles (*see* Vezin, Mrs. Herman)
Young, Roland, 204

INDEX OF PLAY AND SONG TITLES

ABOU HASSAN, 43
Actress by Daylight, An (*see* Anne Bracegirdle)
Adrienne Lecouvreur, 41, 43
Adventure Story, 205
After the Dance, 203
Agnes Sorel, 28, 29
Alcestis, 42, 43

All For Her, 62
"All's Well," 22
All This is Ended, 205
Amazons, The, 121
Ambassador, The, 151–2, 158
Amber Heart, The, 104
American, The, 138
Americans, The, 23
Anastasia, 207
Androcles and the Lion, 183
Andromaque, 41
Anglo-Polish Ballet, 203
Anne Bracegirdle (An Actress by Daylight; Tiridate), 61
Antony and Cleopatra, 206
Aristocrat, The, 187–9
Artaxerxes, 33
As You Like It, 87–8, 97, 147–8, 150, 166
Attack, The, 184
Awakening, The, 159

BARNABY RUDGE, 59
Barretts of Wimpole Street, The, 185
Basker, The, 186–7
Bat, The, 197
"Bay of Biscay", 24
Beggars' Opera, The, 30, 39
Behold, We Live, 201
Bella Donna, 182, 187
Belle Sauvage, La (Burlesque), 59
Belle's Stratagem, The, 51–3
Bells, The, 80, 178, 197
Beside the Bonnie Briar Bush, 166, 193
Big Drum, The, 156, 223
Black Domino, The, 128–9
Black-Ey'd Susan, 77, 78
Black Limelight, 202
Bohemian Girl, The, 89
Brantinghame Hall, 95–7
Brighton, 61
Brittanicus, 207
Broken Hearts, 69
Brontës, The, 205
Builder of Bridges, The, 176
But for the Grace of God, 204
Bygones, 80

CAESAR AND CLEOPATRA, 206
Caesar's Wife, 196
Cape Mail, The, 84
Caprice, 199
Captain Carvallo, 206
Captain Swift, 112
Cardinal, The, 165
Carte de Visite, La, 45
Caste, 66, 116
Charles I, 77
Charley's Aunt, 74, 133, 187, 196, 219
Cherry Orchard, The, 205
Clancarty, 90
Clear Case, A, 29
Colonel Smith, 180
Comedy and Tragedy, 103
Conquerors, The, 150–1, 186
Conrad and Medora, 62
Coralie (Le Fils de Coralie), 84

DADDY LONGLEGS, 191
Daisy's Escape, 80
Dancing Barber, The, 62
Dancing Girl, The, 121
Dandy Dick, 89
Daniel, 196
Danischeffs, The, 62, 64
Dan'l Druce, Blacksmith, 115
D'Arcy of the Guards, 181, 186
Dark Cloud, The, 45
David Garrick, 178, 203
Day Before the Day, The, 186
Dead Secret, 207
Dean's Daughter, The, 93
Dear Ruth, 204
"Death of Nelson", 23
Death of Tintagilas, The, 183
Debt of Honour, A, 158
Decree Nisi, The, 165
Dick Hope, 166

"Did You Not Hear of a Jolly Young Waterman?", 29
Diplomacy, 72
Discarded Son, The (*see* The Queen's Shilling)
Divided Way, The, 142
Doctor Bill, 107–8
Doctor's Dilemma, The, 183
Done on Both Sides, 44
Don't Listen, Ladies, 205
Double Image, 222
Dreams, 70
Drink, 63
Duenna, The, 20, 52
Duke in Darkness, The, 203
Dulcamara, 53

ECCENTRIC LORD COMBERDENE, The, 181
Effie Deans (Burlesque of), 49, 50
Eighteenth Century, The, 178
Elder Miss Blossom, The, 152, 222
Elizabetta, 43
Emma, 196, 204
Enfant Prodigue, L', 114
English Fleet in 1342, The, 22
Escapade, 207
Esther Sandraz, 97
Etienne, 201
Euryanthe, 40
Everybody's Friend (*see* The Widow Hunt)

FAINT HEART NEVER WON FAIR LADY, 44
Fair and Warmer, 196
Falcon, The, 76, 77
Fame, 199
Fantastics, The (*see* The Princess and the Butterfly)
Faust, 42, 105
Faust (Burlesque of), 50
Felicity Jasmine, 204
Fernande, 60
Fils de Coralie, Le (*see* Coralie)
Fils de Famille, Le (*see* The Queen's Shilling)
Forgiveness, 118–9
Formosa, 116
Fox Chase, The, 50
Fra Diavolo, 29
Freischütz, Der, 23
French Company, A, 29
Fridolin, 40
Friends or Foes, 44

GARDEN OF LIES, THE, 165
Gay Lord Quex, The, 93
Gay Lothario, The, 111
General John Regan, 121
Ghosts, 125
Glass Slipper, The, 204
Glitter, 59
Golden Boy, The, 202
Golden Hair the Good, 44
Gondoliers, The (*see* The Village Coquettes)
Grand Duchesse de Gérolstein, La, 57–9
Great Adventure, The, 193
Great City, The, 70
Great Pink Pearl, The, 112
Great Sensation Trial, 49
Green Goddess, The, 198
Grounds for Divorce, 198
Guv'nor, The, 102
Guy Domville, 138–9, 140, 141
Guy Mannering, 32, 39, 140

HAMLET, 78, 80, 147, 148, 205
Happy Ending, The, 197
Happy Land, The, 61
Happy Time, The, 207
Harlequinade, The, 183
Heatwave, 200
Henry V, 17, 178, 194
Henry VIII, 194
Herod, 160

His House In Order, 156, 171–5, 176, 185, 220
His Lady Friends, 196
Hobby Horse, The, 89, 90, 116
"Home, Sweet Home," 23
Housekeeper, The, 166
How He Lied to Her Husband, 166
Hunted Down (The Two Lives of Mary Leigh), 52–5

IDALIA, 55
Ideal Husband, An, 184
Idler, The, 111–4, 116, 117, 118, 134, 141, 159
If I Were King, 162–3, 164
If Winter Comes, 197
Importance of Being Earnest, The, 139–41, 159, 178, 180, 181, 222
Impulse, 85, 86, 103, 116
In Days of Old, 153, 154
"In the Shadows", 108
Inevitable, The, 198
Interference, 198
Ironmaster, The, 88, 103
Is She His Wife? 31
Isle of St. Tropez, The, 44
It's the Geography That Counts, 210, 213

JEANNE QUI PLEURE ET JEANNE QUI RIT (*see* The Cape Mail)
Jenny Lind at Last (Burlesque), 60
"Jephtha's Lamentation," 23
Jeu de l'Amour et du Hasard, Le, 207
John Chilcote, M.P., 166
John Glayde's Honour, 175
Julie Bon-Bon, 191
Julius Caesar, 193–5

KING LEAR, 63, 203
Kingmaker, The, 204
King's Rival, The, 42
Kings and Queens, 185
Kit Marlowe, 124

LADIES' BATTLE, The, 77
Ladies in Retirement, 203
Lady Audley's Secret, 45–9, 50, 51, 53, 55, 135
Lady Flora, 69
Lady of Lyons, The, 84
Lady Slavey, The, 108
Lady Windermere's Fan, 119–22, 123, 130, 134, 137, 182, 183
Lancers, The (*see* The Queen's Shilling)
Last of Mrs. Cheyney, The, 198
Late Christopher Bean, The, 201
Leah Kleshna, 62
Liberty Hall, 122–3, 125, 133, 134, 149, 159, 222
Lights of Home, The, 128
Likeness of the Night, The, 158, 159, 222
Little Sentinel, The, 50
Locandiera, La, 43
London Day by Day, 106–7
Lord Anerley, 118
Lorimer Sebastian, Dramatist, 180
Love in a Village, 32
Love's Carnival, 165, 167
Love's Labour's Lost, 148
Lucky Jim, 187, 219
Lysistrata, 116

MACBETH, 105, 135
"Ma Chère Amie", 20
Mademoiselle de Belle Isle, 41
Madwoman of Chaillot, The, 206
Magic Toys, 42
Magistrate, The, 89
Mahmoud, 21
Maison du Mari, La (*see* Impulse)
Maison Neuve, La (*see* Mayfair)
Maker of Men, A, 166
Man and Wife, 67
Man o' Airlie, The, 63
Man of Forty, The, 157
Man of the Moment, The, 166
Man Proposes, 110

Maria Stuarda, 43
Mariage Forcé, Le, 183
Marie Stuart, 41
Marriage à la Mode, 204
Martyre (*see* The Wife's Sacrifice)
Masaniello, 39
Mask of Virtue, The, 202
Masqueraders, The, 136–7, 138, 141
Mayfair, 88
Merchant of Venice, The, 186
Merry Widow, The, 45, 51
Merry Wives of Windsor, The, 92
Message from Mars, The, 178
"Messiah", 24
Michael and Mary, 200
Michel Perrin, 61
Mid-Channel, 180
Midsummer Day, 123
Miller and His Men, The, 43
Million of Money, A, 114
Misogynist, The, 142
Miss Gwilt, 80
Molière, 117, 118
Mollentrave on Women, 166
Money, 67
Money-Spinner, The, 80–4
Monsieur Beaucaire, 178, 191
Monsieur Jacques, 29
Monsieur le Duc, 75, 76
Monte Cristo, 42
Month in the Country, A, 203
M.P., 67
Mrs. Warren's Profession, 125
Much Ado About Nothing, 149
Mumsee, 196
Murder Has Been Arranged, A, 200
My Old Dutch, 74
Mystery of the Yellow Room, The, 196

NAVAL ENGAGEMENTS, 65
Nervous Wreck, A, 198
New Men and Old Acres, 70
Night of the Party, The, 197
Nine Days' Wonder, A, 69
No, No, Nanette! 196
No Other Tiger, 199
Nos Intimes (*see* Friends or Foes)
Nothing But the Truth, 191
Nursery Governess, The, 180

O, MISTRESS MINE, 220, 224
Oberon, 23
Œdipus, 64
Ogre, The, 181
Old Crimea, 159
Old Heidelberg, 164–5, 167, 223
Old Music, 202
Olivia, 69
On Ne Saurait Penser â Tout, 207
On the Cards, 70
On the Telephone, 63
Only Way, The, 178
'Op o' My Thumb, 165
Open Windows, 183
Othello, 64, 70, 135, 206
Ours, 66
Outsider, The, 198

PAIR OF SPECTACLES, A, 93
Palace of Truth, The, 70
Panorama of Youth, 185
Paolo and Francesca, 160–2, 193
Partners, 116
Passing of the Third Floor Back, The, 178–80
Pattes des Mouches (*see* A Scrap of Paper)
Paul Pry, 60
Payment Deferred, 201
Peg o' My Heart, 185, 187
Pen, 187
Perdita, or The Royal Milkmaid, 50
Perfection, 30
Peter Pan, 108, 149, 196, 197, 200, 220, 224
Phèdre, 41, 43
Play's the Thing, The, 199, 204
Playgoers, 183

Plot of His Story, The, 158
Plus Fours, 198
Pointsman, The, 112
Poll and Partner Joe (Burlesque), 60
Polly With a Past, 196
Polyeucte, 41
Poor Nobleman, The, 44
Pride and Prejudice, 202, 225
Princess and the Butterfly, The (or The Fantastics), 149–50, 171, 231
Prisoner of Zenda, The, 142–7, 148, 153, 155, 159, 186, 221–2
Private Secretary, The, 117
Prodigal Son, The, 166
Professor's Love Story, The, 165
Proof, 116
Pygmalion, 208
Pygmalion and Galatea, 70

QUALITY STREET, 115
Queen's Shilling, The (Le Fils de Famille, The Lancers, The Discarded Son), 73–76
Quiet Rubber, A, 70, 93
Quinney's, 193

RAFFLES, 193
Randall's Thumb, 61
Rapid Thaw, A, 55
Raymond and Agnes, 43
Red Lamp, The, 94
Reparation, 193–4
Repentance, The, 152
Return Journey, The, 199
Richard III, 42
Rip Van Winkle, 127
Rivals, The, 70, 205
Road to Ruin, The, 55
Robert Macaire, 55
Roland for an Oliver, A, 51
Roosters, The, 221
Roxane, 41
Ruddigore, 93
Rupert of Hentzau, 155–7, 159

"SANDS OF DEE, THE", 30
Saving Grace, The, 191
Scar on the Wrist, The, 64
School for Scandal, The, 55, 64, 67–8, 135, 178
Schoolmistress, The, 89
"Scots Wha Hae", 34
Scrap of Paper, A (Pattes des Mouches), 44, 69, 90
Seagull, The, 205
Second Mrs. Tanqueray, The, 125–33, 134–5, 136, 137, 138, 141, 158, 171
Self-Made, 44
Separate Tables (Table By the Window, Table Number Seven), 208–9, 210
Seven Poor Travellers, The, 70
Sham Prince, The, 33
She Stoops To Conquer, 59
Sheila, 189
Shining Hour, The, 201
Sign of the Cross, The, 145
Silent Knight, The, 202
Silver Box, The, 183
Silver King, The, 136
Six Characters in Search of an Author, 208
Sixth Floor, 203
Small Frock, A, 62
Snow White and the Seven Dwarfs, 207
Snowball, The, 101
Society, 65
"Soldier Tired, The", 20
S.O.S., 199
Spanish Dancers, The, 42
Speckled Band, The, 197
Spitalfields Weaver, The, 32–3
Squire, The, 84–5, 90, 158
Still Waters Run Deep, 77
Strange Gentleman, The, 31
Struggle for Life, The, 108

Student Prince, The, 165
Sultan of Mocha, The, 223
Sunlight and Shadow, 108, 109–11, 112, 114, 125, 149
Swan, The, 200
Swan and Edgar, The, 43
Sweet Peril, 207
Sybilla, or Step by Step, 50

TABLE BY THE WINDOW (*see* Separate Tables)
Table Number Seven (*see* Separate Tables)
Tartuffe, 207
Ten Little Nigger Boys, 203
Thief, The, 175–6
Those Who Sit in Judgment, 185
Threads, 196
"Three Fishers", 30
Thunderbolt, The, 176
Tiridate (*see* Anne Bracegirdle)
Tom Cobb, or Fortune's Toy, 62
Tom Pinch, 165
Top of the Ladder, 206
Towards Zero, 210
Tradesman's Ball, The, 33
Treasure, The, 112
Treasure Island, 219
Tree of Knowledge, The, 149, 150
Triumphs of the Philistines, The, 141
Truant in Park Lane, 204
Trying it On, 62
Turandot, 183, 191
Turning Point, The, 182
Turning the Tables, 49
£200 a Year, 80
Two Lives of Mary Leigh, The (*see* Hunted Down)
Two Roses, The, 102–3
Two Virtues, The, 184

ULYSSES, 160
Uncle Ned, 195
Uncle Tom's Cabin, 70
Under the Red Robe, 153
Uninvited Guest, The, 207
Union Jack, The, 94
Up At the Hills, 44, 50

VAGABOND KING, THE, 162
Valentine, 191
Venus Observed, 206
Village Coquettes, The, 31, 32, 33
Vinegar Tree, The, 201

WAITING FOR GILLIAN, 208
War, 60
Waterman, The, 29, 32, 39
Weak Women, 115
Wedding March, The, 61
Whip, The, 60
Wicked World, The, 70
Widow Hunt, The, 56
Wife Without a Smile, The, 171
Wife's Sacrifice, The (Martyre,) 89
Wild Duck, The, 183
Wilderness, The, 159
William and Susan, 78–9
Willow Tree, The, 191
Wind of Heaven, The, 204
Winter Journey, 207
Wisdom of the Wise, The, 158
Witch, The, 90, 94, 183
Witness for the Defence, The, 181, 182
Wonderful Woman, A, 44
Worse Things Happen At Sea, 201

YES, MY DARLING DAUGHTER, 202
Young Folks' Ways, 86–7, 103

ZOO, THE, 62

INDEX OF BOOK AND STORY TITLES

(Most of these have been dramatised, though not always under the same title.)

American, The, 138
Barnaby Rudge, 59
Bella Donna, 182
Dame Madge Kendal, by Herself, 69
Emma, 204
Esmeralda, 86
Far From the Madding Crowd, 84–5
Great Wintlebury Duel, The, 31
Happy Time, The, 207
His Lady Friends, 196
Idalia, 55
If Winter Comes, 197
Lady Audley's Secret, 45
Lady Penelope, 187
Martin Chuzzlewit, 165
Mr. and Mrs. Bancroft, On and Off the Stage, 68
Oliver Twist, 31
Pendennis, 39
Pickwick Papers, 31
Pride and Prejudice, 202
Prisoner of Zenda, The, 142
Rupert of Hentzau, 155
Sketches by Boz, 30, 31
Speckled Band, The, 197
Tale of Two Cities, A, 62
Three Men in a Boat, 179
To Tell My Story, 140
Treasure Island, 219
Vicar of Wakefield, The, 69
Waverley, 24
Way Through the Wood, A, 208